Library of
Davidson College

*UNDERSTANDING
COMMUNITIES*

EDUCATIONAL ADMINISTRATION SERIES
William Ammentorp,
*Consulting Editor*

Understanding Communities
*James A. Conway, Robert E. Jennings, and Mike M. Milstein*

Development of Information Systems for Education
*Khateeb M. Hussain*

Educational System Planning
*Roger A. Kaufman*

James A. Conway  •  Robert E. Jennings  •  Mike M. Milstein
*State University of New York at Buffalo*

# UNDERSTANDING COMMUNITIES

**Prentice-Hall, Inc.**
*Englewood Cliffs, New Jersey*

*Library of Congress Cataloging in Publication Data*

Conway, James A.
   Understanding communities.

   Bibliography: p.
   1. Community and school.  2. School publicity.
3. Community organization.  4. Educational planning.
I. Jennings, Robert E., joint author.  II. Milstein,
Mike M., joint author.  III. Title.
LC216.C64      370.19'31     73-22370
ISBN  0-13-936393-9

© 1974 by Prentice-Hall, Inc., Englewood Cliffs, New Jersey

*All rights reserved. No part of this book
may be reproduced in any form or by any means
without permission in writing from the publisher.*

**Printed in the United States of America**

10  9  8  7  6  5  4  3  2  1

Prentice-Hall International, Inc., *London*
Prentice-Hall of Australia, Pty. Ltd., *Sydney*
Prentice-Hall of Canada, Ltd., *Toronto*
Prentice-Hall of India Private Limited, *New Delhi*
Prentice-Hall of Japan, Inc., *Tokyo*

# contents

PREFACE *xi*

**PART ONE**
**building a framework**
**1**

*chapter one*

CHANGE: THE IMPETUS FOR UNDERSTANDING 3

Understanding: What and Why  *6*
What: The Climate of Expectations  *6*
Why: For Community Decision-making  *10*
Summary  *15*
References  *16*

vi    Contents

*chapter two*

**SPECIFYING THE UNCERTAIN: PROBLEM IDENTIFICATION**　　　　17

What Is a Problem? *17*
A Need for Problem Specification *21*
A Process for Problem Specification *22*
Summary *33*
Reference *34*

*chapter three*

**IDENTIFYING THE UNKNOWN: METHODOLOGIES**　　　　35

A Way of Thinking about Methodologies *36*
Criteria for Selection of Methods *39*
Selecting Methods: A Case Study *42*
Summary *48*
References *50*

**PART TWO**
**getting the information**
**51**

*chapter four*

**USING DOCUMENTS**　　　　53

Purposes of Document Search *53*
Document Search and Analysis *54*
Document Analysis and Summary *58*
Locating Documents *60*
Summary *63*
References *64*

Contents vii

*chapter five*
## ASKING THE RIGHT QUESTIONS 65

Question Development  *66*
Question Format: Open-ended and Structured  *70*
Wording the Questions  *75*
Instrument Construction  *77*
The Pretest  *80*
The Final Instrument  *82*
Summary  *82*
References  *83*

*chapter six*
## ASKING THE RIGHT PEOPLE 85

Purposeful Selection  *86*
Random Selection  *88*
What Size Sample to Draw  *103*
Summary  *109*
References  *109*

*chapter seven*
## ASKING IN THE RIGHT MANNER 111

Objectives in Fieldwork  *112*
Basic Preparation  *113*
Fieldwork for Questionnaires  *119*
Interviews  *123*
Summary  *130*
References  *131*

## PART THREE
## the process of analysis
## 133

### chapter eight
### COLLECTING AND CODING DATA          135

Data: The Object of Analysis  *135*
Collecting and Coding  *136*
Computers in Analysis  *144*
Summary  *146*
References  *147*

### chapter nine
### ARRANGING AND DESCRIBING DATA          148

Approaches for Depicting Structured Data  *148*
Depicting Unstructured Data  *160*
Summary  *161*
References  *161*

### chapter ten
### INTERPRETATION AND STATISTICAL ANALYSIS          163

Interpreting  *163*
An Introduction to Chi-Square  *166*
How Significant Is Significant?  *182*
Summary  *183*
References  *184*

## PART FOUR
## putting it all together
## 185

### chapter eleven
### DATA STORAGE AND RETRIEVAL          187

Anticipating Needs  *188*
A School-Community Data Bank  *188*
Sources  *198*
Summary  *203*
References  *204*

*chapter twelve*
**SHARING THE FINDINGS**  205

The Policy Process and Information  *205*
Possible Audiences  *207*
Organizing the Report for Information Feedback  *208*
Some Writing Concerns  *213*
A Few Parting Words on Understanding Communities  *214*

*appendix a*
**DATA AND INFORMATION SOURCES**  217

*appendix b*
**TABLE OF RANDOM NUMBERS**  225

*appendix c*
**TABLE OF CHI-SQUARE**  231

**ANNOTATED READINGS**  235

**INDEX**  243

*preface*

The basic premise of the authors is that public opinion is important to policy-makers, especially in a society steeped in a tradition of democratic participation in decision-making. Publics do influence policy, whether or not policy-makers request their input. In the end, policy-makers are held accountable for their activities. It is infinitely better to have a feeling for the positions of individuals and groups in the community regarding policy matters *before* a course of action is decided upon than to make decisions and then be abruptly and unhappily confronted by community dissatisfactions. In short, it is our belief that public administrators will increasingly be called upon to display a firm well-grounded understanding of their communities. The contents of this book are intended to provide them with the basic tools for developing that understanding.

Although the procedures discussed in the book should be useful to any public administrators, they are specifically directed to the needs of a particular group of public decision-makers — educational administrators. Of all public administrators, those in the educational domain are probably in most immediate need of the tools which are discussed herein. Even the staunchest supporters of the public schools would find it difficult to refute the fact that public education today is experiencing one of the most difficult periods in its history. Administrators and teachers are being challenged by many sectors of the community, most of which previously had passively accepted the schoolman's views. Old citizen alliances in support of the schools have begun to fall by the wayside and schoolmen are finding it difficult to develop new ones to replace them. Communities formerly composed of a handful of active school supporters, a great mass of passive school supporters, and a few identifiable critic groups can now more characteristically be portrayed as ever-changing in sentiment and highly concerned about the debate over the direction of public education. It is becoming clear that large segments of our communities intend to become actively engaged in the debate. If the educational administrator does not have the tools at hand to gauge the many changes taking place in his community, he will not be able to seize the initiative and move his school district toward better educational programs.

The changes occurring are multidimensional and complex. The American people are highly mobile, in both the physical and the social sense. Thus it is not surprising that the pluralistic nature of our society, which leads to clashes of values and viewpoints concerning racial, economic, and social issues, is manifested in nearly every community. The thrust toward greater participation in decision-making by formerly submerged groups such as ethnic minorities, the impoverished, and college and high school students, heightens and accelerates the processes of change. It could be said that such activist movements have generated a societal syndrome of participation.

The increase in participation has had multiple impacts upon educational systems. Student unrest, which began in the colleges and universities, has reached down into the high schools, but it would be erroneous to assume that high school students are merely imitating college student activism. In truth, these students are seriously questioning the relevance of high schools in a rapidly changing society. Community pressure groups have stepped up their activities, and their influence and power are increasing. Their ability to reach people has been magnified by the use of modern communications which, in turn, adds many more opinion-forming voices to the change process. At the same time, there remains a large number of people who seem to keep their own counsel, shunning an active role, *until they go to the polls.* The so-called taxpayers' revolt which has resulted in an increasing rate of school budget and bond setbacks is the culmination of many strands of discontent, of uncertainty, and frustration.

The school administrator needs to be aware of the changing nature of his community if he hopes to be able to modify the impact of this continuous change on the schools. National polls that explore citizens' attitudes concerning public education, such as the annual Gallup poll on education, are helpful in establishing a general picture, but to understand the rapidly changing shifts in attitudinal positions within individual communities, more discrete information is required. To get this information the administrator must systematically assess (1) citizens' attitudes and opinions about the schools; (2) how they are changing; and (3) to what degree they are changing. To continue to be an effective local educational leader in curricular change, in fiscal policy-making, and, above all, in planning for education, the administrator must have a continuous flow of this information *in usable form.* To be a molder rather than a follower of public opinion, he needs to be able to refine his problem, determine the information required to pose or test alternative solutions, obtain the information, sort it, and analyze it.

Every school community is a readily available and important data bank. The local community usually has been slighted by schoolmen as a prime data source, largely because they have not had the techniques available to tap it in a logical, coherent manner. They have been apprehensive about searching documents, designing instruments, drawing samples, doing pilot studies, and performing other seemingly "sophisticated" research tasks. Given a guide to action in which the mysteries and myths of school-community study are stripped away, the administrator can proceed with confidence to obtain the information he needs and utilize more fully the concepts of community he already knows from reading, training, and experience.

There is no room today or in the future for crisis school administrators; administrators noted for their inability to foresee emerging community demands and needs. Certainly problems will always arise if for no other reason than because of our nation's commitment to open involvement of citizens in their schools. But problems can be monitored *before* they become major school-community confrontations. Wise administrators will not wait for crises to develop. Regular monitoring of community opinions is clearly required to avoid such crisis administration.

It might be argued that since there are persons from universities and other research centers who specialize in monitoring communities, it would be logical to commission such persons to seek the necessary information rather than for the schoolman to do so. Certainly this procedure is employed by many school systems seeking community-related information. Our posture, though, is to encourage educators to carry out such activities using school system personnel and community members whenever possible. Not only are the mysteries and myths of school-community study overrated, as noted earlier, but when studies are performed by outside agents the results tend to be shelved and few efforts are made to adopt the recommendations. It is our belief that school personnel and community members should be centrally involved in formulating the problem, specifying the procedures, and implementing and analyzing the results if an impact is to be expected.

Realistically, given his many role activities, the superintendent cannot give adequate attention to the complex task of monitoring his community. In most school systems this would not be necessary or appropriate at any rate. It is most likely that such activities would be directed by central office personnel such as the director of school-community relations or the research director. Many of the specific methodological considerations discussed in the book are written specifically for this audience. However, to be able to play a part in the major policy decisions related to monitoring efforts, it will be necessary for the superintendent to have at least a general familiarity with the concepts and processes associated with understanding communities.

The purpose of this book is to place in the hands of the school administrator alternative means for systematically obtaining information about his school community. The intent is to increase his ability to monitor community change. More specifically, this book will help him to detect impending problems; define them; select appropriate methods for gathering needed information; and analyze and report findings which can help in the resolution of problems. This is not a new concept; administrators typically process their tasks using such problem-solving approaches. All that is hoped for is that in using techniques described herein, administrators will be able to obtain more complete information about their communities before making critical decisions.

## organization of the book

The book is organized to be used as a manual. That is, the various sections of the book take the reader from problem identification, through information gathering, to information sorting and analysis, and finally to the point where he can bring the findings together in a coherent fashion which can be of use in resolving questions that affect policy-making issues. Brief case studies are included to give some sense of immediacy to the discussion of methods. These cases are based on actual events with which the authors have had direct involvement.

Part 1 should be of particular interest to the superintendent because it builds a framework for problem defining and provides a guide to methods which are available to help him understand specific local problems. Chapter 1 explores the need for understanding the community, referring especially to the climate of expectations for schools, and the development of opinions and policies in communities. Chapter 2 explores the ways in which the administrator can go about establishing his or her specific information needs. The focus in this chapter is upon problem specification. Without a clear and concise problem statement, it is unlikely that subsequent information-seeking processes can be effective. Chapter 3 overviews various ways the administrator can go about getting access to information required to resolve a problem. A number of approaches which center on document search and survey research are presented as potentially suitable for the reader's purposes.

Part 2 is geared to the administrators who will direct the monitoring since it focuses on basic procedures for going about the task of securing needed information. Chapter 4 includes guidelines for searching documents and a list of potentially useful document sources. Chapter 5 is the first of three chapters which deal with survey research. In this chapter, development of questions and construction of survey instruments are discussed. In Chapter 6 the reader will find useful suggestions for identifying the most appropriate persons to respond to a survey instrument. Step-by-step processes related to purposeful and random selection are outlined to ensure that appropriate populations are included and those sampled reasonably reflect community views. Finally, in Chapter 7 the reader is given suggestions for maximizing the potential that persons selected will be cooperative and respond candidly. The chapter is a compilation of sound advice for getting information with the minimum of trouble and the maximum of effect.

Part 3 presents ways to organize and analyze the information collected and is aimed directly at those administrators who will be responsible for these tasks. Organization and analysis of data is not nearly so difficult to pursue as most educational administrators seem to believe. Chapter 8 describes techniques for collecting, scoring, coding, and storing the information. Ways of translating unstructured information into structured information are explored. Chapter 9 presents alternative ways of arranging the information which has been coded into visual forms. Finally, in Chapter 10 use of statistical procedures is explored. The focus is on chi-square; an analytical approach that can be very useful to the administrator.

Part 4 should be of immediate interest to the chief school officer because it explores ways of bringing the results obtained to the attention of others and storing them in usable form for future use. Chapter 11 suggests ways of storing and retrieving the information collected for future needs which might arise. The reader is introduced to the concept of the data bank and given advice concerning how to establish one. The last chapter, Chapter 12, focuses on a most important task; writing up the findings for appropriate distribution. The payoff of the search effort is highly dependent upon the ability of the administrator to put the findings together in a clear and concise manner. The findings must be fed back into the system if appropriate action is to be taken. The chapter closes with a review of the process of understanding communities.

The book is rounded out by the inclusion of pertinent appended materials. An annotated bibliography is also provided to help the reader who is interested in further study and exploration. References are organized around specific categories so that the reader can delve deeper into those methodological and conceptual considerations which are of most interest to him. Further appended materials include tables of random numbers to help the reader select respondents for surveys; a table of chi-square values to help him compute significance; and a list of sources which we feel might be useful to the schoolman as a basis for keeping on top of changes at the local, state, and national levels.

Due to immediate and pressing needs, some readers may choose to focus on one or more particular chapters. It is possible to do this, since chapters are structured to be basically self-contained. However, it is hoped that most will read through the book as an entity to gain full understanding of the logical processes that must be followed from problem identification and specification to information-gathering and data analysis. In any case, it is the hope of the authors that use of the book will assist the administrator in his efforts to understand the environment and more effectively meet the educational needs of the community which he serves.

We are indebted to the Literary Executor of the late Sir Ronald A. Fisher, F.R.S., to Dr. Frank Yates, F.R.S., and to Oliver & Boyd, Edinburgh, for permission to reprint the Table of Chi-Square from their book *Statistical Tables for Biological, Agricultural and Medical Research.*

We would also like to recognize the extremely useful assistance of John Bruce Francis who read through a draft of the manuscript and offered many suggestions which have helped to shape this final product. Finally, we are most appreciative of Ms. Pat Martin for her patience and typing skill. The suggestions we have received from students and colleagues have been incorporated where possible to improve the work. All errors or inconsistencies must be the final responsibility of the authors.

*J. A. C.*
*R. E. J.*
*M. M. M.*

# BUILDING A FRAMEWORK

# PART ONE

In the close and continuing relationships of school and community, of educators and citizens, mutual understanding is necessary for the development of a sound school system.

Administrators know that many facets of present-day school operation require increased information and knowledge about the school community. Conversely, if citizens are to make sound decisions about their educational system they need information about the schools. It has been said that differences of opinion are what make a horse race. This idea can be applied to the school-community situation in that differences in expectations and understandings bring about school-community problems.

Part One develops a framework for thinking about these problems, not as obstacles to be overcome, but rather, as differences to be investigated and resolved reasonably. Chapter 1 indicates the larger needs for school-community understanding in terms of citizens' expectations for education. The process by which expectations become policy, through the interaction of community and school system, is outlined. At various points in that process, the school administrator's need for information, as well as the steps he should take in informing the community, have been delineated.

Careful delineation of problems arising from the policy process, as well as other relationships between school and community, is the first step in problem-solving. Chapter 2 focuses on the means of problem specification. Without this essential step it is impossible to identify the information which will be needed. Successful problem delineation provides clues for choosing processes by which the needed information can be sought. In Chapter 3, the final element of the framework, the means of gaining access to needed information, is discussed. Document search and survey research methods are outlined and their potential for obtaining needed information is explicated. Criteria for selecting the appropriate method are presented and illustrated by the use of simple diagrams and summary sheets.

The three chapters are intended as an orientation for any school administrator who has the task of developing school-community understanding. More specifically, however, these chapters are intended for the chief school officer who has the responsibility for leadership in school-community relations and for delineating the task areas in which his associates and staff should focus their activities.

# Change:
# The Impetus
# for Understanding

*one*

Social change today is rapid, uneven, and widespread. Events and their consequences occur with such rapidity that there is often inadequate time to prepare for them either mentally or physically. The result, to use Toffler's (1970) term, might be called "future shock." Change is uneven, reflecting the fact that technological advances take place before people are physically prepared or ready to comprehend the concomitant changes in values. Birth control pills, for example, have been on the market for a number of years and society is still struggling with their impact on family life and social relationships. The widespread diffusion of change is simply recognition that developments in one place quickly spread to other places. Modern means of communication, the mass media, and particularly television, provide people with an instantaneous view of the new and novel occurring elsewhere. Ideas, as well as the visual impact of change, converge on the receiver without regard to his present state of readiness or his setting.

While it is difficult to discern a predictable pattern of change, it is possible to outline some of the larger areas of concern under which many changes and desires for change may be loosely grouped.

One of the most prevalent areas of concern, to use an example, may be called "the quality of life": the belief that the human side of things in society can be improved. As Reich (1970) and others have noted, concern with the quality of life has developed out of a growing realization that the advantages of modern technology are not being directed at solving human problems and sometimes generate new problems. This concern not only hinges on questions such as what beneficial activities people can undertake in leisure time but also raises the question, how can the society tolerate urban blight side by side with wealth and splendor? Concomitant questions have to do with the elimination of the drug problem and the eradication of crime, as well as with the cultivation of the arts. What the concern for the quality of life is, then, is a matter of shifting social values; a movement toward a more people-oriented perspective.

Closely allied with the concern for the quality of life are heightened expressions of pluralism in the society. Various social and ethnic groups are creating new self-images of dignity and social power. Based on their enhanced self-concept, they are pressing for equality of opportunity in the economic and social life of the nation. A simple cataloging of movements in the early 1970s indicates the breadth of this phenomenon: black power, women's liberation, student unrest, chicano dignity, resurgence of the American Indian, and poor people's rights. These are all manifestations of desires by diverse groups to be full-fledged members of society while, at the same time, retaining and expressing certain distinct social and cultural differences.

Coupled with expressions of pluralism is the increased desire of people to participate in those decisions which directly affect their lives. Students and poor people, for example, want the power and authority to make a greater range of decisions for themselves and to command the resources which can produce the desired end results. They demand equal participation with other groups in decisions which affect everyone. Formal authority or status authority derived from external measures such as the whiteness of one's skin is no longer to be acceptable. New forms of social power such as mass actions of protest and boycott, confrontations, and exposures have come into being to support these demands. In addition, the traditional means of increased political consciousness and participation are being renewed.

However, almost as counterpoint to these clearly developing concerns and trends, there are forces in the society which are resistant to these changes. For example, many of our values continue to emphasize the sanctity of property as being as least equal with the rights of people and the confinement of political action to the voting booth. There is also a strong belief in society that all groups can "make it" by hard work. Cultural pluralism may be expressed in old-world dances but not through different life styles, for this has been a society dedicated to an apparent oneness in its cultural basis.

The result, of course, is an increasing clash of values. On many issues the struggles are between the proponents of change and the advocates of status quo. It is very difficult to distill out of this maelstrom the directions which organizations that acculturate youth and transmit social heritage, such as schools, should take. These changes cannot be dealt with merely at a philosophical level for by the time the ongoing struggles resolve themselves into something which gives a clear indication of what to do, it is already too late to change the organization. Waiting for that resolution or for some expert to pose a solution is to risk missing the problem altogether.

The implication of social change for organizations has been the perennial problem of how to survive in a rapidly changing environment. Efforts at solving the problem through research and reallocation of resources have been somewhat effective but need constant attention and improvement.

In business enterprise, a good deal of effort is expended in keeping up with the environment, changing with it so that the final product is satisfactory and acceptable to the public. Business organizations systematically look for ways to improve their organizational processes to satisfy the demands of the environment. On the input side they research new materials. They spend a good deal of effort locating men and women with high degrees of skill in the latest technical processes. On the output side, such corporations conduct extensive market research to determine what people think about their products and what they would like to see improved. Beyond that, many corporations go into what may be called "market development," that is, they try to ascertain, in advance of actual demand, which people would be potential customers if a company's products were changed in any one of several ways.

What these corporations have learned is that they cannot just react to the environment and survive. They know that they must change as various elements around them change. To react only, or to react in limited terms, say, through a new advertising campaign, is to leave the organization, not to the mercy of its competitors, but to the merciless advance of change.

The public schools face a similar problem in coping with change. They must learn to anticipate change within the environment rather than merely react to it. They must develop processes for examining the environment, observing changes in it, and analyzing the long- and short-range implications which these changes might hold for education. Over the past decade some school systems have devised ways of assessing and adopting new materials for use in the classroom. Many administrators have become quite adept at utilizing people with new skills and the latest ways of thinking about schools. However, much of this effort has been directed to improving the usual school program and has tended to obscure the implications of larger changes taking place in the society surrounding the school.

More recently, schools have been moving toward greater systemization of educational and managerial functions. Concern for the outcomes of education has increased, outcomes which are measurable against inputs. Accountability, the assumption of specified responsibility for specified performance in a task area, has become a watchword. Systems approaches such as planning, programming, budgeting systems, designed to meet these ends, require fuller specification of objectives and inputs from both the community and the professional educators. By far the greater emphasis is on determining what shall be achieved, what shall be produced. In an area of public endeavor such as education, the patrons and clients have much to say about what should be accomplished.

It seems clear that schools should be expending greater effort in determining the impact of societal change and the clash of values in the school-community environment.

## understanding: what and why

If an objective of public schools is to provide communities with educational programs that fulfill and serve the communities' needs, then the concerns of the communities for education must be recognized in the schools' decisions about programs. It is the school administrator who must bring order to the diverse and changing concerns. What issues do the concerns generate? What are the ideas which people have from observing and participating in our changing society? What seems to be needed is for the school to reach out to determine how the larger concerns seem to be affecting people's expectations for education. For the school administrator it comes down to the question, "What information do I need to understand my community?"

As already indicated, the people are the community. It is their values, beliefs, and opinions that must be ascertained. What expectations do the people of a community have for the schools? What beliefs are held about the goals of the schools as well as how the schools should operate? The administrator's ability to obtain relatively accurate information about such questions directly affects the decisions he will make about the organization and operation of school programs; decisions which will go toward either (1) matching the expectations of the community, or (2) changing the expectations of the community. Under the first, his decisions will be those which bring the school operation more in line with the wants and needs which people have. Under the second will be decisions to actively reach out into the community and aid in the formation of new sets of attitudes and opinions about schools and education. The initial problem is to determine what these expectations consist of and to develop processes for continually monitoring them. Following this, the problem is to assess the effect of these expectations on community decision-making.

## what: the climate of expectations

The climate of expectations within a community is made up of traditions and values which people have about an area of endeavor such as education (see Carter, 1960). It is immediately observable that there is a spectrum of views within the climate of expectations. For example, many people hold to the tradition that schools are places where young people learn to read, write, and behave; others believe that schools should be instruments of social change, helping youngsters to develop new values. Expectations also deal in ideologies. For some, government enterprise should be limited to a minimum role in the affairs of the citizens and hold to a norm of low taxation. For other people, however, government enterprise should be designed to do the things which people want done, efficiently and at costs which are comparable to those of private enterprise.

As institutions and agencies operate over the years their history of past actions, or record of failure and achievement, enters into people's expectations. A poorly constructed school, inadequately educated youngsters (e.g., college dropouts or secretaries who cannot spell) are perceived as examples of deficient educational policy and operation. On the other hand, a high number of scholarship winners or a successful football team are often taken as evidence of effective school operation. Of course, both sets of expectations resulting from these conditions can exist side by side in different segments of the same community.

The expectations which people hold become yardsticks by which they measure present performance and form opinions about future performance of their schools. For example, where does a proposed sex education program fit within the tradition of teaching reading, writing, and behaving? Has the school board really examined the necessity for a building which will add $5.80 per thousand to the tax rate? Has the school done so well in its college preparatory program that it should expand the language department to include both Spanish and French? How can parents make judgments about youngsters' work if letter grades are abolished? When a policy is proposed these are the kinds of questions people ask themselves and each other. Discussion focuses on the comparisons of past and present performance versus expectations and then predictions are made about future action.

Where past and present performance meets expectations, the tendency is toward support of new school proposals. School officials can capitalize on this support for approval of policies and have a higher probability of gaining community consent and cooperation in their operation. In instances where ballots are cast, it may mean successful passage of a referendum or tax levy.

Where expectations have not been met, support tends to be withheld. This condition indicates that the climate of expectations is such that serious conflict may be generated by proposed policy changes. This is not to say that conflict per se is bad and must be avoided. Certain levels of conflict seem to produce a creative atmosphere for bringing out new ideas, increased activity, and greater understanding of the problems. Properly handled in an open situation, conflict can result in genuine improvement of the schools. The conflict situations to be avoided are those which destroy confidence and result in the shutting down of communication between the schools and the community. Deciding major policy changes in executive or conference sessions of the board of education is one example.

The school administrator faces a real problem in that the usual arrangements for school government do not include structures for regularly monitoring community opinion, determining alternatives, and handling conflict. The public schools provide an example of a public agency built and operated without the expectation of serious conflicts over its nature and task. The governance of American schools was developed on a belief of sameness in values and thus a high degree of consensus of educational objectives within the community. School boards were created as nonpartisan bodies to see that schools were maintained and operated. Whether elected or appointed, school boards have varied and extensive powers for the operation and control of the schools. However, their members do not generally represent a well-defined set of community values for schools and schooling. At most they may reflect, very loosely and informally, an amorphous predominant ethnic group, a limited segment of the socioeconomic scale, or ill-defined geographic portions of the district. Different members may also embody different viewpoints on any issue from taxation to sex education. Beyond the board's authority there are several large decisions often reserved to the voters of the district; that is, approval of the budget or tax levy, decisions about the purchase of sites and the issuance of bonds to pay for land or buildings. Between the authority of the board to operate schools and the types of major decisions left to the voters, there is a tremendous void of formal structures for examining issues and making decisions about education (Bendiner, 1969).

A variety of limited means have been employed to fill the void. In many communities, various groups have found ways to bring pressure on school boards and superintendents for the purposes of having certain of their expectations met. These interest groups generally appear when there is something to oppose as with a tax increase, the employment of a controversial teacher, or the start of a new curriculum incompatible with one value scheme or another. When no overt issue exists these groups lie dormant and invisible in the community, but ready to become active if their interests are threatened.

Other efforts to fill the void have been made by district officials themselves. School administrators attempt to reach out to their communities with programs of information and explanations of school activities. These efforts consist of news releases, parents' nights, and other activities which, to one degree or another, essentially open the school to community observation. The most intense activities of this nature are usually related to campaigns for the passage of bond referendums or annual budgets. In these situations citizens' advisory committees are established, open discussion meetings arranged, and, in general, greater efforts are made to achieve a modicum of two-way communication with the community (Carter and Odell, 1966).

These methods often fail to reach beyond immediate crises. Pressure groups and school campaigns have not been effective for bringing about significant change or facing the larger, more basic, problems of schools. More heat than light is generated as little is done in the way of systematically developing and using information. Beyond that, such methods do not even bring into being appropriate forums through which issues can be fully defined, points of the conflict taken up, and viable alternatives proposed.

As a result, the schools' response to criticism is usually gross and efforts at determining new policy directions, based on the expectations of the community, are minimal or nonexistent. When action is taken, it is often based on assumptions that expectations have not changed and that consensus exists (Mogulof, 1969).

Issues and alternative solutions have probably become more important to citizens than their generalized understanding of the schools and school quality. The relationship of public opinion to officials' policy options seems to be on a continuum and each issue can be considered separately for popular constraints on policy action. At one end, in issues where people have little interest and information, they exercise no important constraints. Officials are quite free to choose the policy. Next there are issues in which people have interests but the constraints they generate permit officials a wide range of policy options. In this situation, the option chosen will be judged later as to its outcomes. (This is the classic view of the voter as an astute appraiser of official actions.) Finally, there are issues in which peoples' opinions severely restrict the policy options. Four conditions are observable in this situation:

1. Large numbers of people are intensely interested in specific policy alternatives.
2. Officials' views on the issue are well known.
3. Opinions cannot be manipulated in a short time.
4. Opinions are so well balanced the officials' choice of position on the issue directly affects the outcome at the polls (Boyd, 1972, pp. 446-49).

Policy processes for local education have not yet developed to the point where analyses can be made along these lines.

It seems safe to say at this point in time that great changes have occurred and are continuing to occur in the expectations which people hold for public schools. The high degree of mobility of people makes communities more heterogeneous than ever before. Newcomers often bring new and different values with them. Formerly submerged groups in our population demand and are obtaining a voice in the affairs of the community. These groups, particularly minority people, often have their own sets of expectations for education which differ from those of established groups. Other segments of society form new expectations for the operation of public schools when their particular vested interests seem to be under attack. The most obvious examples are taxpayers' groups or businessmen's associations opposed to the expansion of government enterprise. In addition, as the barriers of tradition have eroded, other groups seek to share what was formerly closed to them. For example, church groups seek public support for the educational system they provide. All of these changing conditions mean a greater range of opinion and constraints on policy alternatives in a vast number of educational issues.

The intensity of these expectations should not be underestimated. Many groups are willing and able to close down schools by protest action if their expectations are not met. Many have the means available to investigate and expose what they believe to be discriminatory or unfair practices. There is little hesitation about utilizing the mass media to make their views and findings known and to bring pressure to bear on the schools to meet their demands.

In short, there is no longer a single set of expectations for many areas of public education. To respond grossly to demands in the community is an ineffective way of solving problems. To wait for consensus to develop in the community is to invite disaster. The administrator must determine the expectations of the community and assess their impact on schools and community decisions about schools. Such decisions are not based in the merit of a proposal measured against some timeless value scheme, but more on the fit of the action with the expectations of various groups in the community.

How do these expectations affect an idea as it moves from proposal to consideration to embodiment in public policy? How are the choices made between the alternative lines of action at several different points in this process? What is the role of the administrator in the community decision process?

## why: for community decision-making

Community decisions, according to Rossi (1960), are choices among alternative lines of action directed at affecting community-wide institutions. The actual decision is a choice among modes of action made by an authoritative person or group within the community institution with the objective of change or maintenance of the institution. To qualify as a community decision the choice must be made by an authoritative person or group, one which has a legitimate right to make the decision, by either law or custom. Such choices run the range from voter decisions in local elections to decisions made by control boards of community agencies. Secondly, the decision must involve community-wide institutions such as schools.

The major point here is that most decisions of wide consequence for a community will at some point in the process be legitimated by a recognized authoritative group. Undoubtedly a majority of decisions, having community-wide consequences, will be legitimated by formal government bodies, i.e., voters, elected officials, or appointed administrators. This, however, does not exclude other participants from the process. It very definitely includes input from various socioeconomic groupings, including power structures, from associations and organizations whether relatively permanent or ad hoc and, of course, individuals. The actions of many of these participants may be covert rather than overt but they are not ruled out as influences even though they are nonauthoritative in the process.

The policies of public agencies evolve from government response to human needs and wants, according to Hennessey (1965). Policy most often begins as a private or individual idea. These ideas, when shared by large numbers of individuals, become proposals. When proposals are adopted by authority they become public policy. It is necessary, however, to expand this simple three-stage policy process to permit analyses and show at different points where individuals, groups, formal organizations, and government agencies exert influence and to demonstrate the role of the administrator at various points in the sequence.

Ideas may simply arise as two individuals discuss some past events or examine a problem. Ideas may also originate in organization meetings. In public schools ideas often originate with the professionals, the administrators and/or teachers. The expectations which people have about action which an organization should take, the values which they hold in terms of community services, the traditions of the society or given institution, all generally contribute to an idea. The dissatisfactions which people have with an organization or its services also contribute to an idea. When this idea has been transmitted to others and discussed and numbers of people have some knowledge about it, when there is public notice taken of the idea, it may be called a proposal. There is no clear line of demarcation between these two stages.

At some point within the proposal stage public agencies and their administrators become officially involved as agencies and officials. That point is where there is a request, either stated or implied, for action by government. Once there is a suggestion that government action is required the administrator's task begins.

The decision-making process for government agencies is exposed to political, economic, and social forces of community groups and individuals. Thus, it is essential to assess their impact at several points in the process. In order to provide a framework for this analysis, the process between policy proposal and implementation has been divided into six stages. These stages, adapted from Knill (1964) and Agger, Goldrich, and Swanson (1964) are:

1. policy formulation;
2. policy deliberation;
3. organization of policy support;
4. authoritative consideration;

5. policy promulgation; and
6. policy effectuation.

Just as an idea is discussed and emerges as a proposal, these six stages are not discrete and distinct but flow one into the other in a constant process of evolvement. At each stage, the administrator must seek information which will help the system remain in touch with and influence the policy process. Descriptions of each stage follow and are summarized in Table 1.1.

*FORMULATION*

The process begins with proposals, or dissatisfactions, from the community. At the policy formulation stage the task of the administrator is to create a policy response or policy alternatives in the area suggested by the problem or proposal from the community. Much of the task involves clarifying with various groups and organizations and various forces in the community what the proposal means and what some of the hoped-for outcomes are. It also involves determining why something needs to be done and what the expectations are for action by the agency. There can be no doubt that there are other influences at this point — the authority of the agency to act under state law as well as the political feasibility of the agency entering into the issue.

*DELIBERATION*

At the policy deliberation stage many points of view come into being and forces begin to coalesce around them. Conflicts begin to arise as public and private discussions take place involving individuals, groups, and organizations. The mass media plays a role reporting and examining the different views. Issues and alternatives come up for discussion, choices are delineated and become alternatives or competing demands. Around these possible outcomes various groups and individuals begin to gather. Among the choices are the policy responses or alternatives put forth by the public agency.

The role of the administrator at this stage is to know thoroughly the position of the agency and the meanings, or implications, of the alternatives which it has proposed. Secondly, the administrator must gauge with considerable accuracy the effects of other alternatives and competing demands. Doing so requires him to know and understand the community and utilize some relatively scientific means of information and opinion gathering.

*ORGANIZATION OF SUPPORT*

In the third stage, the organization of policy support, individuals, groups, and interested agencies bring influence to bear for the acceptance of particular

Table 1.1

The Policy Process in Community Decisions

| | 1 | 2 | 3 | 4 | 5 | 6 |
|---|---|---|---|---|---|---|
| Community information needs | How well is the school performing? | How does performance fail to meet expectations? | When will the choices be clarified? | Why should the agency alternative be chosen? | Who made the choice? voters? agency? power group? | What improvement has resulted? |
| COMMUNITY ACTIVITIES | Initiation of idea or proposal | Develops various points of view, counter demands; forces begin to coalesce | Groups bring influence to bear behind particular proposals; consensus begins to appear | Selection of choices to be supported | Learns of choice made | Begins to give feedback on results of new policy |
| Policy Process Stage | FORMULATION | DELIBERATION | ORGANIZATION OF SUPPORT | CONSIDERATION BY AUTHORITY | \*DECISION POINT\* PROMULGATION | EFFECTUATION |
| AGENCY ADMINISTRATOR ACTIVITIES | Develops policy response or policy alternatives | Explication of agency alternatives | Revision of policy stand in terms of community opinion proposals, influences, agency objectives | Determines choices to be proposed, campaigns for agency choice | Announces choice made | Puts new policy into action in the organization |
| Administrator information needs | What is being proposed? What is the problem? | Who is proposing? coalescing? | Why is there coalescence? around which alternatives? | When to press for a decision? | How to best publicize choice made? | How to communicate results of changed policy? |

policies or competing demands. Some alternatives become merged with others through processes which are moving toward consensus. At the same time, however, other alternatives come into sharper conflict. The administrator, at this stage, is still involved with revision of the agency's policy stand. The decisions involved at this point may be to expand or contract the policy statement as well as the area which it may ultimately affect. This is often done through compromise with concerned groups and forces in the community, but more often it is done in terms of administrative decisions, based on understanding of community expectations. At this point the administrator needs very definite information about the community and the positions of various segments within it. Where consensus has been achieved, in terms of a proposal, this is an essential piece of knowledge. Where greater conflict has developed, particularly between the agency's developing policy and other alternatives, there must be some accurate assessment, not only of the intensity of that conflict but also of the particular groupings on either side of the question. If appropriate public relations activities are to be undertaken by the agency, this knowledge and information is needed to target the groups to be reached. It must be remembered that members of a community obtain most of their knowledge and understanding of public issues through the communications processes with which public relations concerns itself. Any communication from the agency must bear on those facts and opinions which have been obtained from the communication of others, communications that have already helped form and shape his attitudes and opinions.

## *CONSIDERATION BY AUTHORITY*

Stage four, authoritative consideration, is the point where one set of alternatives is selected for authoritative decision or legitimatization. The selection of one set of alternatives can come about in several ways. On the one hand, it may be made by an administrative officer or by the control board of the public agency, or by balloting of the citizenry. On the other hand, the selection at this point could be made by an informal group or groups through informal methods influencing the public school, its control board, or administrators. The latter situation pertains when there is no public balloting or other formal proclamation about policy change and where there are power structures operative and active in this area of community endeavor. Elections, of course, are at the other extreme. Here the decision is to pose alternatives for placing on the ballot, one of which is to be selected by the voters.

It is at stage four that the administrator can take positive action and press for the decisional outcome which he prefers. Obviously this is the point at which the final policy alternatives are examined both within the formal organization and within any power structure operating in its area of endeavor. This power group also operates between the point of choosing outcomes for a ballot and the actual day of voting, in a process of persuasion, aimed at the voters. So may the agency through its own campaign. Where the decision is not made by ballot, the choice is made by authority, unless influence groups have the power to decide and do so informally.

*PROMULGATION*

The fifth stage, the promulgation stage, is the point at which the new policy is enunciated. Under some conditions, such as in a ballot, time of promulgation may be defined within the proposal which was approved. On the other hand, if the majority voted against the proposed policy change there is no promulgation. If the decision was administrative or resided with the control board, the official statement may be made at almost any time. Where the decision was made informally there may never be a promulgation publicly but only within the informal group.

*EFFECTUATION*

Finally, the sixth stage of decision-making is the effectuation of policy within the organization. This is a task of the administrator and, as he moves from policy statement to action, it is to this end to which the entire process has been directed. The process itself is not complete until actuation takes place, actuation which hopefully has built-in feedback mechanisms to monitor the effects of the new policy, not only in terms of the clientele served but also in terms of meeting the larger expectations within the community.

How well the school fares in this process is closely related to the ability of the administrator to determine the climate of expectations in the community with regard to the activities of the schools and people's expectations as to how the school will act in the particular issue at hand. At each of the several stages along the way the administrator and other members of the organization have opportunities to make input to the community about the prospective policy. The purpose is to modify the climate of expectations by raising or lowering them as need be among the several segments of the community.

summary

Effective decisions about school organization and operation under evolving conditions of social change can only come about through a knowledge of the community and its expectations for education. As the community environment changes, its impact on the schools must be assessed by the administrator.

Community attitudes and opinions need to be continually monitored as ideas become proposals and proposals move into the policy process. There are several points in the process where the systematic collection and collation of information are needed.

Yet the question remains, whose expectations is the administrator seeking to modify? What is the problem at issue and how can it be identified? How can the administrator gain sufficient information about his community and elements within it in order to get at the critical groups with an appropriate explanation made by the appropriate means? What information does he need to fully define the problem? We will be concerned with just these topics in the next several chapters. The next chapter turns to problem identification, offering the administrator some means of determining and analyzing problems.

## references

AGGER, ROBERT E., DANIEL GOLDRICH, and BERT SWANSON, *The Rulers and the Ruled.* New York: John Wiley, 1964.

BENDINER, ROBERT, *The Politics of Schools.* New York: Harper & Row, 1969.

BOYD, RICHARD W., "Popular Control of Public Policy: A Normal Vote Analysis of the 1968 Election," *American Political Science Review,* LXVI (June 1972), 429-49.

CARTER, RICHARD F., *Voters and Their Schools.* Stanford, Calif.: Institute for Communications Research, Stanford University, 1960.

_____, and WILLIAM R. ODELL, *The Structure and Process of School Community Relations: A Summary.* Stanford, Calif.: Institute for Communication Research, Stanford University, 1966.

HENNESSY, BERNARD C., *Public Opinion.* Belmont, Calif.: Wadsworth, 1965.

KNILL, WILLIAM D., "Community Decision Processes: Research Strategies," in *The Politics of Education in the Local Community,* eds. Robert S. Cahill and Stephen Hencley. Danville, Ill.: Interstate Publishers, 1964.

MOGULOF, MELVIN D. "The School as an Opening System," *Urban Education,* IV (Oct. 1969), 231-42.

REICH, CHARLES A., *The Greening of America.* New York: Random House, 1970.

ROSSI, PETER, "Theory, Research and Practice in Community Organization," in *Social Science and Community Action,* ed. Charles R. Adrian. East Lansing, Mich.: Michigan State University, 1960.

TOFFLER, ALVIN, *Future Shock.* New York: Random House, 1970.

# Specifying
# the Uncertain:
# Problem Identification

*two*

The first chapter has elaborated on the need of schoolmen for "understanding the community," for ascertaining the "climate of community expectations." To meet that need the schoolman must, in essence, adopt a problem-solving posture. The first and most important step in problem-solving is to recognize that a problem exists and then to specify it so that it can be answered. It is the purpose of this chapter to aid the administrator in that first step in the process, that is, to help him in translating the broad concerns of the system and the opinion-community into a problem or set of problems that are answerable. It is not an easy task to transform "gut level feelings" into a format that will lend itself to specification and investigation. Our emphasis in this chapter is to approach this task as a systematic process for problem recognition, specification, and action.

### what is a problem?

It may be useful to think of a problem as a deviation. To clarify, imagine that the norm or expectation of parents is that their children will achieve one grade level in arithmetic for each year of schooling. While it is beneficial if they achieve somewhat more than that, it is not too upsetting if their children fall slightly below norms. In fact, if the children increase their arithmetic achievement by one year ± 2 months (that is, if a student in grade X who tests at that level at the start of a year increases as much as 14 months or at least 10 months when tested at the beginning of grade Y) then the achievement progress is considered satisfactory by most parents. However, when children begin to fall below that expectation, that is outside of the ± 2 month *band of tolerance,* then a significant educational deviation or *problem* may be identified by parents and teachers alike. This is a simple specification or translation of someone's feeling or belief that "there are problems in arithmetic in this school" into a demonstrable or measurable picture.

In particular, then, a problem exists when there is a deviation that exceeds some established *tolerance limits.* "Deviation" implies a moving away from something, in this case a norm or expectancy. Figure 2.1 depicts a hypothetical deviation from some undefined expectancy. This type of specification facilitates or at least aids in the future identification of the person or persons manifesting the problem as well as the severity of the problem.

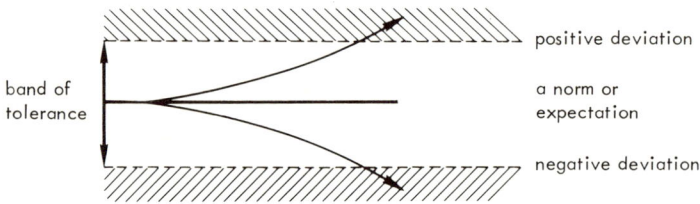

**Figure 2.1**

Deviations from a norm.

To clarify this further and also to put it into the context of "understanding community" we will give an example for visualizing the deviation. Suppose that over time it has been observed that the annual budgets (or bond issues) have been approved in a certain school district rather consistently. Furthermore, the votes in favor have always exceeded the negative votes by at least five percentage points, but never by more than ten percentage points. These observations provide an historical norm or expectancy and an accompanying *band of tolerance* as depicted in Figure 2.2.

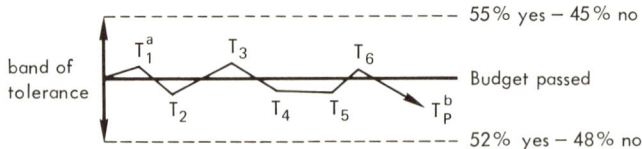

**Figure 2.2**

Deviations within tolerance.

$^a T_1$ = time that the *first* budget vote was recorded.
$^b T_p$ = *present* record of budget vote.

In this case the tolerance limits were established by historical precedent. The limits could also have been set in other ways, for they are man-made placements. They could be established by administrative fiat, by a vote of the board, or by some other decision-making mode, even by a toss of a coin. The *limits* are important only insofar as they are useful for identifying problems. If the *limits* are set too far from the norm then significant deviations will almost never occur; if set too close to the norm then almost any chance fluctuation will indicate a problem and the usual flurry of activities associated with problems will occur. Practice, judgment, and sound argumentation may aid in establishing limits, but they should remain set at one place only as long as they aid in administrative decision-making. No matter what limits are set, they must be examined frequently.

To return to the hypothetical school district and the budget-vote-limits in Figure 2.2, it is obvious that any budget that failed to pass would be well below the lower tolerance line and would constitute a problem. Perhaps not so obvious would be a vote that passes, but only by the narrowest of margins. Suppose, for example, that this year's annual budget received 50.2 percent favorable votes and 49.8 percent of the votes were in opposition. The fact that the budget passed is important. But if the tolerance limits were rationally established, and if that vote falls outside those limits, then a problem has been identified. A significant deviation from the norm has been witnessed. The reasons for such a deviation must be known if the school system is to avoid the risk of a further negative deviation and rejection of future budgets. The vote is shown in Figure 2.3 and its position on the chart is an alert to the need for additional information.

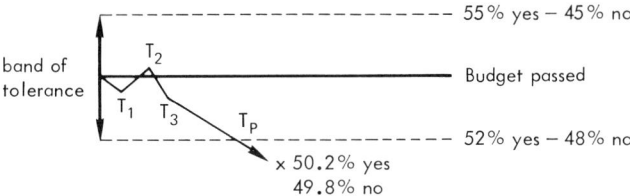

**Figure 2.3**
A significant deviation.

What factors were associated with the narrow passing of the budget? The usual course of action is to make some guesses to explain the event: e.g., "the voters were angry at recent increases in taxes and were merely expressing that dissatisfaction through a convenient outlet"; or, "the introduction of a sex education program has upset some members of the community." *Assuming* such intuitive guessing is accurate, the superintendent might want to begin a systematic consideration of what to expect if taxes continue to rise or other programs enter the curriculum. That is, he might want to determine what his action alternatives might be should the phenomenon continue.

A preferred set of behaviors, though, is that the superintendent start from a position of learned skepticism. Such an attitude is judicious *if* there is still time to assume that posture. If a systematic procedure for specifying and identifying problems is followed, then there may be ample time for preparation. Too often, however, the schoolman is in a position where immediate action is needed, where time is no longer available for collecting information. What is being urged here is that a continuous monitoring of the system be established, maintained, and attended to, so that the number of times the latter situation occurs is minimized.

There is one final aspect of the problem deviation that needs to be examined. To this point consideration has only been directed toward *negative* deviations. It is also advantageous to view *positive* deviations as problems. In the usual sense "problems" are seen as negative events, but in the perspective presented here the term "problem" is neutral. A problem is simply a deviation from a norm, positive or negative, beyond some band of tolerance. If the deviation, whether positive or negative, is unwanted (not valued), then it conforms to the usual conception of a "problem." But rather than operate strictly from a *value position,* the more general approach is to consider *all* significant deviations as problems. To clarify this, the example of budget votes will be examined again.

Suppose that a budget is passed by a very wide margin. For purposes of argument, consider that the community expressed approval for the budget with 72 percent voting favorably and only 28 percent casting negative votes. In this case the graph would depict an increasing deviation on the positive side of the norm (Figure 2.4).

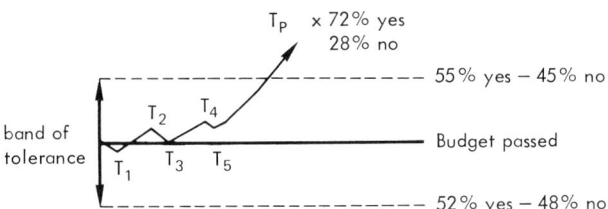

**Figure 2.4**
Significant positive deviation.

Accepting the notion that "problem" is a neutral term, then Figure 2.4 depicts a deviation and, therefore, a problem. Specifically, there is an unusually high deviation on the positive side of the norm. This is a problem in the sense of being worth the schoolman's concerted attention. The concern is to determine what factors might be associated with that deviation. What was special about this event that gave rise to such an extreme vote? If those associated factors can be identified, then perhaps the desires or expectations of the community can be better interpreted. At least the schoolman will be aware of *what* appeals to the community and *why.* When faced with a positive deviation the strategy is to discover the associations and to interpret them for action.

In addition, a positive deviation may signal the possibility that the community expectations are becoming more polar and, in some cases, may result in a significant *negative* deviation with the next referendum. Schoolmen are familiar with the "pendulum" or "action-reaction" nature of polarized districts and should be sensitive to any significant deviation as a warning of potential community reaction.

## a need for problem specification

When faced with significant deviations, positive or negative, the administrator has two basic alternatives: (1) if the deviation is not desirable he can take "corrective" action to return the deviation to the norm; (2) if it is desirable, then "progressive" action can be taken so as to increase the deviation. In most cases the actions will be corrective for negative deviations and progressive for the positive ones. Another way of viewing corrective and progressive actions is as *norm-maintenance* and *norm-transformation*. These are two basic functions for any organization. The preponderance of administrative time is usually spent on the *maintenance* function. But if the administrative emphasis is on maintaining the norms as opposed to transforming norms, then how can the school expect to keep abreast of the changing society? The school system must be alert to positive deviations so as to capitalize on them and move toward new norms or expectancies. Before a norm may be changed it is necessary to ascertain what has been associated with the deviation. Only with that new information can practices be adapted so as to maximize the probability or repeated occurrences of desired actions or events. The same information is needed if norm-maintenance is to persist in areas of negative deviation.

The ascertaining of associated factors is, in essence, an attempt to determine the variables related to the deviation noted. The concern is with the practical events of running a school or school system and of performing that task in a systematic and logical fashion. Finding the related factors to a deviation will facilitate that goal. The administrator must delimit or narrow the problem so that he can identify those factors (events, persons, or attitudes) associated with the deviation. Then and only then will logical action prevail. Perhaps the following case will help clarify the significance of identifying related factors.

*THE CASE OF THE
ASSUMING SUPERINTENDENT*

The school board of a small suburban district put a bond issue for a new junior high school before the public. The building, needed to correct overcrowded conditions, was to contain the very best facilities available. Included in those intended facilities were a large gymnasium and swimming pool. The issue was defeated by a narrow margin. Because the margin was so close, the superintendent and school board were convinced that people did not understand the need. They conducted a second campaign offering more information and, for a second time placed the original bond issue before the public. The vote resulted in a more substantial defeat.

The superintendent and school board returned to the voters one more time. Assuming the rejections were for economic reasons they removed the gymnasium and swimming pool from the requests, thus lowering the cost. This new bond issue was passed by a wide margin.

Actually the superintendent made a poor adjustment based on erroneous assumptions. He would never have learned how poor his assumptions were had a series of events not occurred soon after. He was asked to address the parents and faculty of a large local parochial school. At that meeting he learned that these parents were quite willing to support public educational facilities (as indeed was indicated by the third vote). But, they were opposed to the recreational facilities for public education. Did this opposition arise from a desire to economize? No! On the contrary these parents indicated that such facilities would be welcome, but only if their youngsters could also profit from them.

A separate issue for a gymnasium and pool was once again presented to the community. This time the vote was preceded by a campaign explaining how facilities would be made available to the total community so that all might benefit. Though this issue was considerably more costly than the original request, it passed with an overwhelming vote.

Had the superintendent been able to discover the attitudes of certain substantial segments of the community (in this case the "high school parochial parents" and those who were sympathetic to their position), he would have been able to achieve the original goal by the second vote. As it was, he was quite fortunate in discovering the "cause" or associated factors at the time he did. To reduce that type of determination from a chance occurrence to a systematic likelihood is the purpose of "problem specification."

## a process for problem specification

Problem specification is essentially a two-stage process that helps to narrow-in or focus attention.[1] The narrowing continues until there is sufficient specificity for action. The first stage involves the accumulation of relevant data associated with the problem and helps to limit the problem as to location (where), time (when), and the actors involved (who). The second stage is one of analysis. The accumulated preliminary information must be compared and contrasted to ascertain *why* particular factors may or may not be associated with

---

[1] The process described is similar to that described by Kepner and Tregoe (1965). However, their work concentrates on *material* factor identification in business and industry.

the problem, with the deviation that was noted. This general process of specification is designed to reduce the likelihood of those quick and erroneous assumptions that were described earlier.

## STAGE ONE:
## ASSEMBLING RELEVANT DATA

Assuming that a significant deviation has been identified, the next task is to limit the problem, that is, to determine:

1. *Where* the deviation is occurring and where it is not occurring;
2. *When* the deviation is occurring and when it is not occurring; and
3. *Who* is involved in the occurrence and who is not.

These probes may provide insights and facilitate the first-level identification of "factors" associated with the deviation. To demonstrate these initial steps the sample deviation depicted in Figure 2.3 (see page 19) will be examined. This example involves a bond issue that was passed by a small margin (50.2 percent in favor and 49.8 percent opposed). Having accepted this vote as a significant deviation, it is necessary to assemble relevant information for analysis.

**Where.** A first probe may be to ascertain *where* the deviation is occurring, for example, were the proportions of positive and negative votes the same in all major geographic sectors of the community? To answer this the administrator must first visualize what is meant by "major sectors."

Any geographic area (in this case the particular community where the referendum occurred) may be divided in any number of ways. Certain of the divisions may be advantageous or convenient for the analysis of the problem, that is, for ascertaining the vote-pattern. Following are three examples of such divisions. Figure 2.5 shows a school district divided according to elementary school boundaries within the district. This is a convenient division when votes are recorded or cast in elementary school districts. The second example (Figure 2.6) shows the same school district divided according to the type of living area. If votes could be examined relative to the areas, then certain useful comparisons might be made. To illustrate, if the district transcends a metropolitan area, the suburban voters might be contrasted with urban and rural voters to determine whether or not the issue is perceived similarly in all such areas. Most useful in this type of analysis would be a division of the district in terms of *census tracts*.[2] Figure 2.7 depicts a symmetrical division of the district. Such divisions appear logical but rarely are they practical. The drawing of school district lines was not, historically, a logical process and symmetrical divisions do not coincide with other data-producing sources.

[2]Census tracts as a source of information are considered in the chapter on data storage and retrieval (Chapter 11).

**24** Building a Framework

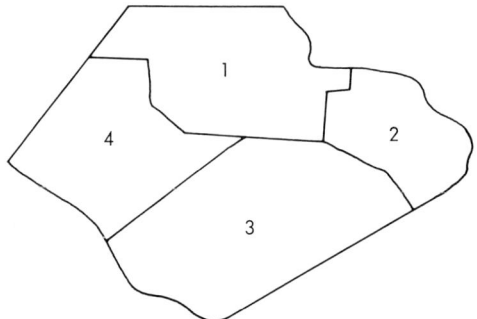

**Figure 2.5**
Elementary school districts.

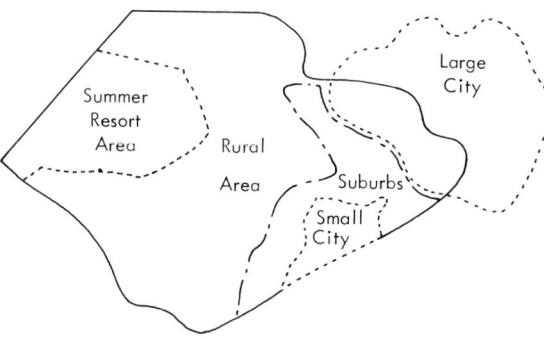

**Figure 2.6**
Type of living area.

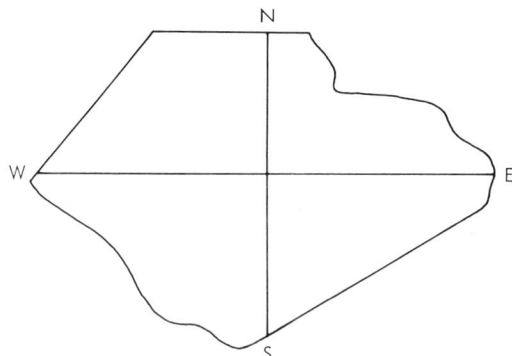

**Figure 2.7**
Simple geographic division.

To elaborate further we will consider the division of the district into elementary school districts. In a real situation the administrator would probably use multiple schemes for narrowing his problem, but this division will be useful for our purposes. It might be convenient, for example, to see if the proportion of votes for and against were approximately equal in each of the elementary districts. Three possible distributions have been developed to demonstrate some of the differences that *may* occur when employing this mode of analysis (see Figures 2.8, 2.9, and 2.10). The total district vote is 8,000 with 50.2 percent (4,106) casting favorable votes and 49.8 percent (3,984) casting opposing ballots. For sake of simplicity let us say that each case also has the same number of subdistricts (four) and the same total vote within the subdistricts when comparing across the three cases. Thus, the number of voters in Elementary School District 1 is the same in Figures 2.8, 2.9, and 2.10. However, by changing the distributions of votes within subdistricts, three divergent community patterns emerge.

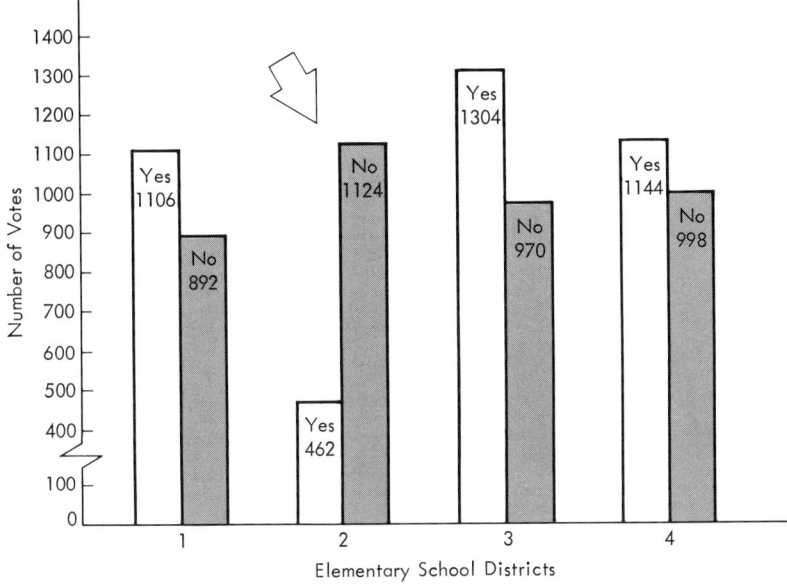

**Figure 2.8**

Voting pattern 1.

The first case, Figure 2.8, shows a community with an identifiable pocket of dissent[3] (see the arrow in the figure). District 2 is strongly opposed to the issue in contrast to the other three districts which show strong support for the bond issue. What is it that is peculiar to that dissenting district? Is this a district that will continue to oppose? And, if so, why?

The next two figures depict a split community with the opposing factions distributed in different patterns. Figure 2.9 shows a split with Districts 1 and 3

---

[3]There is an assumption behind these analyses that in past years the voting patterns of the districts were known and differ from that depicted. If District 2 in Figure 2.8 was always dissenting, then little could be learned from this year's vote since it continued that pattern.

## 26  Building a Framework

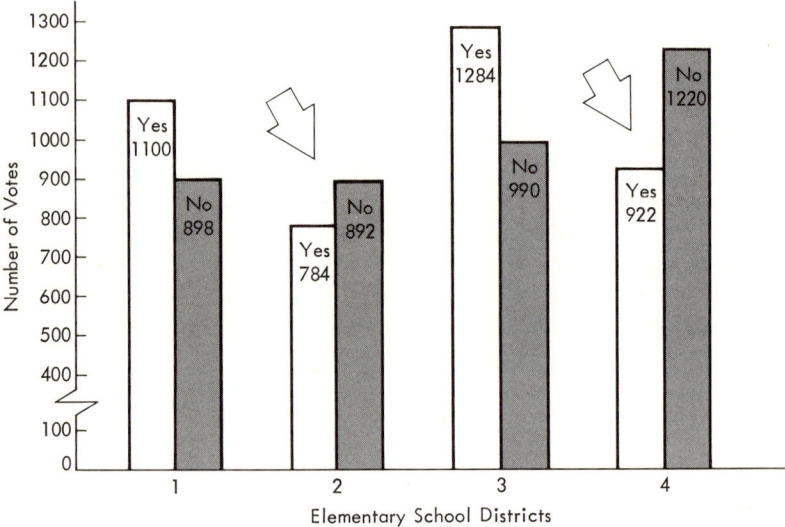

**Figure 2.9**
Voting pattern 2.

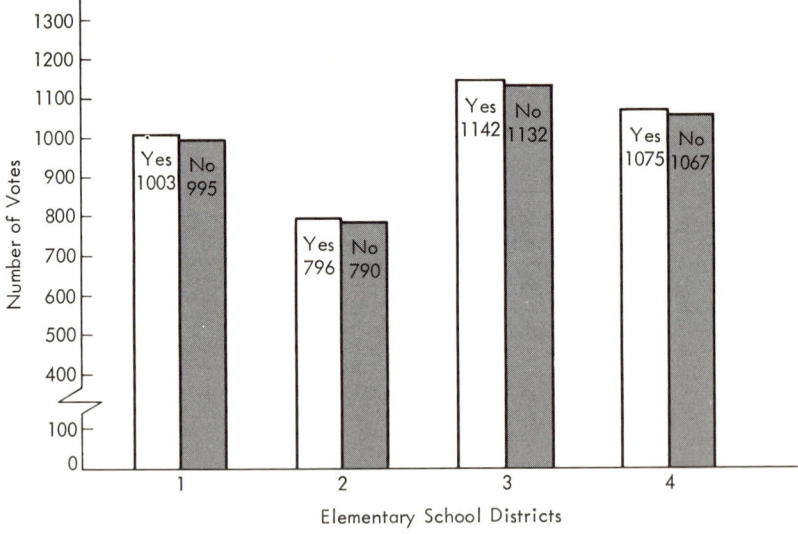

**Figure 2.10**
Voting pattern 3.

favoring the bond issue and Districts 2 and 4 opposing it. With this type of outcome the strategy may be to concentrate on the similarities and differences in the opposing districts. What factors are common to Districts 1 and 3 and are not common to Districts 2 and 4? For example, are there large parochial school populations in two of the districts that are not found in the other two? Are there economic differences? Are there clusters of blue-collar or white-collar workers? Are there any other distinguishing features that can be found?

The split that is indicated in Figure 2.10 crosses all of the district lines. An attempt to view similarities and differences among districts would probably not be a fruitful endeavor for this pattern. The division of the community into Elementary School Districts did not lead to significant differences in the patterns of voting. When this occurs some other geographic division (such as depicted in Figures 2.6 and 2.7) may be attempted or this line of inquiry may be suspended and the *time* area may be examined.

**When.** *When* did the deviation, that is, the vote, occur? This would probably be most helpful where a history of voting was available so as to allow for comparisons and contrasts over time to observe trends. Was there some event or situation that occurred prior to the present vote that did not occur prior to other votes? For example, was there an unusual tax increase, whether state, county, or local, that might be a clue as to a possible precipitating factor? Was there rapid growth in the community or a segment of the community accompanied by the introduction of a new industry or plant? Any such factor of considerable magnitude could be a lead for further investigation.

**Who.** Whether or not the temporal (time) questions uncover possibilities or leads for investigation, the area involving the *people* participating in the deviation should definitely be pursued. *Who* were the voters in favor and who were those opposed? Were there voting differences between males and females? Did the older, middle-aged, and younger voters react differently? Did those with children in the public school vote differently from those without children or those whose children go to private schools? These questions by no means constitute an exhaustive list.

A somewhat longer list of possible questions for each of the probe areas of *where, when,* and *who* is offered below. This list may aid the investigator in identifying possible probes or aid him in generating his own questions. No single set of questions will suffice for all communities and all problems as each community has its own, unique "social mapping." The genesis and development of that mapping is the heart of this first stage of problem specification.

*SUGGESTED QUESTIONS*

Where is the deviation occurring?
1. Throughout the community?
2. In some elementary school districts?
3. In urban areas? Rural areas? In the suburbs?
4. Near certain buildings?
5. In apartment dwellings?

28     Building a Framework

    6. Near recreation areas?
    7. Near the airport? The river? Railroad?
    8. In the streets? In the schools?
    9. In the industrial district? The business section?

Use this space to expand the list for your community:

When is the deviation occurring?
    1. At all times? At regular intervals?
    2. During election years?
    3. During times of crisis?
    4. During inflationary periods?
    5. After a tax increase?
    6. After an opening or closing of a factory?
    7. After the transfer of a golf course?
    8. After condemming of properties?
    9. After a school closing?
    10. After moving to double sessions in a school?
    11. During lunch hours? After school hours?
    12. During summer? Winter? Vacation times? A holiday?

Again, expand the list:

Who is involved in the deviation?
    1. All adults? Certain clusters only? Parents?
    2. Those with school-age children?
    3. Retired persons?
    4. Widows or widowers?
    5. Separated parents?
    6. Business people? Blue-collar workers?
    7. Certain religious groups?
    8. Certain ethnic groups?
    9. Certain racial groups?
    10. Certain age groups?
    11. Those with certain political interests?
    12. Those belonging to service clubs? Fraternities?
    13. Women? Men? Both?
    14. Local garden clubs? Civic associations?
    15. Delinquents? Returning veterans?
    16. The wealthy? The poor?
    17. Those who move frequently?
    18. Those living in the community the longest? Shortest?
    19. Those receiving certain newspapers? Or magazines? Or school publications?

20. Absentee owners? Renters? Homeowners? Mobile home owners?
If these suggest others write them in:

Answering the questions given above requires considerable information. Some of it is readily available. More may have to be collected and organized. In either case, the next step in the process of problem specification is to assemble the information in a systematic way for analysis, for ascertaining *why* the deviation occurred.

*STAGE TWO:*
*ASCERTAINING THE WHY*

To assist in discovering the "most plausible explanation" for a deviation, it is suggested that a *form* or *model* be employed for systematically recording what is known. The purpose of using a model is to organize what is known, aid in analysis of that arranged information, and thus enable the user to ascertain what information is still necessary to explain the particular deviation. There are many models that might be appropriate and we encourage experimentation and adaptation of such models to fit individual styles. For illustrative purposes two models will be described here; the first by Kepner and Tregoe (1965) and the second developed by the authors. To clarify the use of these models we will apply them to the "Case of the Assuming Superintendent" described earlier. It should be noted, though, that the models described have general applicability and are not restricted to such bond referendum or vote-type problems as depicted in the case we are using. We have employed these models with a diversity of problems ranging from student disturbances outside a single classroom to enrollment projections for a district's adult education programs (see Chapter 9). The important point is that models can be helpful! Here are two that merit attention.

**Model 1: Kepner and Tregoe.** The Kepner and Tregoe model for recording and analyzing information stresses the building of parallel lists of information about the deviation for comparison and contrast analyses. Central to the listing is a column indicating where the deviation IS occurring and a parallel list of where the deviation IS NOT to be found. For example, if the Assuming Superintendent had used the Kepner-Tregoe model to try to identify those groups that voted negatively on the bond referendum, he might have completed his form like that in Figure 2.11. He would then search the two lists for similarities or a common thread in the IS column that is different or not to be found in the IS NOT column. His intent would be to isolate possible factors related to the deviation.

What is similar about "citizens without children," "Catholics without children," and "Catholics with children in parochial schools"? One possible similarity might relate to financial burden: that is, citizens without children may be older and live on restricted incomes while Catholic parents may also have

**Figure 2.11**[a]

Form 1, Deviation: negative votes for a bond issue as completed by the "Assuming Superintendent."

| Is | Is Not |
|---|---|
| Deviation is found among: | Deviation is not found among: |
| many citizens without children, many Catholics, most Catholics with children in parochial schools. | some citizens without children, some Catholics, most Catholics with children in public schools, most citizens with children in public schools. |

[a]Adapted from Kepner-Tregoe, 1965.

restricted finances as a result of heavy tuition burdens. However, before accepting this speculation the superintendent would examine the IS NOT column to see if that similarity was also to be found there. Once again, if the group identified as "some citizens without children" are mainly younger persons with an income that is not fixed, then possibly that type of financial burden may be missing. What this analysis would have led to is a "best guess" explanation or an *hypothesis*. But is it the best explanation? Is it the only hypothesis? Are there competing explanations or hypotheses that might explain the deviation?

A second look at the list would have indicated that there is another similarity. The groups in the IS column appear to have little access to existing or proposed school facilities. Either those groups have no children or are using nonpublic educational facilties. Is this missing from the parallel column? If the groups noted as "some citizens without children" do make use of the public school facilities (possibly through adult education) then the similarity is missing. This, then, becomes an alternative hypothesis. Perhaps still others could be generated. Every hypothesis generated must be tested for acceptability. Information must be gathered for that purpose.

**Model 2: Possible-Probable.** The second model has been found useful by the present authors for identifying leads for investigation. Figure 2.12 depicts a *form* where the headings "probable" and "possible" are provided so that the user may indicate, based upon his best judgments and preliminary analysis, those areas that are likely leads for further study. The "probable" category indicates a lead that appears to have a first priority. That is, the probable leads indicate highest potential explanatory payoff. The "possible" heading, while indicating a lead, is a low or second-order priority and thus indicates the lowest potential explanatory payoff. Speculations concerning causes which have not been uncovered in the "what, when, where, whom" exercise of *stage one*, but which

**Figure 2.12**
Form 2, Problem specification.

| What is Known | Probable Lead | Possible Lead |
|---|---|---|
| What is the deviation? | | |
| When did it occur? | | |
| Where? | | |
| With whom? | | |
| Hunches | | |

the schoolman feels might be related to the deviation, should be listed separately under "hunches."

The *process* of completing the form is as important as the information listed on it. It is recommended that the user cross-check his perceptions or responses to the questions on the form by asking individuals in various roles, both within and outside of the school system, for their observations. Thus, a superintendent might query board members, principals, teachers, and parents for their perceptions of the deviation — where it occurred, when, and with whom. Where the perceptions differ, the several observations should be recorded with the initial of that person following his statement. The initialed perceptions enable the user to identify who he differs with so that he may check back with such sources at a later date if such proves necessary.

To demonstrate the use of the form, we have completed it as the superintendent might have in the "Case of the Assuming Superintendent" (Figure 2.13). The superintendent would indicate on the form that the bond issue was defeated in July immediately after the public information campaign was completed. Since this was the procedure and timing for previous issues it does not seem likely that it is a high priority lead. Nevertheless, it is still a potential lead since there may be something in that timing that is just not yet evident.

**Figure 2.13**

Form 2, as completed by the "Assuming Superintendent."

| What is Known | Probable Lead | Possible Lead |
|---|---|---|
| What is the deviation? <br><br> Defeat of Bond Issue <br> Higher negative vote than expected | | |
| When did it occur? <br><br> In the month of July. After distribution of campaign brochures. After series of meetings. | | ✓ <br> ✓ <br> ✓ |
| Where? <br><br> Throughout the district (S) <br> Many negative votes in certain neighborhoods (P) | ✓ | |
| With whom? <br><br> Many Catholics <br> Many citizens without children | ✓ <br> ✓ | |
| Hunches <br><br> General pattern of bond defeats in the area | | ✓ |

Next on the form the superintendent would indicate that *he* perceived the negative votes as spread throughout the district (initialed "S." for superintendent). If that was so, then it would not seem that location or geographic area of the vote would be a high priority lead for further study. However, he has noted that a parent (initialed "P.") observed an unusually large number of negative votes in his neighborhood. This divergence of perception warrants further investigation.

In the section dealing with people involved in the deviation (*With whom?*) the superintendent would indicate that his analysis leads him to believe that this is an important area for further investigation. He suspects that a substantial percentage of Catholics as well as citizens without children have cast a large proportion of the negative votes. It might be easy for him to dismiss these persons as people who always resist taxes or tax increases, but he is wary and alerts himself to leads for further study. What he needs now is further information to help trace the leads. He would have to know if, in fact, the majority of Catholics did vote against the referendum. Or, might it be that only certain identifiable groups of Catholics voted against it?

Some hypotheses can be tested without developing sophisticated and expensive probes. For example, if, with information already at hand, the superintendent could determine whether the group of "most citizens without children" was predominantly young or old, then he should pursue that course of action. However, if information did not exist to test the competing hypotheses, the superintendent would have to gather further information. His initial analysis, as demonstrated through the two models, would have enabled him to narrow his questioning so as to maximize responses and minimize expense. He is now faced with finding ways or methods that will enable him to get the information he needs.

## summary

This chapter focused on the specification and identification of problems. A problem was identified as a deviation from a norm or expectancy. The deviation is seen as significant or requiring attention when it passes an established band of tolerance. Since a problem is viewed as a neutral term, it is possible to depict a problem as a deviation in either a negative or positive direction. Using this conception of a problem, the alternatives for the administrator are to seek to return a deviation to the norm (norm-maintenance) or to increase and continue the deviation (norm-transformation). For either action there is a need for delimiting the problem so as to identify possible factors associated with the deviation.

The identification of associated factors, that is, problem specification, is viewed as a two-stage sequential process of narrowing the problem. The initial stage is a process of accumulating and arranging information as to *where* the deviation is or is not occurring; *when* the deviation is or is not occurring; and *who* is or is not involved in that deviation. Suggested questions for each of these probe-areas are also included.

For the second stage of analyzing to ascertain *why* a deviation is occurring two models were described. The first was a format for comparing and contrasting which can lead to hypotheses; the second was a form for generating leads for further study. In both cases the process helps to draw initial parameters around the deviation, a critical step in problem-solving. If specification is done well — funneling the fullest possible scope of information obtained from all sources into the deviation framework — it is possible to identify the information needed to understand the reasons for the deviation.

With the information-needs identified, the schoolman must determine which method for data collection he might pursue. To be able to do this he must have some knowledge of the methods available, the benefits, costs, and purposes of each. Which methodological approaches will best fulfill his information needs? What outcomes can be expected from using a particular method? The next chapter introduces methodological approaches and details the information the schoolman needs to make a logical and rational choice of methods.

reference

KEPNER, CHARLES H., and BENJAMIN B. TREGOE, *The Rational Manager: A Systematic Approach to Problem Solving and Decision Making.* New York: McGraw-Hill, 1965.

# Identifying the Unknown: Methodologies

*three*

Thus far the discussion has focused upon ways of specifying probable and possible factors related to deviations. This specification process helps draw the initial parameters around deviations; a critical step in problem-solving. If specifications are done well — funneling the *fullest* possible scope of information obtained from *all* potential sources into the deviation framework — it should be possible to identify what further information will be needed to ascertain which of the probable and possible leads might help the schoolman to understand the deviation.

It now becomes necessary to seek information that can lead to understanding the deviations and thus provide a rational basis for decision-making. To be able to do this the schoolman must have some knowledge of the methods available and the benefits and costs of each. Which methodological approaches will best fulfill information needs? What are the costs, in terms of time, manpower, and dollars, of the various methods? What outcomes can be expected from using each method? How much skill is required to carry out the various methods? The chief school officer will want to know enough about these considerations so that he can, in concert with the administrator in charge of the monitoring effort, make intelligent decisions regarding the understanding process.

The purpose of this chapter is to introduce methodological approaches which may be used by school administrators as they seek to answer the problems they have specified. A framework will be provided to help schoolmen develop an understanding of the several methods available after which each method will be briefly described and criteria for methods selection will be presented. A case will be developed to illustrate how schoolmen might select among the methods and use them to understand deviations in their school districts.

*TWO CAUTIONS*

Before putting on his "research glasses" the reader is reminded that problems often call for more than one information-seeking approach if full and sufficient information is to be attained. In general it is probable that several techniques employed in tandem will provide greater breadth and depth of information than will any single technique. Human problems are complex and all methodologies have their advantages and disadvantages. Therefore we urge our readers to familiarize themselves with as many potentially useful methods as is possible.

Further, as information is collected, understandings about the problem will increase. As these understandings are developed they will lead to further questions to be answered and thus necessitate that additional information be gathered. Eventually, as specification of the deviation increases, information needs will decrease, but, in all probability, the schoolman will have to seek information several times during the process of deviation specification and problem resolution.

## a way of thinking about methodologies

Methods which might be used in seeking to understand discrepancies can be grouped under two general headings: *document search* and *survey research*.[1] Document search is basically "an attempt to find out what has happened in the course of time and to correlate the events, within the limits of available materials on the one hand and of the researcher's intelligence and understanding on the other, into a meaningful sequence [Rummel, 1964, p. 170]." The schoolman, when carrying out document search, will seek out what is available and put it into a form which is useful for explaining the deviation at hand. That is, he will

---

[1] Another method, *observation,* could be added. However, it is not centrally germane to the purposes of the book, so we have chosen not to deal with it. The interested reader is referred to the following sources for treatment of this topic: Frank W. Lutz and Laurence Iannaccone, *Understanding Educational Organizations: A Field Study Approach* (Columbus, Ohio: Charles E. Merrill, 1969), see especially Chap. 5; W. Richard Scott, "Field Methods in the Study of Organizations," in James G. March, ed., *Handbook of Organizations* (Skokie, Ill.: Rand McNally, 1965), pp. 261-305; and Eugene J. Webb, Donald T. Campbell, Richard D. Schwartz, and Lee Sechrest, *Unobtrusive Measures: Non-Reactive Research in the Social Sciences* (Skokie, Ill.: Rand McNally, 1966), pp. 112-71.

retrieve information which is already in existence but which must be reformulated to meet specific needs.

Survey research differs from document search in a very basic way. While information sought through document search exists but must be reformulated, information sought through survey research does not exist in any form until the analyst develops it. Those who can provide the required information are members of the community. The schoolman is required to actively seek this information by developing questions and asking them of these persons.

These two methods, both of which will be explored in detail in the following chapters, constitute the major avenues for understanding problems in the community. Document search allows the schoolman to delve into the past to discover antecedent events to a deviation. It also helps him understand ways in which the community has responded to similar situations in the past. Survey research helps him to understand the present, clarifying unknowns which cannot be answered by document search, and provides directions for the future. Thus the two methods are complementary: Document search focusing on the past to the present and survey research focusing on the present to the future. The reader may prefer to organize these methods differently than as depicted in Table 3.1 and is encouraged to do so if another scheme seems more useful. It is important only that he be able to recognize methodologies and their uses so that when needed, he can choose the methods which offer the greatest promise of obtaining information necessary to understand a specific deviation.

The two methods lead to different kinds of information to clarify problems. There will be instances when the choice of one of these methods is quite clear. At other times it may be appropriate to use both to good advantage. Generally document search should be pursued first. The search may provide sufficient information to clarify the problem. If not, it will at least help to clarify what should be sought in survey research, often raising questions not anticipated before the document search. In short, document search leads to an understanding of what is known and what is not known.

*Primary sources* consist of reports of persons who have participated in or witnessed an activity or event. *Secondary sources* consist of documents which are developed on the basis of original statements (i.e., primary sources) of an activity or event. Secondary sources may be sufficient if the search is only exploratory in nature, seeking to establish the general picture of a deviation. However, if specification and resolution of problems is to be achieved the administrator will have to test the accuracy of the "general picture" through a review of primary sources.

If it becomes clear that survey research is an appropriate method, the schoolman can choose to use an interview or a questionnaire approach, or some combination of both. Interviews are face-to-face question and answer sessions between a trained questioner and the respondent. Questionnaires require only

**Table 3.1**

**Methods and Sample Content: Document Search and Survey Research**

| Methods | Sample Content |
|---|---|
| Document Search | |
| Primary Sources | Legal papers; school board records; city council minutes; and census data |
| Secondary Sources | Newspaper articles; histories; journals; and magazines |
| Survey Research | |
| Interviews | In-depth, face-to-face encounters with key actors who might have specific information about a deviation: e.g., community leaders; municipal officials; and special interest group leaders |
| | Less frequently, with "typical" citizens-random selection of persons from the community: e.g., parents of children at particular schools or members of minority groups |
| Questionnaires | Large-scale pollings of persons representative of those involved in a deviation: e.g., persons who voted in a recent budget election; students and parents involved in a school boycott; and parents whose children will have to attend an integrated school |

that the respondent read and react to questions on a survey instrument. The schoolman must decide whether he will rely on interviews; some combination of interviews and questionnaires; or strictly on questionnaires. Selection of survey format depends upon many variables including the purposes of the survey; the extent to which the problem is community-wide or relates to a specific subgroup; the characteristics of potential respondents; the fiscal resources available for the project; time constraints; and the skills of the persons doing the surveying. The major advantages and disadvantages of interviewing and questionnairing are summarized in Table 3.2.

An examination of Table 3.2 should indicate that much thought must be given to selecting the most appropriate survey procedures to obtain information through survey research. There is no one "right" way to survey; the choice of approach depends upon the deviation identified and the information required for understanding the basis of that deviation. The discussion found in the next section should help clarify which approach is most appropriate to gain information about a given discrepancy.

**Table 3.2**
**Interviews and Questionnaires: Advantages and Disadvantages**

| Survey Technique | Advantages | Disadvantages |
|---|---|---|
| Questionnaires | Low cost of information gathering. | Relatively little chance that "unexpected" information will be derived (self-administration of the instrument requires that questions be highly structured). |
| | Potential to obtain information from large numbers of the community population. | |
| | Relatively little involvement of high cost personnel. | Limitations on the scope of questions to assure that answers match questions. |
| | Relatively easy to code and store information. | If respondent does not understand the questions asked, there is no opportunity for interpretation by the schoolman. |
| | Relatively short time needed to survey the target population. | |
| Interviews | Potential exists to follow up unexpected information obtained during course of interview. | High cost of information-gathering if using paid interviewers. |
| | Possibility of asking more complex questions due to fact that the interviewer can help the respondent if further clarification is required. | Relatively long time needed to obtain information (often from one-half hour to two hours per interview). |
| | | Relatively high risk that respondent will "turn-off" if interview is lengthy. |
| | | Complex coding process of open-ended information takes much time and risk that coder will misunderstand intent is high. |

## criteria for selection of methods

The process described thus far includes problem specification, gathering of existing information, and identification of unanswered questions. Now the schoolman must select the most appropriate methods for answering those questions. There are several criteria which can guide him to the selection of the most appropriate methods. These criteria include accessibility, relevance, accuracy, economy of resources, and skills and time available. (See Richardson, 1965, for another discussion of criteria for methods selection.)

## ACCESSIBILITY

By which method is the desired information most readily obtainable? For example, it is feasible to ascertain size of family units among households which have children in the school system either through review of the school census data or through a door-to-door saturation survey. Obviously, the former method is more efficient, but in addition the information is infinitely more accessible. Surveying the total population probably would not yield as complete information as a simple review of the census data can provide. In other cases information will only be accessible through one method. For example, citizens' attitudes toward a proposed addition to the curriculum of sex education probably cannot be obtained through document search, but can be ascertained through a survey. Finally, there are times when the information desired will be accessible through the use of two or more methods employed in tandem. For example, how citizens will vote in the next school board election might best be predicted through a combination of analysis of recent board elections and a sample survey of citizens who might be expected to vote in the coming election.

## RELEVANCE

Will the methods employed result in useful and complete information?[2] That is, will they provide information that directly answers the questions? For example, if the schoolman wants to find out how the community feels about the school district's work-study program, collection of data related to the socioeconomic status of the community over time might be interesting, but it probably would be more appropriate to devise a questionnaire to get at attitudes of citizens toward work-study programs and administer it to members of the community. Relevance, in short, should help the schoolman to decide which methodology promises collection of the most useful information.

## ACCURACY

Which method gives promise of producing the most precisely correct information? For example, the administrator might want to know if the community favors a curriculum which emphasizes either preparation for the world of work or preparation for higher education. How would he obtain the most accurate information about the views of citizens on this question? Would document search through the local newspapers to derive statements of community leaders give him this information? Probably not, because community leaders can only make public pronouncements which are based upon *what they*

---

[2]This question relates as much to initial deviation specification as it does to methodology selection. The extent to which the specification process goes beyond the superficial or gross level towards insights which can help to determine the methods to be employed, the more payoff that can be expected from the information-gathering effort.

*think* is preferred by citizens in the community. To increase the accuracy of information, it probably would be necessary to go directly to the community and survey a sample of persons about the question.

## ECONOMY OF RESOURCES

If several methods can be used to obtain the desired information, which among them promises to be the most economical? Questions of economy must be asked at all stages of the information-seeking project. These questions should be concerned with the economies of:

1. Identifying the information sources;
2. Obtaining the information from these sources;
3. Analyzing the resultant information;
4. Putting the findings into usable form.

How much manpower will each method require? What about supplies, travel, and dissemination costs? Although precise figures often cannot be detailed, estimates of costs at the outset should provide useful information for deciding on appropriate methods.

Questions concerning accessibility, relevance, and accuracy should also be considered when thinking about costs. Often the least expensive method is the most inappropriate method, and, therefore not economical at all. For example, if document search is considered because of its low cost features and the deviation at hand calls for surveys, *then document search is inappropriate.* At some point the schoolman will have to balance economy of resources against accessibility, relevance, and accuracy. He wants useful information to understand his community, but at some point costs become prohibitive. He will have to decide the point at which the added accuracy and relevance of information to be obtained is prohibitive given expected costs in manpower, dollars, time, and, possibly, good will of citizens.

## SKILL AND TIME

How well equipped are the schoolman and his staff to use the various information-seeking methods? This is a critical question and should be given considerable thought before methods are selected. For example, what methodological expertise is available? Similarly, is there sufficient time to devote to the project? Assuming that appropriate methods are selected and the administrator assigned is well versed in the techniques to be used, if he is unable to devote the requisite time, it makes no sense to launch an ambitious information-seeking project. Where it is clear that he lacks one of these resources, are there others to whom he can turn who have such skills or available time? These practical questions should not be slighted in the methods selection process.

In summary, then, choice of methods should be made upon multiple criteria. These criteria cannot usually be put into a formula. As Richardson (1965, p. 31) notes, "The ultimate choice of a data-gathering method depends, therefore, not on abstractly matching the method with the problem but on a careful examination of the subject matter, the group to be studied, budgetary limitations, and the characteristics of the investigator."

## selecting methods: a case study

The remainder of the chapter applies what we have discussed about methods, exploring how to narrow in on the selection of procedures for seeking information about communities. In "Milbrook Citizens Reject a Bond Issue" we will follow the superintendent as he clarifies the problem using appropriate staff personnel, and seeks understanding about it. In the process we will present a form which can help the reader as he finds himself faced with the need to select methods for problem clarification.

### MILBROOK'S CITIZENS REJECT A BOND ISSUE

By 1973 it had become clear to the school board and superintendent of the Milbrook School District that a junior high built in 1924 would soon have to be replaced. The building was entirely inadequate to meet the needs of the curriculum of the 1970s. Therefore the board decided to go to the community with a referendum requesting approval for funds to build a new junior high and to renovate the old junior high school for use as an elementary school.

The school board and Superintendent Goodell and his staff conducted a vigorous campaign to explain the proposal. The main thrust of their argument was that the building was obsolete and a more modern structure was needed that would be more suitable for the present and planned curriculum.

The people of Milbrook had, until this time, demonstrated strong and continuous support for their public schools. The school district had never lost a school budget election. Similarly, all 25 bond referendums put to the people from the formation of the school district in 1948, through 1972, had been approved. The total cost of these bonds to the community was $31,500,000.

The bond referendum, held in February, 1973, precipitated the largest turnout of voters in the history of the district. The community, breaking precedent, rejected the bond referendum by a resounding 3,925 against 2,184 for the proposal.

### THE DISCREPANCY

A majority vote was required if the bond referendum was to be approved. Contrary to expectation, this did not occur. As a result the funds required for building a new school plant and renovating an old school plant would not be available. Assuming that the school board wanted to go back to the community for funds in the near future to meet the building requirements which would only become more acute with time, Superintendent Goodell set out to gain as much understanding as possible about the factors associated with the negative vote on the bond referendum.

*PROBLEM SPECIFICATION*

Employing Form 2 ("Problem Specification"), Goodell and his staff started the investigation by talking with as many knowledgeable people as was feasibly possible, both inside and outside of the school system. They recorded the results of these discussions as indicated in Figure 3.1.

Having identified the knowns and best guesses concerning the deviation, Goodell now had to ascertain what information would be required to check out the noted leads. Further, he had to develop specifications regarding what methods would be employed to obtain this information. To do these things, he met with his school-community director and research specialist who would be responsible for carrying out the day-to-day monitoring activities. They used the form "From Problem Specification to Information Gathering" to help them decide on an appropriate strategy. The results of this exercise are summarized in Figure 3.2.

**Information-gathering.** The superintendent and his staff had thus proceeded from deviation specification to listing the information needed and stating the methods which might be required to obtain this information. The exercise led them to the conclusion that they might have to employ both document search and survey research. It was possible that document search might provide sufficient information, so they proceeded with this approach before making a decision about using the survey approach.

When documents were analyzed, Superintendent Goodell possessed information which led to a clearer understanding of the deviation. Some of this information had already been collected for other purposes, so it was not long before the following facts were brought to light:

1. There was a community trend away from support of the schools over the last decade. Bond referendums early in the 1960s received between 70 and 80 percent favorable votes. Referendums late in the 1960s received between 55 and 65 percent favorable votes.
2. During the past year the community had narrowly (by 52 percent) approved a municipal bond for a new sewage system. A state bond request for highway improvements failed to pass in Milbrook (60 percent against), although it was approved state-wide by 55 percent of those voting.
3. School-aged population, which had increased at a rapid rate between 1950 and 1967, leveled off until 1970 when it actually declined by 167

**Figure 3.1**

Form 2: Problem specification: the Milbrook bond rejection.

| What is Known | Probable Lead | Possible Lead |
|---|---|---|
| **What is the deviation?**<br>—Defeat of the Bond Issue (3,925 opposed, 2,184 in favor). First time ever that a bond issue was defeated. | | ✓ |
| **When did it occur?**<br>—February 19, 1973<br>—Following campaign stressing need to remodel plant to meet curriculum requirements (A.S.) | ✓ | ✓ |
| **Where?**<br>—Heavy negative vote indicates a general community-wide discrepancy | ✓ | |
| **With whom?**<br>—High suspicion that community median age is increasing and thus there would be many citizens without children in school (S.) | ✓ | |
| **Hunches**<br>—Fear that new school could be used to integrate the district, bussing in black children from the neighbouring city.<br>—Innovative school design (open class rooms).<br>—Keeping old buildings as a school might have diluted campaign impact. (P.) | | ✓<br><br>✓<br>✓ |

S = superintendent
AS = assistant superintendent
P = parent

**Figure 3.2**

Form 3: From problem specification to information gathering (as filled out by Superintendent Goodell).

| Leads to Deviations | Information Needed to Determine Accuracy of Lead | Methods for Collecting Information |
|---|---|---|
| **Probable Leads** | | |
| 1. Campaign stressing needs for open-school design | Attitudes of citizens toward new school plant concept | Survey representative sample of citizens concerning acceptability of school plant innovations |
| 2. Wide-spread negative note (suspected) | Area breakdown of voting patterns | Analysis of vote returns by precinct (mapping) |
| 3. Citizens without children voting against the issue (suspected) | Demographic analysis of voting patterns | Survey the voters, cross tabulate demographic information with responses |
| **Possible Leads** | | |
| 1. First defeat of a bond issue in the district (also wide margin of defeat) | a) past voting records<br>b) current district votes on other tax issues (e.g. municipal bonds, state bonds) | a) Document search (Reviewed poll records over last decade)<br>b) Comparison of school and other tax referendum votes (form of trend analysis) |
| 2. Innovative school design | Attitudes of citizens toward school design, curriculum, innovation, etc. | Survey representative sample of the community |
| 3. Keeping old buildings in spite of arguing over its inadequacy | Attitudes of citizens toward this campaign strategy | Survey representative sample of the community |
| 4. Fear of racial integration | Attitudes of citizens | Surveys |

students. Recent projections indicated that there would be a continuing steady decline in the school-aged population until 1980.
4. Between 1940 and 1960, Milbrook was a rapid growth area, doubling in population, but now it appears that Milbrook is population saturated. It is surrounded by communities on all sides (on one side by a city). Most housing is individual-owner occupied and existing zoning laws make it difficult to build additional residential housing.
5. The population which, on the basis of income, can be typed as middle class, is highly sedentary. Several possible reasons have been offered for this fact, including a general positive perception of the community and the public schools.
6. The deviation occurred district-wide, but some variations appeared. The highest negative votes came from precincts which were heavily populated by people who were older than the average adult population of the community.

The preceding information, gathered through document search, indicated that many of the initial guesses might, in fact, be related to the present deviation. Further, the new information enabled Superintendent Goodell to modify and add to his initial estimations. The district-wide occurrence of the deviation, the declining level of bond referendum support in the community and the rejection of the state bond indicated that understanding the deviation would require that information be gathered from a broad spectrum of the residents of the community.

Superintendent Goodell, along with the school-community director and the research specialist, next reviewed the criteria for methods selection. They decided that gathering information from "a broad spectrum" of the community in a relevant manner required that an in-depth survey of citizens be conducted. To obtain accurate information in the most economical manner in this instance would require that the survey be of the questionnaire form, as interviewing "a broad spectrum" would be impractical fiscally and time-wise. Finally, having an experienced school-community office and a research office in the system, they felt that there was adequate expertise available to conduct the survey.

Therefore, they decided to proceed with a community survey, using the questionnaire format, to see if these tentative understandings would hold up in the light of broad-based, representative citizen responses. As noted above, a general survey by questionnaire was selected because initial information-gathering indicated that the deviation would indeed by found throughout the community. Where there were suspicions that certain subgroups voted negatively more often than other subgroups, this could readily be tested if appropriate demographic questions (e.g., age, sex, parental status, and income) were included in the questionnaire.

The original leads which had not been satisfactorily tracked down through document search were then reformulated as questions and a questionnaire was developed. The planning group decided to restrict the survey to those who voted in the bond referendum since it was this group of citizens that played a role in the deviation. Therefore, respondents were randomly selected from the poll book of the last bond referendum. Selected respondents received the questionnaire in the mail and were asked to complete it and then return it in an enclosed self-addressed and stamped envelope. Approximately 60 percent of those surveyed did respond. Returned questionnaires were coded and tabulated by personnel in the research office (by hand, since all questions were "choice" probes and thus did not require complex tabulation).

After analyzing the results of the survey Superintendent Goodell was able to present the board with two lists: those factors which seemed related to the defeat of the bond referendum and those factors which did not appear to affect its defeat. In particular, those factors which did appear to affect negative voting included:

1. *Increasing town, county, state, and federal taxes.* Respondents indicated that the school bond referendum was one way of making their dissatisfaction felt concerning this trend;
2. *The innovative school design of the proposed building and the suggested curriculum to be established in it.* Respondents felt negatively about changing from more "traditional" buildings and curriculums to the newer buildings and curricular ideas;
3. *School officials and citizen suggestions.* Respondents felt that the campaign leading up to the bond referendum did not afford them an opportunity to have a say about the proposed school. That is, while school officials appeared to listen to citizen suggestions, in the final analysis, citizens felt that their suggestions were not taken into consideration; and
4. *Need for the school.* Most respondents did not understand why a new school plant was necessary. They reasoned that, since the population of the town had leveled off, there was no further need for expansion of the school district.

Further, significant differences appeared between subgroups on these four factors. An analysis of responses by demographic subgroups showed that parents with children in parochial schools and citizens without children in the schools (mostly older citizens) reacted more negatively to these factors than did other groups.

Factors which respondents felt did not lead to the defeat of the bond referendum, included:

1. *Quality of education available in the district.* Both those in favor of the bond referendum and those opposed to it agreed that the quality of education in the district was high;
2. *Proposed location of the new junior high school.* Respondents felt that there would not be a transportation problem since bussing would be available. No significant resistance to bussing was discovered; and

48    Building a Framework

3. *Proximity to neighboring city and potential for racial integration programs.* School officials felt that citizens might suspect that racial integration would follow if a new plant were constructed. Respondents were indeed opposed to racial integration, but did not feel that integration would result if the bond referendum were approved.

Now that leads had been checked out, the school board and the superintendent were in a much better position to decide what to do about the school district's building needs. One factor, tax increases in other governmental jurisdictions, was beyond their control. However, the other three related factors could be dealt with. Innovative designs and curriculum could be modified and/or more fully explained to the community. School officials could work at establishing greater community involvement in initial decision-making to reduce the lack of understanding. They also probably could create an aura of need for the new facility. Further, knowing which factors did not affect voter behavior would make it possible for them to concentrate their analysis and further campaign — if such were deemed advisable — on those issues which appeared salient. For example, it might be necessary for them to continue to point out the high quality of education available in the school district to *maintain* good will, but not to gain further positive votes.

We are not here concerned with the course of action taken by the Milbrook school board. At this point human preference enters the picture. What is important is that with this information the school board and superintendent were in a much better position to make decisions. They were in a better position because they had systematically listed factors which appear to be related to the discrepancy; gathered existing information (document search) to provide further clarification; and then gathered information which did not already exist in some form (survey research). As a caution it should be pointed out that the time consumed in the process of gathering the information was probably greater than might appear in this capsulated report of the case. There are no shortcuts; collecting information about the community is a major task, but the potential payoffs should make it more than worthwhile.

summary

Means of gathering information about problems were presented. Table 3.1 categorized methods according to document search and survey research. Document search brings together information which exists in some form but must be reformulated. Survey research is employed to collect information which does not presently exist in any form. Limitations and advantages of the two survey approaches, interviews and questionnaires, were presented in Table 3.2.

# Identifying the Unknown: Methodologies        49

Criteria for selecting methods to obtain desired information were presented. These criteria include accessibility, relevance, accuracy, economy of resources, and the ability and time available of the schoolman who is assigned to carry out the information-seeking effort. It should be possible to select the best method or methods to obtain necessary information by matching information needs with the foregoing criteria.

Finally, to illustrate how these criteria and subsequent methods might be applied we presented a case study of Milbrook, a school district which lost a bond referendum election. The steps through which the superintendent went from initial definition of the discrepancy to the collection of necessary information were summarized.

Cautionary notes were given in the chapter. First, the need for adequate specification of the deviation cannot be over-stressed. If initial specification is incomplete or erroneous then the information gathered will also be incomplete or erroneous. Therefore it is recommended that the widest possible group of school-district members be involved in the initial specification process. Second, the schoolman should be aware that usually no single method will suffice to achieve full understanding of discrepancies. Employing two or more methods will usually result in more and different types of information than will the use of one method. Finally, as new information is fed into the system, the discrepancy should be further specified accordingly. More likely than not, as new information is developed and the discrepancy form is updated, it will be discovered that new leads appear and more information will be required. When new information no longer leads to the call for further information, it is probable that the schoolman has completed the information-seeking tasks.

The authors assume that all schoolmen attempt to understand deviations in their district. What we do not assume is that schoolmen, because they lack time or skill, account for all factors in their analysis. The reader can test this assumption by completing a discrepancy exercise. Recall a discrepancy situation in your own school district. Then fill out the discrepancy form in Figure 3.3.

The reader, after concluding the discrepancy form, might ask himself these questions. Does he feel that the form would have been more completely filled out if other persons who know of the discrepancy were involved in the exercise? Does the form lead to the development of leads which can be followed up through the use of document search and/or survey research? Would two or more methods provide more information than one method? If most of these questions can be answered affirmatively, the reader is probably ready to move on to a detailed presentation of methods. The purpose of the next several chapters is to acquaint those who will be responsible for the day-by-day leadership of the monitoring effort with ways of searching documents and conducting surveys. Chapter 4 deals with document search while Chapters 5–7 will focus on survey research.

**Figure 3.3**
Form 2: Problem specification.

| What is Known | Probable Lead | Possible Lead |
|---|---|---|
| What is the deviation? | | |
| When did it occur? | | |
| Where? | | |
| With whom? | | |
| Hunches | | |

# references

RICHARDSON, STEPHEN A., BARBARA SNELL DOBREHRWEND, and DAVID KLEIN, *Interviewing.* New York: Basic Books, 1965.

RUMMEL, J. FRANCIS, *An Introduction to Research Procedures in Education* (2nd ed.). New York: Harper & Row, 1964.

# GETTING THE INFORMATION

# PART TWO

In Part One, we have explored ways of specifying problems. With this initial thinking about the deviation completed it is next necessary to decide upon the appropriate methodological approach to pursue. While the chief school officer should be generally acquainted with the approaches available, it is most likely that the detailed and ongoing chores associated with the monitoring activities will be directed by his support staff (e.g., the director of school-community relations, the director of research, computer service personnel, and other central office personnel). It is to these staff members that the four chapters in Part Two are directed.

In Chapter 4 we explore document search. Documents, both primary and secondary, are treated as evidence to be examined. How these should be examined and critical questions which must be asked about them are described to help the administrator extract useful information. In addition, sources which might prove useful are presented. These sources, most of which can be found in the schoolman's own school district or the community which he serves, provide an inexpensive and often critical input into problem resolution.

The following three chapters center on the several aspects of survey research. Instrument construction is the focus of Chapter 5. Initially we discuss ways of posing appropriate questions; questions which promise to provide information that answers the original purposes of the survey. Next we present ways of logically organizing and sequencing questions so that respondents will be willing and able to provide needed information. Finally it is urged that the survey instrument be pretested on a population which approximates the population for which it was constructed and, on the basis of the pretest, appropriate modifications be made in the instrument.

In Chapter 6 guidelines for selection of respondents are presented. Respondents can be chosen either purposefully or randomly. How to decide which approach to use is clarified in this chapter. Approaches to random selection of respondents are described and guidelines for the number of persons to survey are offered.

Finally, in Chapter 7 the field work required in the survey process is described. There are many ways in which the staff responsible for the monitoring activity can increase the potential for obtaining information from respondents, either in interviews or through questionnaires. The suggestions in the chapter should facilitate achieving this goal.

We fully realize that carrying out these tasks will be complex and time-consuming. While it may be tempting simply to turn the monitoring process over to an outside agency, there is good reason for attempting to carry out these activities using local personnel and community members. As noted earlier, such studies performed by outsiders tend to have minimum impact on the system because school personnel and community members do not play active roles in clarifying and resolving problems. The methods described herein are *not* so difficult to learn. Further, we firmly believe that the impact which results will be greater if local persons play major roles in the understanding process.

# Using Documents

*four*

Existing documents are an important but often neglected source of information in any problem-solving situation. Documents are defined here as reports of past events, observations or activities made for the purpose of transmitting information. This definition includes written summaries or reports, memos, films, charts, recordings, tapes, and other similar items. The information contained in documents is useful for determining what is known about the problem and in clarifying what is not known. This chapter deals with ways of examining documents and extracting pertinent information. It also indicates where the schoolman and his staff might locate documents to aid them in problem-solving.

## purposes of document search

Document search is usually conducted with a specific problem in mind. As no problem is entirely new, the results of the efforts of others to solve similar problems or elements of the same problem can often be found in documents. The reports or records of their activities, the related research, and the literature developed in the problem area are the objects of document search (Conway and McKelvey, 1970).

The purposes of document search and the subsequent analysis are fourfold:

1. Documents provide background information about the problem. Previous experiences with the problem locally or in other places are part of this background. There is a need to know who was affected by the problem, where, when, and to what extent. It would also be helpful to know under what conditions the problem occurred in the past. Then, too, it is important to know when the present problem was first noted. What were the indicators or manifestations that were observed? And, finally, is there other background information available in studies or experiments reported in the literature of the field?
2. Documents are useful in delineating the present manifestations of the problem. Is the problem observable in one place or in several? How are these manifestations being measured? Who is being affected? Have any attempts been made to solve the problem and, if so, what was done?
3. Documents provide information about previously applied methods for delineating or solving the problem. What were the conceptual bases used in approaching the problem? What factors seemed to be critical and how were they isolated? What steps were taken in attempts to solve the problem? In what sequence? What were the results?
4. Further sources for examination can be identified through documents. Who has reported about the problem: teachers, supervisors, citizens? Are there studies of the problem currently underway? As materials are examined, they will provide leads to further sources.

Through document search, the administrator begins to separate what is known about the problem from what is not known.

## document search and analysis

The search of documents for answers to these and other questions is conducted in an organized manner. It begins with the identification of what is wanted by way of information. As the documents are obtained, they are examined and evaluated for their authenticity and usefulness. Finally, the information that has been obtained is organized and analyzed for what it can contribute to problem delineation or solution. Each of these steps in the process will be discussed in turn.

### WHAT INFORMATION IS WANTED

The several topic areas suggested by the problem provide key words and ideas under which to begin document search. The listing should be as specific and as exhaustive as possible given the present understanding of the problem. For example, the problem of defining educational goals might be investigated through topics such as objectives for youth, purposes of elementary education, preparation for living or the world of work, educational policies, home-school cooperation, and other categories. These topics can be reorganized and broken down as follows:

*GOALS FOR EDUCATION (GENERAL)*

*Goals for youth and children*
1. Young people as people
2. Young people as future adults
3. Socialization and society's goals for youth
4. Development of the intellect
5. Skills and knowledge in recreation, health, social interaction

*Goals for life and living*
1. Preparation for marriage and family life
2. Intelligent consumerism
3. Use of leisure time
4. Health
5. Human relations

*Goals for work and economic well-being*
1. Defining a productive life
2. Occupational choices and changes
3. Obtaining needed skills

*GOALS FOR EDUCATION (IN THE SCHOOLS)*

*Elementary grades (ages 4-11)*
1. The child as a child
2. Basic communications skills, including social relationships
3. Skills in computation

*Secondary school (ages 11-17+)*
1. Relating high school to life
2. Student goal-setting
3. Skills refinement

*Home-School cooperation*
1. Parents' expectations for the schools
2. Schools' expectations for parents

The initial listing could be refined further and probably will be as work begins and new insights come to mind.

What kinds of documents are being sought under each topic? In general, any recorded statement, account, summary, or figures which will contribute to understanding or solving the problem. If the district is defining (or redefining) educational goals, the search would be for documents summarizing goals set by curriculum committees or parent-teacher groups, board policies pertaining to courses or student conduct, and student requests for courses or programs. Implied goals should not be overlooked in documents such as transportation policies, co-curricular offerings, adult education brochures, and student handbooks of school regulations.

Beyond the school, goals for education should be searched out in state board of education policies and regulations, the literature of curriculum theory and planning, as well as journal articles about community expectations, youth, and subject-matter areas. Not to be overlooked are descriptions of goal-setting methodologies, the means of separating actual goals from professed goals, and how to involve people in goal-defining activities.

Another part of the task of finding what information is wanted is the clear separation of facts about the problem from opinions or commentaries on the problem. In document search, this can often be handled by separating primary sources from secondary sources. Primary sources are those reports of people who participated in, or were eyewitnesses to, an activity or an event. These usually contain the facts of the event: times, places, persons, and occurrences. Secondary sources are any further evidence developed on the basis of original statements or from records of the activity or event. Very often opinions or interpretations of what happened are found in these sources. To illustrate, a curriculum committee report to the board stating local school goals for the decade of the seventies is a primary source document. If the history of local curriculum development were recounted in the superintendent's annual report, that recounting is a secondary source. Facts about the establishment and operation of the school program can only be derived from primary sources such as the original recommendations of superintendents and resultant board actions as recorded in minutes, authorizing funds, appointing supervisors, and setting policies on content, and so on. This would also be true for later data, such as course objectives, policies governing textbooks, and other facts about the program change and development.

But there can also be primary and secondary sources of opinion. Primary sources of community opinion about school goals would be the alumni, parents, and citizens. Their feelings about school goals are facts in this situation. Thus, the documents necessary to establish how people feel about them would be letters from parents or records of statements made by a person interviewing alumni. Secondary sources of opinion about school goals might be found in editorials in the local newspaper, the statements of a taxpayers' group spokesman, or a summary of observations by the curriculum coordinator.

Whether a document is treated as a primary or secondary source often depends on how it is used. There is no hard and fast rule. However, the user must be prepared to justify his use in regard to the topic being investigated.

## *AUTHENTICITY*

Each document must be tested to prevent specious data from being included in the analysis. Such tests are needed since items are often found which bear rather imprecise dates or have been developed by a group rather than a single author. The reports of ad hoc committees or drafts of proposals for federal aid are examples of this kind of material. Reprints of articles or reports made without the complete bibliographic information being attached fall into a similar category.

Finding out who wrote the document and how soon after the events reported in it can help in establishing its genuineness. Was the writer there and was the writer qualified to report on what occurred? Was the document produced immediately after the event or the activity? How does it relate to other materials about the same event or activity? Finally, where was the document found? Acceptable answers to these questions will establish the document itself as authentic (Good, 1966, p. 161).

Whether or not the contents of the document are trustworthy must also be determined. While some judgment can be made on the basis of the writer's competency, the facts reported should be checked against other sources where possible (Good, 1966, pp. 169-70). The internal consistency of the document should also be examined. The ideas or thoughts of earlier sources mentioned in the document should be examined for their consistency with the state of the field at the time the material was written.

These tasks are time-consuming but necessary where doubts exist. However, in examining school-community problems exhaustive authentication of documents will probably not be necessary in a large number of cases.

*COMPARABILITY AND COMPLETENESS*

The usability of documents in examining school-community problems is a major consideration. Usability involves two questions. First, is the information contained in the document readily comparable to information already known? Second, is the report complete enough in its contents so that it may be integrated with other materials to form a complete picture?

The data found in documents should be comparable to what is known or easily converted to a comparable form. For example, in looking at the record of job placement for school graduates, the most usable documents would be those which use standard categories, such as those of the National Census of Occupations. It is obvious that this material is easily compared with state or national figures. Documents which report data in percentages should be examined to determine the number of cases used. Without this information the document is less usable for comparative purposes. Knowing the number of cases facilitates easy conversion to raw frequencies, usually a more usable form. There is also the matter of comparability in geographic or population coverage. For example, county-wide data on average family income reported by a government agency may not be applicable to the school district if a major city in the county is outside of district boundaries. Similarly, real property tax data might better be searched out in documents on a town basis for the several portions of the district rather than taken from documents containing county figures. Whenever documents deal with populations there should be a clear identification of the segment included in the data in order to facilitate comparisons. For example, reports of some government agencies may exclude Indians, migrant workers, or youth under eighteen from certain population studies. The school system, on the other hand, may need this very data for examining the problem at hand.

The completeness of data and information in a document is an additional consideration. For example, a curriculum committee report on reading achievement in the school system is much more usable if it includes the recommendations of the committee as well as a critique of deficiencies in the reading program. Similarly, a report on tax delinquent properties and their valuation from the school business office is probably more useful if it contains the location of the properties in addition to their dollar value.

*BIAS*

Finally, there is the matter of bias in documents. Some information is biased from the beginning by the way it is collected, while other information is biased by the point of view of the reporter. An example of information biased by its manner of collection would be parent conference summaries from the pupil personnel office. These statements would be representative only of those parents who had conferences, not all parents in the school system. Examples of information possibly biased by the reporter's point of view include summaries of the requests and justifications of teacher salary committees or the statements of a candidate for membership on the board of education. In these instances, the expression of a point of view is a major purpose behind the document. Facts and words have been carefully selected to express that point of view. Before such documents are used as background information for a problem, the biases in them would have to be noted and limitations placed on their use.

## document analysis and summary

Once documents have been searched, the material gathered should be reformulated to present a total picture. This work begins with a simple diagraming of the data obtained under each topic. Table 4.1 illustrates this technique with the example of educational goals used earlier in the chapter. Information for each topic has been categorized under the headings: who, what, when, where, and why. Other headings may be more appropriate for other problems or headings may be developed out of the information discovered in documents.

Diagraming has the advantage of highlighting pertinent points uncovered in the document search. It also has the advantage of clearly indicating where information is lacking, thus giving direction to further searching. In the example, it should be noted that there is still a need to obtain placement figures for seniors after 1949 in order to make comparisons with the data from previous years.

The analysis of the material gleaned from documents is structured by what has been found in relation to the kind of information and data needed. In some instances, there will be very little analysis necessary as the display of the data

Table 4.1

Sample Document Summary Form
Xville Public Schools Document Search: Educational Goals, Xville Schools 1944–1973

| Topic | Where | Who | When | What | Why |
|---|---|---|---|---|---|
| Goals for Youth | Xville Schools, Supt.'s Memo on Post-War Education December, 1944 | Harry Williams, Supt. (1939–1945) | Board meeting December, 1944 | Outlined need to set goals compatible with a shrinking world and emphasizing human rights | Response to Xville Chapter of One World and PTA requests of November, 1944 |
| | Xville Schools Board Resolution on College Preparation October, 1950 | A.C. Thorpe, Board Member (1950–1960) | Adopted at Board meeting, November, 1950 | Called for development of math, sciences, languages in high school | College education deemed essential in modern world. Xville college placements were only 10% of senior class whereas 35% applied (1945–1949) |
| | *Young Children* May, 1955 pp. 19–25. | John Hadley, Professor of Education, Michigan | 1954 survey of goals for children at play, 30 schools, grades 1–3 | Only 2 schools had goals. 20 believe play is play, 8 felt the children should set own goals | Hadley believes goals for play should be set in conjunction with other goals of schools |
| Goals for Work, Economic Well-Being | Xville *Clarion* June 2, 1960 | Editor | On reading State Board news release on the lack of vocational programs | Editorial calling for vocational programs in schools at Xville | Believed terminal education should be for specific work skills |
| | Xville Schools Report of Curriculum Committee May, 1960 | Jim Williams, Chairman | Xville Citizens Advisory Committee meeting May 10 | Outlined proposed consumer education program for seniors | Goal of making discriminating consumers; extend beyond Home Economics classes into economics elective |

will make the situation quite clear. In other cases, however, conflicting or missing information may have to be accounted for by making careful comparisons with other materials or clearly delineating what cannot be found through the document search. The point is that, through the examination of the material found in documents, a fairly complete picture of the situation should be developed.

The results of the search should be presented in a brief written report. The findings of the report would consist of summaries and abstracts of the documents read. Copies of pertinent charts or maps should also be included. The analysis is probably best presented in a narrative form accompanied by summary charts or outlines where they will lend clarity. A list of the documents used by title, author, and date should be appended to the report. Thus, if there is a need to return to these sources they can be quickly located.

## locating documents

Documents useful in the examination of school-community problems can be found in many places. A number of these places, some obvious, others not so obvious, will be highlighted in this portion of the chapter. It is hoped that school administrators will more and more begin to anticipate their needs for data and information and take the logical step of establishing a school-community data bank as outlined in Chapter 11.

### SCHOOL DOCUMENTS

The local school system itself generates many documents which are useful in problem-solving. There are reports for the state education agency on expenditures, pupil accounting, staffing, and the condition of buildings prepared by the chief school officer or school business official. The district clerk has charge of board minutes, records of elections and, in some states, tax records. From the pupil personnel office, an administrator can usually obtain the results of school censuses, placement records, summaries of parent interviews, and attendance records. Building principals may keep data on transfers, home school groups, and standardized test results. Increasingly, staff committees are studying aspects of curriculum or instructional organization and develop information for these purposes. There are also proposals for federal or special state programs which have been prepared and filed. Many of these documents may be utilized as primary sources, yielding information which is directly applicable to certain problems and providing context or background for other situations. There are a number of other items which may be useful sources of opinion, such as the annual report of the superintendent, reports of committees of the staff, memoranda and abstracts prepared by the administrative staff, and school publications, such as the newsletter. Making an inventory of school offices or officers responsible for the development or custody of these materials provides a simple guide to locating the documents themselves.

### COMMUNITY SOURCES

The school community and the governmental jurisdictions which serve it are rich sources of information useful in the examination of school-community

**Figure 4.1**

Sources of information in the community.

### Public

| | | |
|---|---|---|
| city manager | planning board | board of elections |
| mayor | recreation or parks board | other special authorities, com- |
| town supervisor | board of public safety | mittees, commissions |
| city council | welfare board | occasional consultants |
| county executive | bureau of vital statistics | |
| town board | transportation | |
| county legislature | water board | |
| board of supervisors | civil service commission | |
| treasurer or comptroller | sanitation department | |
| town or city clerk | public works | |
| board of assessors | youth board | |
| tax collector | housing authority | |
| city or town engineer | libraries | |
| | soil conservation district | |
| | extension service | |
| | colleges and universities | |

### Private

| | | |
|---|---|---|
| chambers of commerce | historical societies | civic organizations |
| retail merchants association | newspapers | service clubs |
| better business bureau | churches | educational organizations |
| banks | | |
| corporations | | |
| unions | | |
| utilities | | |

problems. The many reports and records of local governments can be examined and analyzed for their contributions to understanding the problem. Private organizations and associations should not be overlooked in thinking about the location of documents within the community. Figure 4.1 lists offices, bureaus, and other organizations where pertinent materials might be located.

Examples of some of the documents which might be obtained from public sources will serve to illustrate their value. The bureau of vital statistics records births and deaths. The tax division compiles and corrects tax rolls. Local boards and authorities issue the results of studies or consultant reports on topics of community concern, such as transportation, land use, recreation, and population change. Many agencies make monthly or annual summaries for distribution to other agencies. The office of the mayor or city manager may develop and periodically update descriptive material about the community to help local businessmen examine markets or to attract new industry. The local planning board provides projections in population growth and change, and forecasts the needs for many community services.

In the private sector, numerous organizations and groups develop information for their clients and the general public. For example, banks may send their depositors advisory information on business conditions or publish a brochure for general distribution. Chambers of commerce compile lists of retail and wholesale businesses, issue reports on business trends, or assess the impact of taxation on local business activity. Local historical societies have archive holdings on community events and development. Organizations such as the League of Women Voters provide fact-filled pamphlets on issues of the day with the objective of voter education. Newspapers maintain voluminous files of publicity releases and reports from many sources to aid in developing background for their news stories. The files are often open to interested persons for their own research. Many newspapers provide clippings free or at nominal cost.

These examples are by no means exhaustive of the kinds of documents available within the community. With a few inquiries by telephone or in person, documents containing information which bear on school-community problems may be located and examined.

*OTHER DOCUMENT LOCATIONS*

Locating documents on the state or national scene is probably best done through the use of reference material, such as indexes and catalogs (see Chapter 11). At this point, some of the more familiar locations will be reviewed (along with a few unique ones) in order to illustrate the breadth of coverage possible in document search.

First of all, the most familiar location of documents is the library. The school system itself may have a professional library or curriculum research center which should not be overlooked as a source of documents. The local library is an excellent source of information about the community and, in addition, may have the advantage of being part of a county or regional library system. This means that documents and publications housed in other libraries including the state library or university libraries can be obtained by the local librarian for use by the schools.

Second, there are a number of publications of particular help to school people in document search. One of these is the ERIC (Educational Resources and Information Center) journal, *Research in Education,* which contains abstracts of recently completed research in education. By using the word descriptors listed in each monthly issue the reader can locate items which may be useful in document research. These can then be ordered by following the directions printed in each issue of the index.

Some state education agencies distribute checklists of the materials which they publish. These materials consist of reports, studies, and publicity materials developed by the agency and, in some cases, summaries of studies conducted in local school systems. Many school systems receive these checklists automatically and they are well worth perusing as a part of document search.

In addition, there are the leading journals in the several fields of education, such as *Educational Leadership* in the field of curriculum, and *Educational Administration Quarterly* in the field of educational administration. The indexes of these journals should be perused in conducting document search in order to find out the latest data and information as developed by scholars and thinkers in each field. Of course, teachers and administrators are familiar with the *Education Index* and the *Readers Guide to Periodical Literature* which are monthly indexes to articles published in leading journals and magazines.

Finally, there are some unique materials available which should not be overlooked. For example, an annual survey of public attitudes toward the schools is available through the Kettering Foundation subsidiary, CFK, Ltd. By the use of a national survey designed by the George Gallup Organization, a cross-section of opinion by lay citizens is obtained. There are two parts to the survey: one on continuing educational questions, such as the objectives and costs of education; the second on current topics or issues in public education. The results are published by CFK, Ltd., and are also reported in the *Phi Delta Kappan* magazine. This survey may be administered locally and the results compared with the national figures. Manuals for administering the survey are available from CFK, Ltd., and announcements of the survey are made each fall in the major educational journals.

## summary

Document search and analysis is an essential part of problem identification and solution. Through the critical examination of existing documents, the necessary background of a problem can be developed, the current status of the problem can be delineated, and previous means of problem solution and their results can be ascertained. In order to assure the authenticity and usability of documents certain tests should be applied. The results of document search should be summarized in a written report which answers the several questions being investigated.

Locating documents essential to understanding the problem is not a difficult task. School systems generate much useful material, and agencies and organizations in the school community provide a wealth of material for examination. Identifying the major producers of reports and records is the key to locating useful material. In the larger scene, the publications of state and federal governments, as well as the major journals in the field of education, are rich sources of data and information which can be easily investigated. There are numerous checklists and indexes which provide guides to locating pertinent information.

There will be times when little or no information about a school-community problem is available to the school system. It is at this point that the decision is taken to go to the community to obtain the needed answers.

## references

GOOD, CARTER V., *Essentials of Educational Research.* New York: Appleton-Century-Crofts, 1966.

CONWAY, JAMES A., and TROY MCKELVEY, "The Role of the Relevant Literature: A Continuous Process," *Journal of Educational Research,* LXVIII (May-June 1970), 407-13.

GOTTSCHALK, LOUIS, *Understanding History.* New York: Knopf, 1950.

# Asking
# the Right Questions

*five*

Assuming that it is decided that the survey approach is appropriate to obtain information, it then becomes necessary to construct a viable survey instrument and select respondents. These two tasks usually proceed concurrently. Time is of the essence and the administrator assigned the activity will probably want to match the right questions with the right people as quickly as possible. For sake of presentation, we will first deal with the active development of survey instruments. In the following chapter the reader will find an extensive discussion of respondent selection.

The schoolman will want to be sure that questions included in the survey instrument are relevant to the questions he has raised through problem specification and subsequent document search, and are asked in such a way that they will result in the collection of accurate and complete information.

It may be tempting to turn to "packaged" instruments that are already available for measuring attitudes and perceptions (cf., Lake, Miles, and Earle, 1973; Robinson, Rusk, and Head, 1968; and Robinson and Shaver, 1969). These instruments may be of some use for deriving ideas for locally-constructed instruments. But by their very nature, these "packaged" instruments are constructed to be universalistic and thus will not be sufficiently focused to permit a full range of responses to specific deviation specification needs in particular communities.

To provide assistance to the schoolman who will direct this process, the contents of the chapter are centered around the following major tasks associated with the construction of survey instruments: developing questions; sequencing questions on the instrument; and pretesting the instrument to see how well it accomplishes that which it was revised to accomplish.

## question development

As he begins the task of developing questions, the schoolman will have to consider (1) the *types* of questions which can be asked; (2) the *forms* in which these questions might be asked; and (3) the actual *wording* of the questions.

### TYPES OF QUESTIONS

Three basic types of questions can be posed for inclusion in the survey instrument: demographic, factual, and opinion probes. Most survey instruments include some combination of these types of questions. Review of the following discussion should help the reader in deciding the possible uses they may have for his deviation specification needs.

**Demographic Questions.** Demographic questions seek vital statistics about respondents which might aid in explaining their answers. In most surveys several respondent subgroups are included (e.g., men and women; wealthy, middle class, and poor; old, middle aged, and young; property owners and non-property owners). For analysis purposes the investigator must often be able to differentiate responses according to subgroups. For example, in analyzing the bond defeat, the "Assuming Superintendent" needed to contrast responses of "citizens with children in public schools" against responses of "citizens with no children in public schools" to ascertain whether there was a variation in the level of support for school needs between these two groups. To be able to establish this, demographic questions concerning the presence of school-age children in the homes of survey respondents would have had to be included in the survey instrument.

There are many demographic questions which might be included in a survey instrument, but those actually used should be restricted to the information required. The schoolman might include demographic questions formed from categories in the lists presented in Table 5.1. In each of the three categories found in the table the reader will find space where, depending upon his particular interests, he might want to extend the list. The table is organized according to descriptive information about the person, his family, and his place of residence.

There are several criteria for choosing demographic questions to include in the instrument. First, they should be relevant. If demographic questions do not serve a clearly useful purpose (i.e., result in obtaining necessary information), they should not be included. Second, they should not interfere with the

**Table 5.1**

**Demographic Information**

| Demographic Categories | Specific Demographic Information |
|---|---|
| The Person | Age |
| | Sex |
| | Educational attainment (level completed and whether public or private) |
| | Income |
| | Political preference |
| | Occupation |
| | Employment status (self-employed or work for others) |
| | Place of employment (in community or elsewhere) |
| | Organizations |
| | Race |
| | Religious preference |
| | Other: _____ |
| | _____ |
| The Family Unit | "Habits" (reading, TV, etc.) |
| | Marital status |
| | Head of household (male/female) |
| | Children in household (number in public and/or private schools) |
| | Other: _____ |
| | _____ |
| The Place of Residence | Length of time in district |
| | Reasons for residence in district (e.g., good schools, employment) |
| | Neighborhood of residence |
| | Type of dwelling unit (home owned or rented, apartment) |
| | Value of home (if owned) |
| | Other: _____ |
| | _____ |

probable cooperation of respondents. For example, information about religious preference and income may be desired but might also result in respondents' refusal to cooperate. Such sensitive questions should be included *only* if they are vital to the information needs required. Third, demographic questions should not require excessive response time which might reduce the probability that respondents will fully answer opinion and fact questions. These descriptive questions should require only a minor portion of the time needed to complete the survey instrument. Those demographic questions which can be completed by the investigator through observation should not be asked of the respondent. For example, sex, marital status, and neighborhood can usually be recorded by the investigator (unless a mail or telephone survey is used). Places should be reserved on the survey instrument for the investigator to record such information.

It is usually a good idea to organize demographic questions as checklist items (e.g., "Our family income is in the following range:" ___ a. $0-$4,999, ___ b. $5,000-$9,999, ___ c. $10,000-$19,999, ___ d. $20,000 or more). This serves three purposes. First, it anticipates analysis needs by providing built-in coding categories on the survey instrument itself. Second, it helps respondents by clarifying how you would like the question to be answered. Third, it reduces the potential that they might refuse to respond to an item. For many people it is much less threatening to circle a response item which, for example, represents the family's income range rather than to record the family's exact income in a space provided.

**Factual Questions.** Factual questions establish what respondents know about the problem. While these kinds of questions are not found as frequently on survey instruments as are demographic and opinion questions, there will probably be times when specific fact questions are desirable. For example, in more than a few instances the opposition to sex education in school districts by community groups is based on emotions and not related to actual facts. If he suspects this to be the case, the schoolman will probably want to test his assumption in the survey instrument before becoming committed to the time and expense of mounting an educational campaign. If so, he would then construct a few questions which seek this information (e.g., "At what grade level is sex education taught in the schools?").

Factual questions should be used only as needed. Keep them to a minimum in the survey instrument to avoid making respondents feel that they are being "tested." Testing is not a central purpose of the survey, but even more important, respondents may refuse to cooperate if they feel that they will be embarrassed by their ignorance.

**Opinion Questions.** Opinion questions seek information concerning how respondents feel about an issue, idea, or object. Opinions, or dispositions, are the result of a person's past experiences, group memberships, and value system. Because peoples' backgrounds vary in experiences, memberships, and values they can have diametrically opposing opinions even when they possess the same facts. For example, given the same factual information, citizens' opinions may still vary considerably on the prospect of a community swimming pool as part of a proposed school facility. Some citizens may react negatively because they have access to other swimming pools or feel that such "frills" should not be supported by the public treasury. Others may view education in ways which make a pool in the proposed school seem logical or may feel that attendance at the pool can help their children to make new friends. In short, predispositions may cause citizens to respond differently to the same issue stimulus, even though they possess the same information.

Whether based upon fact or not, it is important to ascertain opinions to clarify community preferences about deviations. Opinions are often difficult to verify with a single item, so there are usually many opinion questions asked in surveys. These questions often have opening phrases such as the following.

How do you feel about . . .
Do you think that . . .
How important is . . .
In your opinion, do you believe . . .
Do you feel that . . .
Would you be willing to . . .
Are you in favor of . . .
Are you satisfied that . . .
How do you rate the following . . .

At times it may be relevant to *probe* to establish further information about an issue. A *probe* question is one which seeks further information about a topic from the respondent. There are three reasons to probe: (1) to clarify a respondent's views; (2) to find out if the views he expresses are based on fact; or (3) to establish the intensity of his opinions. Probe questions can be open-ended in form. "Would you explain further?" might clarify an opinion. "How is that?" or "Why?" may bring forth the factual base of opinions. And, "Do you really feel strongly about that?" may elicit the intensity of the opinion. More often, however, it is a good idea to provide direction by asking specific probes. For example, a question such as "Were you in favor of the last bond referendum put up by the school district?" might well be followed by a probe question which gets at *why* the respondent was in favor of or against the bond referendum. Such a probe question might be, "Were there particular issues involved in the last bond referendum which led you to take this position on its passage?" The intent of the question is to discover whether the respondent has based his opinion upon factual knowledge and, further, what factors were most relevant in forming his opinion.

In summary, surveys usually include demographic, factual, and opinion questions. Demographic questions seek vital statistics that describe the respondent; factual questions establish his knowledge base about an issue; and opinion questions elicit feelings or attitudes central to an issue.

## question format: open-ended and structured

There are two basic formats for stating questions: *open-ended* and *structured*. Open-ended questions invite the respondent to formulate his own answer as he wishes whereas structured questions require that he respond within

Table 5.2

**Open-Ended and Structured Questions: Advantages and Disadvantages**[a]

| Question Format | Advantages | Disadvantages |
|---|---|---|
| Open-ended Questions | Assure complete choice of responses when there are only limited ideas of the probable answers; Assure complete choice of responses when a wide range of answers are anticipated; Allow for unexpected information when there is particular interest in what respondents will volunteer; and Allow for further specification when it is necessary to probe into respondents' motivations. | Cumbersome: If the instrument is an interview schedule, much skill is required in recording responses. If the instrument is a questionnaire, open-ended questioning requires much space, limiting the possible number of questions to be asked or requiring a lengthy questionnaire, increasing the danger that respondents may skip such questions; Require interpretations in recording responses if the survey is of the interview type and in analysis regardless of the survey format employed; and Developing coding categories is difficult. |
| Structured Questions | Questions are pre-coded, requiring only that appropriate responses be selected from set choices. Thus they are relatively easy to administer; and Because respondents' answers are pre-coded, much of the difficult translation task is eliminated and analysis is made easier. | Difficult to capture the intensity of respondents' answers; and Force respondents to fit their answers into predetermined categories or to omit questions. |

[a] For a more complete discussion of advantages and disadvantages of question formats, see Charles H. Backstrom and Gerald D. Hursh, *Survey Research* (Evanston, Ill.: Northwestern University Press, 1963), pp. 72–76, from which several of the above ideas have been adapted, by permission of the publisher.

some predetermined answer format. Though both forms can be used for either interview schedules or questionnaires, generally questionnaires tend to include more structured questions while interview schedules tend to include more open-ended questions.

The choice of question format, open-ended or structured, will often be dictated by the kind and extent of information needed, but sometimes either question form might be used. Therefore, it may be helpful to review the advantages and disadvantages inherent in structured and open-ended questions. A review of Table 5.2 should help the reader to make decisions about which format his questions should take.

Knowing his information needs and the limitations inherent in the open-ended and structured question formats for coding and analysis, the schoolman is in a better position to select the most appropriate question format. Open-ended questions allow for more complete responses, but increase the possibility of misinterpretation of responses and require much skill to code and analyze. Structured questions cannot get at the intensity of response that is possible with open-ended questions, but they are easier to administer, code, and analyze. Frequently, the two are combined – structured questions followed by open-ended questions. This assures some data for comparisons and may lead to the discovery of unanticipated information.

For many purposes the structured question format is sufficient for information-gathering needs, but at other times open-ended questions will more likely lead to the collection of necessary information. For example, a structured question is probably sufficient for ascertaining a respondent's view about optimal class size:

> *Question:* How many students do you think can be adequately taught by a single teacher?
>
> *Answer:*[1]    1. Less than 10
>             2. 10–15
>             3. 16–20
>             4. 21–25
>             5. 26–30
>             6. 31–35
>             7. More than 35

---

[1] A caution: whenever possible checklist items such as this should exhaust all possible responses. If this is impossible, a catch-all "Other" category should be added as the final item. For example:
> *Question:* Who do you think will win the election for the vacant school board seat?
> *Answer:* ___ 1. Sam Brown
>          ___ 2. Harry Smith
>          ___ 3. Dorothy Kilmer
>          ___ 4. Other _____
>             (The line after "other" may lead to unexpected information.)

The schoolman may need to have more information than this structured question can obtain. For example, he may want to know if respondents feel there are times that class size should vary. Because there may be multiple answers that respondents could give, obtaining this information probably necessitates that a structured question such as "Are there times when class size should vary?" be followed by a probe question such as "Why do you think so?" if the respondent answers affirmatively. In short, information needs may dictate whether it is better to limit respondents to fixed-choice answers or allow them to volunteer answers of their choice.

*STRUCTURED QUESTIONS:*
*VARIATIONS*

Open-ended questions are fairly straightforward as to format. They usually are articulated as questions rather than as statements (e.g., "How do you feel about the education children in this school district receive?"). The exception is when respondents are asked to finish an incomplete statement (e.g., "The School Board spends most of its time...."). They can be answered in a word, a sentence, or a phrase. Structured questions, however, vary in form, depending upon such criteria as the type of information required; the amount of information required and the expected willingness of respondents to take a substantial amount of time to complete the instrument; the educational level of the respondents; and existing time and manpower limitations for coding.

**Dichotomous-Choice Questions.** There are two basic forms in which structured questions may be posed: dichotomous-choice and multiple-choice. Dichotomous-choice questions are those which require the respondent to choose one of two answer options. Examples of dichotomous-choice responses include: yes/no; right/wrong; high/low; and true/false. These responses are appropriate if there are only two possible choices *or* if you want to *force* the respondent to make a choice. However, when there are more than two possible or desired choices, a multiple-choice response form should be used.

**Multiple-Choice Questions.** Multiple-choice questions permit respondents to select from three or more responses. These responses should be mutually exclusive *unless* it is specifically desired to permit respondents to choose more than a single response. For example, the question "To which, if any, of the following community organizations do you belong?" could lead respondents to check more than one answer if they belong to more than one community organization. Within the "multiple-choice" category there are two forms: scaled and nonscaled items.

**Scaled Multiple-Choice Responses.** These are questions which seek to place the positions taken by respondents along a continuum of possible positions. That is, they seek to clarify how intense respondents feel about an issue, idea, or thing. These questions most often have three, four, or five possible responses.[2] For example, if the schoolman wants to discover how important respondents feel it is to establish a work-study program in the schools he might choose a three-response scale such as:

> Important
> Undecided
> Not Important

A four-response scale for this same question might look as follows:

> Very Important
> Important
> Not Very Important
> Not Important

A five-response scale might be as follows:

> Very Important
> Important
> Undecided
> Not Very Important
> Not Important

The number of responses offered for a scaled multiple-choice question depends on the information required. How discrete must the resultant information be? How much knowledge is desired concerning the intensity of respondents' opinions? Further, it is a good idea to think ahead toward coding and analysis. How difficult will it be to code the responses? How much time does the administrator have to analyze the results? How much space will the information require in the report of findings? Such long-range planning for activities which will have to be pursued once the information is collected should influence the decisions concerning number of responses on multiple-choice items as well as for other questions on the instrument. Thinking ahead at the outset can save a good deal of work later in the process.

It should also be noted that odd-number response scales (3 and 5 responses) have middle-point responses which should always be neutral positions on the scale so that there is an equal choice factor for the respondent. The even-numbered response scale (4 responses), on the other hand, has no middle position. Even-numbered response scales require the respondent to take a pro or con position on the question. If the schoolman believes that the respondents will

---

[2] A notable exception is the Semantic Differential Scale noted on page 74.

**Table 5.3**

**Samples of Three, Four, and Five-Scaled Multiple-Choice Response Items**

| Three-Response Items | Four-Response Items | Five-Response Items |
|---|---|---|
| Agree | Strongly Agree | Strongly Agree |
| Undecided[a] | Agree | Agree |
| Disagree | Disagree | Undecided |
|  | Strongly Disagree | Disagree |
|  |  | Strongly Disagree |
| Important | Very Important | Very Important |
| Undecided | Important | Important |
| Not Important | Unimportant | Undecided |
|  | Not Important at all | Unimportant |
|  |  | Not Important at all |
| Good | Very Good | Very Good |
| Undecided | Good | Good |
| Bad | Bad | Undecided |
|  | Very Bad | Bad |
|  |  | Very Bad |
| Favorable | Highly Favorable | Highly Favorable |
| Undecided | Favorable | Favorable |
| Not Favorable | Unfavorable | Undecided |
|  | Highly Unfavorable | Unfavorable |
|  |  | Highly Unfavorable |

[a]The neutral "Undecided" could be replaced by "No Opinion," "Neither," "Don't Know," or any other neutral term, depending upon the logic of the scale itself.

have taken a position on the question and wants to force them to articulate this position then he should use an even-numbered response scale.

There are many ways in which a three, four, or five-scaled response item can be stated. A few examples of these possible statements are represented in Table 5.3. The choice of scaled response items will depend upon the particular information being sought by the question. The four and five "response choices" provide some indication of the intensity or strength of opinions which cannot be obtained from a three "response choice." However, these must be treated with some caution in interpretation for many people are reticent about revealing a strong position even though this may be their actual feeling.

There are other scaled response forms which can be used in surveys. These include the Semantic Differential Scale (Osgood, 1952); the Guttman Scale (Guttman, 1944); and the Likert Scale (Likert, 1938). However, these scales are beyond the scope of the present discussion. While they may add further refinements to the survey instrument, they are more complex to construct and to analyze than those response forms discussed above. For most needs the schoolman will find the simpler scaled response forms adequate. If he feels that he must use scaled information of a different form *and* he has the skilled manpower available to construct such items and analyze them, he might want to refer to the sources noted in this paragraph.

**Non-Scaled Multiple-Choice Responses.** These are similar to scaled responses in that they should be mutually exclusive unless the investigator specifically wishes to allow multiple responses. They differ from the scaled responses in that they do not seek to establish the intensity of responses along a continuum. For example, the schoolman might want to know where members of the community would like to have a proposed middle school built. If so, he might list several alternatives and ask respondents to select the one they prefer. Similarly the schoolman might ask respondents to select, from among a list of choices, the most important single curricular offering which should be included in a child's school experience.

There is a variation, the *ranking of responses* which can be devised for non-scaled multiple-choice questions. For example, using the ranking of responses variation, the schoolman might ask respondents to rank-order curricular selections from most to least important. This gives the schoolman more information. It also makes coding and analysis more difficult, but the purposes of the survey may necessitate more information than a single response to a multiple-choice question can provide.

## wording the questions

A discussion of the do's and don'ts of question wording could fill an entire book. In fact, a useful book on question writing, *The Art of Asking Questions,* has been written by Stanley Payne (1951). All that can be done in this short space is to briefly point up some of the most important general guidelines for question writing. They should be drawn upon as needed.

*The overriding concern should be clarity.* Keep uppermost in mind those for whom the questions are being constructed. The language used and the way it is arranged must be understandable to those who will be requested to respond to the survey instrument. In pursuit of this objective there are five major question-writing problems which should be considered. First, questions are often *too long.* Lengthy questions tend to require respondents to work hard at interpreting what is expected of them. Often they "turn off" to the survey if this problem persists. When responding becomes a great effort most persons will refuse to continue to cooperate unless they have an exceptional commitment to the purposes of the survey. Further, our experiences indicate that most questions can profit from being restated in a shorter version than that which was first constructed.

Second, the level at which the language of questions is being pitched is sometimes either *too simplistic* or *too difficult* for many respondents. Question writers should consider who the probable respondents will be. Generally the language should be such that the *least educated* expected respondents will be able to understand the survey questions. Question writers often overestimate the sophistication of respondents. A pretest of the survey instrument (discussed later in this chapter) can help to correct language difficulties.

Third, questions are often stated in an *ambiguous* manner. For example, the question "Do you participate in school affairs?" contains several distinct ambiguities. Participation may have *different meanings* to different respondents (e.g., participation may imply taking part in PTA activities to some, belonging to community pressure groups to others, and voting in elections to still others). There is no measure of *intensity* of participation in the question (i.e., how many participations over what period of time?). Finally, the question is *incomplete.* It does not indicate which schools are being discussed nor does it fully define "affairs."

Fourth, some questions are really *two questions within one.* An example might be "Should the school district adopt the open classroom concept or should it adopt a nongraded approach?" If a respondent says yes to this question the schoolman does not know if the schools should adopt one or both of the two possibilities. This kind of question-writing error can usually be dealt with easily. The preceding question, for example, could be divided into two separate questions or one of the two choices could be eliminated.

Fifth, sometimes questions are stated in a manner that seems to favor a particular response over other responses. This question-writing problem is often referred to as *loading questions.* There are several ways in which questions can be loaded. The question, "It costs too much to support the schools in this district?" (Yes/No), presents a *value position.* Respondents may be swayed by the wording of the question and say they agree with the statement even if they really do not. The same question could be worded neutrally: "How do you feel about the money it takes to support our public schools?" Another way to load a question is to *state only one alternative.* For example, take the question, "Some people say that the best way to increase the efficiency of our public schools is to hold classes all-year round. What do you think?" In this case if the respondent had no thoughts on the topic before the question was asked, he might now. Further, he may feel that the alternatives that he might suggest could not possibly be as good as what "some people say." Finally, using *emotional words* also results in loaded questions. Bussing, integration, discipline, remedial education, and slow learners are but a few of the many words which might trigger emotional reactions in respondents. Unless such reactions are purposely desired, the question writer would do best to avoid such words.

The reader may want to add to this list of common question-writing problems. It is impossible to foresee all such problems, but these general comments and others which the schoolman makes note of as he encounters them, should help to minimize such errors.

Thus far the discussion has focused upon question development. At some point the questions which have been framed must be put together as an interview schedule or a questionnaire. This process is usually referred to as instrument construction.

## instrument construction

Instrument construction is the critical process of bringing together the questions developed into a unified questionnaire or interview schedule. If the questions posed are inappropriately sequenced, all the efforts spent on their development will have gone for naught. "Inappropriate" instruments are those which result in inaccurate, incomplete, or otherwise misleading information and, often, in angry respondents. Following some basic guidelines concerning the sections of the instrument and other instrumentation concerns should help to minimize these problems.

### SECTIONS OF THE INSTRUMENT

Survey instruments have introductory sections, central sections, and closing sections (though not so labeled). The *introductory section* sets the tone of the questioning and should build rapport. Usually a brief description of the purposes of the survey is presented to the respondents, either verbally by an interviewer or in descriptive statements on the questionnaire. This establishes the legitimacy and importance of the project, thus helping to assure that respondents will cooperate. After the purposes are established any instructions required to be able to complete the instrument are presented. Following this opening, respondents should be put at ease by being asked questions, usually demographic, which are fairly non-threatening (e.g., "How many years have you lived in this school district?" or "Are you married?"). As the respondents' confidence and trust are secured, then it is possible to move on to questions which may have more potential threat for them (e.g., "What is the income in this household?"). The introductory section should be kept short so that the major portion of the time required to complete the instrument is reserved for obtaining required information.

The *central section* contains the factual and opinion questions which the schoolman hopes will answer the initial hypotheses or research questions. Once respondents have been introduced to the instrument and are sufficiently willing to complete the task, it is possible to move on to more difficult questions with some assurance that they will continue to cooperate. Topics treated in this section should be carefully sequenced so that there is a logical thought process development and the respondents' initial cooperation continues.

The *closing section* is nothing more than a way to complete the interview or questionnaire. The intent is to exit gracefully and, further, to avoid leaving a traumatized respondent behind. There are several things which might be treated in the closing section of the survey instrument. For example, this section might provide an opportunity to seek information which was not anticipated when the instrument was constructed. This might be done by simply asking the respondent: "Do you feel that there is anything else that we ought to know about . . .?" Such a question can often lead to attitudinal responses which might be particularly relevant. Further, the closing section can provide an opportunity to seek information which was asked for earlier but which respondents were either unwilling to divulge or could not formulate at the time. Finally, the closing section can let respondents know that their cooperation has been appreciated and that their inputs are important if the school system is to accomplish its objectives. A positive closing section is an important component of the survey instrument.

## OTHER INSTRUMENT CONSTRUCTION CONCERNS

Survey instruments should not be viewed as standardized or mechanical. The sequence in which questions are asked should be such that there is assurance that respondents will understand them and be willing to cooperate so that the purposes of the study can be accomplished. There are several guidelines to consider to enhance this potential.

**Begin With the Least Threatening Questions.** Questions should be ordered so that they move from least to most threatening. The respondent's trust and cooperation must be established before it can be expected that he will share facts or opinions which he might not otherwise divulge. He should be put at ease at the outset. Asking non-threatening questions serves this intent.

**Include Questions All Can Answer.** Be sure to include questions which all respondents should be able to answer. This is necessary not only to assure that information will be obtained, but also to make respondents confident that they do know things or have views which are important to the surveyor. If a respondent is unable to answer most questions on the instrument it is probable that he will be left with a feeling of personal inadequacy about the subject matter at hand and resent the embarrassment it causes him. This resentment could lead the respondent to be negative about the issue from that point onwards.

**Use Well Chosen Demographic Questions.** Usually demographic questions are best asked in the introductory section. These questions help to gain the initial cooperation of respondents. An exception is when the demographic information being requested is threatening to the respondent (e.g., seeks information about his religious preference, annual household income, or value of his home). If it is suspected that a demographic question will be threatening to the respondent, it might better be moved towards the closing section or omitted entirely.

**Emphasize Opinion Rather Than Fact Questions.** It is more difficult to establish respondents' opinions than to establish their knowledge about facts. For this reason opinion questions should usually constitute the vast majority of questions on the instrument.

**Limit the Length of the Instrument.** The instrument must be kept sufficiently short so that respondents do not feel that they are being imposed upon. Therefore only questions which are clearly related to the purposes of the survey should be included on the instrument. Often the schoolman will find that he has developed some interesting but not pertinent questions. These should be eliminated to minimize the length of the instrument. Similarly, questions which result in information already obtained through another question should be eliminated. The exception to this rule is when the schoolman feels that substantial additional information will result by asking a question in several forms. For example, the question "What do you think that school board members do?" might be followed by the question "What other things do you think that they do?" if it is expected that respondents can offer substantial further information.

**Minimize Anticipation.** Questions should be so stated that respondents do not anticipate answers which are "expected." It is useful to lead respondents to anticipate the next question, but not the next answer! For example, it may be necessary to establish whether a general favorable attitude toward racial integration of society is transferable to a willingness to integrate schools in the community. In this case, questions related to the topic will probably have to be scattered throughout the instrument so that respondents do not anticipate the direction of questioning. Further, most respondents want to cooperate and help the investigator. If they are able to anticipate what they believe are the schoolman's "favored" responses, they may choose to answer as they think he would like to have them respond rather than as they really feel.

**Provide Adequate Transitions.** Transitions should be provided within and between sections of the survey instrument. Never assume that respondents will be able to make transitions for themselves. When moving from the introductory section to the central section and on to the closing section, statements should be devised to alert respondents so that they will be at ease. In addition, transitions are necessary when moving from topic to topic within sections. Statements such as "Next you will find a few statements about . . ." or "In this part we would like to . . ." are examples of transition statements or connectors which bring questions together into a coherent whole for respondents.

These hints for the questionnaire format may seem trivial on first reading, but they are derived from experience and may help the reader to avoid unnecessary construction problems.

### the pretest

Once the instrument has been constructed it is ready to be administered. Or is it? Thus far the schoolman has been writing questions and sequencing them in a manner which he feels should insure that required information will be obtained. However, he does not know if the survey instrument will actually meet the purposes for which it was constructed. The only way to establish this is to try out or "pretest" the instrument on persons who are much like those to whom it will be administered. Such a "reality test" may indicate shortcomings which otherwise may not have been discovered until it was too late.

As a result of the pretest the schoolman should have answers to several important questions: Are the questions asked in appropriate forms? Is the wording of all questions clear? Are some questions ambiguous? Are some questions loaded? Is the sequencing of questions logical to respondents? Have clear and sufficient transitional phrases been provided? Does the same information result from asking different questions? Do the responses obtained provide full and complete information, both within individual questions and concerning the overall purposes of the survey?

Care should be taken to replicate expected survey conditions as closely as is possible. If an interview has been constructed then the pretest should be an interview which approximates expected interview setting conditions and respondents as closely as possible. For example, if the interview calls for asking low socioeconomic blacks in their homes about their satisfaction with their children's public schools, then the pretest should be administered to comparable low socioeconomic blacks in their homes. This can be done by surveying blacks who live in the same school district but who will not be part of the actual interview sample.[3] An alternative might be to interview comparable blacks in other school districts. Preferably however, pretest respondents should come from the same school district if there are questions on the instrument which relate specifically to that district.

The same holds true for questionnaires. They should be pretested under conditions which are comparable to those to be employed in the actual administration of the instrument. For example, if the questionnaire is to be mailed to randomly selected respondents, then it should also be mailed to randomly selected respondents in the pretest. If the questionnaire is to be

[3]Sample selection has not yet been discussed. This is the focus of the next chapter. In all probability, as was noted earlier, the schoolman will have selected the sample before the instrument is completed. If so, it should be easy for him to determine appropriate pretest respondents.

self-administered by respondents, this should also hold true for pretest respondents.

In any event, whether the instrument is an interview schedule or a questionnaire, pretest sample respondents should be selected in the same manner as are those who will be asked to respond to the instrument in its final form. Consistency in the selection process helps to establish the effectiveness of the sampling procedures used to identify respondents. In addition, if pretest respondents are actually representative of those to be surveyed, the probability that the pretest will be relevant is increased. That is, on the face of it, it is possible to ascertain if the instrument can actually elicit the information being sought.

It is usually a good idea for those who have developed the survey instrument to participate in administering the pretest. Because they wrote the questions they are in the best position to understand whether the instrument has indeed been so developed that the purposes of the survey can be achieved. They should know whether responses which were expected are actually obtained by specific questions. (Chapter 10, which deals with analysis, should be referred to for ways of performing item analysis.)

Further, it is often useful to ask pretest respondents to express the feelings they experienced in answering the survey instrument. Suggestions obtained from pretest respondents regarding things such as clarity and appropriateness of questions, logic of progression, sequencing of questions, and length of the instrument are often pertinent. Besides discussing reactions with respondents orally,[4] it is a good idea to provide a form at the end of the instrument which pretest respondents can use to provide responses to questions such as:

> Were instructions for completing the questionnaire clear?
> How long did it take you to complete the questionnaire?
> Were the questions clearly stated?
> What do you think the purpose of the questionnaire was?
> Were there questions which were threatening to you?
> How did you feel about answering the questionnaire?

When the information derived from the pretest indicates that there is one or more shortcoming to the survey instrument, the schoolman should work to improve it. A debriefing session attended by those who administered the pretest survey instrument is helpful in clarifying specific shortcomings which might exist. Survey instruments which are returned to the drawing board for improvements in wording, sequencing, transitions, format, and completeness are usually significantly improved.

---

[4]Follow-up with mail-out and telephone pretest survey respondents to gain complete information on instrument shortcomings may require face-to-face discussions. This follow-up need should be considered when contacting pretest respondents.

### the final instrument

Once modifications are incorporated in the instrument as a result of the pretest, it should be finalized and readied for administration. To make the respondents' task as manageable as possible the instrument's format should be clear and instructions should be explicit. In addition, to help him understand the questions asked the instrument should be sectioned into logical parts; preferably questions should be typed on one side of the paper only; and there should be extensive blank white space on each page. To avoid a bulky instrument when the final draft is very long, it is a good idea to have it printed, using a photo-reduction technique.

There are also ways of making later tasks more manageable by careful construction of the survey instrument. Responses to structured questions should be lined up on one side of the page. This makes information transfer and coding much easier. If the instrument is to be administered by interviewers, instructions should be typed directly on the instrument, set off by parentheses and (WRITTEN IN CAPITAL LETTERS) so that the interviewer is able to easily distinguish his instructions from statements he should be reading to the respondent.

### summary

This chapter centered upon asking the right questions. Question construction was discussed under three topical headings, the first of which explored the types of questions usually included in surveys: demographic, fact, and opinion questions.

The formats in which questions might be asked were treated next. There are two basic question formats: open-ended and structured. Open-ended questions usually allow respondents to react as completely as they wish to questions asked, but also increase the potential for misinterpretations and complicate the coding process. Structured questions minimize coding problems and interpretation errors by the schoolman because they provide set choices from which the respondent must select an appropriate answer. However, they have potential for inaccuracy because respondents may desire to answer differently than any of the set choices permit. Structured questions can be either dichotomous in choice of response or multiple-choice. Multiple-choice structured questions may be scaled or non-scaled. Scaled items seek intensity in responses whereas non-scaled items seek choices among alternatives which are not phrased in levels of intensity.

The third question construction topic was question wording. In wording questions the schoolman should *always* be concerned that respondents will understand what is expected of them. Wording difficulties include level of language used; length of questions; ambiguous statements; questions which may have different meanings to different respondents; questions which are really two questions posed as one; and questions which are loaded because they take a value position, favor a particular alternative, or include emotional words.

With types of questions and formats selected and the actual wording accomplished, it next becomes necessary to put the questions together in a logical manner. This is referred to as instrument construction. Survey instruments should have opening, central, and closing sections. Specific guidelines have been presented to assure that these sections are well constructed by appropriate sequencing; moving from least to most threatening questions; considering space allocations for opinion and fact questions; avoiding preconditioning respondents' answers; providing appropriate transitional phrases; and spartan selection of the most pertinent questions.

Finally, it is advisable to pretest the prepared instrument on persons who are very much like those to be surveyed. Pretesting the instrument helps the schoolman to ascertain whether respondents will understand what is expected of them and will be willing to share the desired information. The schoolman who wrote the questions should be involved in the pretest phase as he is most knowledgeable about expected responses. On the basis of the pretest, if necessary, the instrument should be appropriately modified to increase its potential usefulness.

If the schoolman has done an adequate job of posing and ordering questions, the instrument is now ready to be administered. The next question becomes: To whom shall it be administered? How can the schoolman isolate appropriate respondents? How can he select from among potential respondents to assure that the information obtained adequately represents the community? These questions will be addressed in Chapter 6.

## references

BACKSTROM, CHARLES H., and GERALD D. HURSH, *Survey Research.* Evanston, Ill.: Northwestern University Press, 1963.

FOX, DAVID J., *The Research Process in Education,* Chap. 18, pp. 524-69. New York: Holt, Rinehart & Winston, 1969.

GUTTMAN, LOUIS, "A Basis for Scaling Quantitative Data," *American Sociological Review,* IX, 2 (1944), 139-50.

LAKE, DALE G., MATTHEW B. MILES, and RALPH B. EARLE, JR., eds., *Measuring Human Behavior.* New York: Teachers College Press, 1973.

LIKERT, RENSIS, "A Technique for the Measurement of Attitudes," *Archives of Psychology,* No. 140 (1938), 5-55.

OSGOOD, CHARLES E., "The Nature and Measurement of Meaning," *Psychological Bulletin,* XLIX, 3 (1952), 197-237.

PAYNE, STANLEY I., *The Art of Asking Questions.* Princeton, N.J.: Princeton University Press, 1951.

ROBINSON, JOHN P., JERROLD G. RUSK, and KENDRA B. HEAD, *Measures of Political Attitudes.* Ann Arbor: Institute for Social Research, University of Michigan, 1968.

―――, and PHILLIP R. SHAVER, *Measures of Social Psychological Attitudes.* Ann Arbor: Institute for Social Research, University of Michigan, 1969.

SAX, GILBERT, *Empirical Foundations of Educational Research,* Chap. 9, pp. 201–40. Englewood Cliffs, N.J.: Prentice-Hall, 1968.

# Asking
# the Right People

six

To get the necessary information the right questions must be matched up with the right respondents. The process of respondent selection, which probably will be going on at the same time as the survey instrument is being constructed, is explored in this chapter. In particular, two basic approaches for finding the right people to respond to the right questions are described; these are purposeful and random selection of respondents.[1]

Which of the two selection approaches is appropriate *depends on the purposes of the survey.* These words, "the purposes of the survey," are repeated time and again through the book for they stand for a principle which should guide the schoolman as he makes important decisions regarding the survey. This principle, that the unique needs for deviation specification encountered in his situation should govern methodological considerations, applies especially to respondent selection. To help the reader make these respondent selection decisions the chapter highlights the various purposes that each of the selection approaches might serve.

---

[1] These approaches apply equally to selection of respondents for interview or questionnaire surveys. Both survey formats require that the right persons be selected either purposefully or randomly. See Chapter 3 for a discussion of interview schedules and questionnaires as alternative vehicles for use as survey instruments.

## purposeful selection

Purposeful selection, as the name might indicate, is the deliberate choice of specific individuals or groups to respond to the survey questions. Purposeful selection is required when the needs of the survey indicate that respondent selection *should not be left to chance.* There are at least two occasions when this may be the case: when there is little information available about the problem and a pilot study is necessary, and when "key participants" are the only persons who can supply required information.

### PILOT STUDIES

There may be times when the schoolman is unable to construct the "right" questions because he does not have sufficient information regarding the problem at hand. The reader may recall the models described in Chapter 2 which emphasized the identification of information that can help explain deviations or problems. One of these models (Figure 2.11) included a space for "Other Hints (Unknowns)." When a review of a problem results in many "unknowns" being recorded, this might indicate that these knowledge gaps should be filled before the community is surveyed. One way such gaps can be covered is to run a pilot study. In most communities there are persons or groups who can be identified as having a particular interest in school-related issues. These persons or groups often have valuable insights into school problems and into the views of the community about the problems. If they can be identified and asked about their perceptions regarding the issues, it may be possible to fill enough of these knowledge gaps ("unknowns") to be able to construct a relevant and complete survey instrument. Thus this variation of purposeful selection, the pilot study, would add further specification before asking questions of the community. When he feels that he is ready to survey the community, the administrator in charge of the project can then turn to a random selection procedure.

### KEY PARTICIPANTS

There may be occasions when an issue is precipitated by specific individuals or groups. These individuals or groups can be referred to as key participants. If a person or group plays a critical role in an issue the schoolman must know that person or group's position to be able to understand the causes of the issue. If they can be identified, these key participants should be surveyed. For example, a boycott of the school lunch program may be organized by parents because of their negative feelings about the lack of adequate supervision in the lunch room. If the key participants in the boycott can be identified it would be important to seek information from them. They are, after all, the opinion leaders who caused the parent group to take the action in the first place. Therefore their views about the issue must be known if the issue is to be alleviated.

## HOW TO SELECT PURPOSEFULLY

By now, it should be apparent to the reader that there is no one way of purposefully selecting respondents. Nor is there an optimal number of purposefully selected respondents to survey. Both the "who" and "how many" questions of purposeful selection are dependent upon the needs of the survey.

If the need is to obtain further information (a pilot study) before conducting the survey in the general community, the schoolman will have to know who are the most knowledgeable persons in the community concerning school issues. This will probably require that the superintendent, with the assistance of his staff, keep an up-to-date file of community members who have demonstrated their interest and knowledge about school matters. This group could be expanded by simply asking members of it if they can identify others who might be knowledgeable about school issues. If the need is to select key participants, the administrator will have to review pertinent documents and newspaper reports as well as talk with persons who are acquainted with the issue so that these key participants can be identified.

Political scientists have been carrying on an active debate for the past several decades concerning the most accurate way of identifying community influentials. Those who agree with Hunter (1953) believe that individuals in the community who are influential can be identified through *nomination* by persons actively interested in public affairs. Those who agree with Dahl (1961) and Polsby (1963) insist that influentials can only be identified by a thorough *review* of the decision-making process; i.e., who participates *and* plays decisive roles in the eventual decision.[2] As indicated above, we believe that the nomination and the review approaches are both valid and that they may have to be pursued in tandem to accurately identify purposefully selected respondents.

The number of persons surveyed in a pilot study depends upon the schoolman's ability to identify the persons with particular interest in school issues and the extent of "unknowns" about the issue itself. If he can identify appropriate respondents and the "unknowns" are relatively limited, he should only have to survey a few persons. The number of persons responding to a key participant survey is entirely dependent upon the number of individuals who are clearly identified as key participants in an issue.

## A LIMITATION

The administrator should take care to avoid drawing conclusions about the views of the community on the basis of information derived from respondents

[2] These approaches to the identification of community influentials are criticized by political scientists who argue that "the scope of actual decision-making" that can be observed is limited because the majority of potential issues are subverted *before* they ever reach the public forum stage (cf., Bachrach and Baratz, 1963). The administrator will have to be sensitive to the activity of those community influentials who influence the withdrawal of an issue (a "non-decision") as much as he is to those who influence issues that do reach the public arena.

who are purposefully selected. It cannot be assumed that persons and groups selected purposefully reflect the views of others in the community. Persons responding to a pilot study *may* reflect such views, but this is mere conjecture unless other citizens are surveyed. Key participants have access to information which outsiders to an issue cannot possibly have. As a result, they will probably feel more intensely, and probably differently, about the issue than will others in the community. Further, generalizations cannot be made from one small group to another. If the same issue became relevant to another small group, it too would have to be surveyed to ascertain how it would react. Thus purposeful selection restrains the administrator from generalizing survey findings to others in the community or to later issues.

## random selection

When the purposes of the survey require that generalizations be drawn from those responding to the survey instrument to others in the community, the second approach to respondent choice — random selection — should be pursued. The group whose views the schoolman wants to understand is referred to as the *population* or universe.[3] The persons he selects to respond to the survey instrument constitute a portion of that population and are referred to as a *sample*. To enhance the potential that the sample respondents are *representative* of the views of the population, they must be selected *randomly*. These key terms — population, sample, representative, and random — will be defined and described in some detail. Following that, different ways of selecting respondents randomly will be discussed. Finally, guidelines for determining the size of the sample will be provided.

### *POPULATION*

The first task in the random selection approach is to identify the group, or *population*, about which the administrator wants to develop understandings. A population is defined as all the individuals, subgroups, objects, aggregates, or items in a specific group. Note that this definition of population includes "things" as well as people. Given the needs of the survey, it may be appropriate to consider "things" such as organizations or classes as the basic units of interest. For example, the administrator may want to further his understanding of the positions taken by community organizations with interests in the public schools or he may want to know more about the achievement level of students in algebra classes.

The intent of the investigation will dictate the definition and composition

---

[3]The terms "universe" and "population" are used interchangeably in the literature. The term "population" will be used exclusively in the present discussion to minimize possible confusion.

of the population. Thus the population might include all residents in the school district or it might be composed of specific identifiable subgroups within the larger group. Examples of possible subgroups include all whites or blacks; males or females; parents or non-parents; and teachers and students by subject matter or grade level.

Geographically the population may come from all parts of the school district or it may be spatially limited. For example, the population may be spatially limited if it is defined as all of the eligible voters in a single school attendance area. On the other hand, it may be geographically dispersed if it is defined as all parents in the school district whose children are eligible to participate in a work-study program. These examples should make it quite clear that the "population" does not always include all the people in the district. The basic units and the specific compositions of populations will vary from problem to problem. Therefore, with each new problem of interest, the administrator will have to take care to redefine the population. This must be accurately done if appropriate units are to be randomly selected from the population. To be able to define the population regarding a specific problem, the schoolman will have to know something about the *characteristics* of populations and have access to complete *listings* of the basic units of the population of interest.

**Characteristics of Populations.** The first step in random selection is the identification of the population about which information is wanted. The identification is made by listing the characteristics that are known about the population. The more that is known about the characteristics of the population, the more capable we are of choosing a sample that is representative. Once the characteristics are known, we can sort out who is in the population (and eligible to be part of the sample) and who is not in the population (and not eligible to be part of the sample). Only when the sample is representative of the population can one be confident that what one finds out from the survey applies to the larger group.

The characteristics to look for depend on the information being sought; the generalizations or comparisons to be made from the survey results. A major consideration is identification of the people who have the opinions we want to find out about or who have knowledge of the topic being investigated. For example, if we want to find out how parents feel about school bus safety precautions, it would be the parents of youngsters who ride the buses that would make up the population. If information is wanted about local post-high school employment patterns for the past five years, it is the public, parochial, and private school graduates and dropouts of the past five years who make up the population. There will also be less clear-cut instances where choices will have to be made. For example, if the school wants to find out what will make its newsletter more appealing, should readers or nonreaders be sampled? If the district wants to predict how its voters might react to a proposed bond issue, would the population be defined as all eligible voters or just those who usually vote?

Other characteristics have to be thought of too. These are the usual traits by which populations are grouped: age, sex, socioeconomic class, and geographic location. Some examples follow. The voter population should frequently be grouped by age and sex. Persons below minimum voting age should be excluded, but all others must be included. If one sex outnumbers the other, that fact must be represented in the sample. Further, if the school wants to know the impact of school taxes across the community's households, then socioeconomic characteristics and geographic locations must be considered in defining the population. All income brackets would have to be sampled as well as residents in housing subdivisions, trailer parks, and apartments. Again there will be instances where choices will have to be made. If the school system wants to know the attitudes of older residents toward its pupil promotion policies, would a key characteristic be age of respondents or length of residence in the district? Or both? The clear definition of purposes for the survey can help determine which characteristics are paramount in defining the population.

**Sources of Population Lists.** The next question is where to find the names and locations of members of the population in order to draw the sample. Usually the administrator will find that there are a number of usable listings in existence, but each list should be examined carefully to find out how it was compiled, for what purpose and when. Knowing how the list was made will help to judge its completeness and accuracy; knowing the purpose for which it was assembled will indicate some of the population characteristics included; and knowing when it was made will help to determine if it is still usable.

The first place to turn is to the school district's own resources and to public records. Pupil registration records would yield lists of parents and guardians of children in school. The mailing list of the school-community relations or school business office are other sources. Care should be exercised to make sure that such lists are not just property owners or made up on a subscription basis. Then there are specialized lists such as school alumni, community organization officers, and youth group leaders which should be available and which may comprise the specific population wanted or at least a portion of it.

There are other sources within the community. A city or area directory compiled by a local company or by a directory publisher in the region is usually a reliable up-to-date source. For example, the J. L. Polk Company of Detroit, Michigan, publishes some 1,300 directories covering about 7,000 communities in the United States. Polk listings are developed by a door-to-door canvass and include all residents eighteen years old and over. There are usually two sections of directory entries, one by street addresses and one by name and address. Occupations are often listed with the names.

Local government agencies may be able to supply mailing lists or maps which will yield names and/or addresses. Be sure, however, that the names are residents and not, for example, the owners of property or automobile owners. Some fire districts keep records of occupied dwellings by name of householder and number of occupants. Charitable organizations often develop listings for campaign purposes. Specialized listings, such as newcomers to the community or retired persons, are maintained by organizations which serve them, for example, welcome wagon, newcomers, and golden age clubs. Such lists may be useful if the people on them comprise the population or a portion of it.

From experience, there are several sources to avoid. Churches, by and large, do not keep accurate records of parish members. The telephone directory is not as usable as might be thought. Unlisted numbers and nonsubscribers make it a biased source. Names and addresses supplied by an organization or obtained by the school on the basis of confidentiality should not be used. State laws may prohibit the use of pupil records for such purposes.

Finally, there may be occasions when it is necessary for the school district to create original lists for survey purposes. This is not as difficult a task as it may seem. The annual or biannual school census can be used as a base. A few additional notes about each household, such as other adults living there and occupation of head of household, would round out the listings sufficiently for most purposes. Such a list is easily updated. It may also be possible to have a directory company supply a list even though its printed directory does not include the community. The cost of such a service will vary by the amount of data wanted, size of the population, and the extent to which the company has the information already in hand.

Once a usable list has been developed from sources, it should be carefully labeled as to the characteristics and sources utilized, dated, and a copy stored. Copies of the original list should be made available for use in drawing the sample.

**When to Survey Populations.** In most instances it will be sufficient and appropriate to survey a portion, a sample, of the population, but there are two exceptions to this generalization. First, an issue may affect a small and well-defined group. For example, when a curricular innovation is a significant departure from traditional practices and it is to be tested in a single classroom, the "issue" immediately affects only the parents and students in that classroom. With a population this small it is difficult to assure representativeness of a sample without surveying virtually every member of that population. It probably would be easier in the long run at any rate to survey every member of the group. A second exception is when the schoolman wants to use a survey to disseminate information or to serve a public relations purpose as well as to gather information. If these other purposes are relevant, it may be well worth the cost of surveying the entire population.

*SAMPLE SURVEYS*

When the population is not small and well defined or public relations aspects are not relevant, it is more logical to survey a sample of the population rather than the entire population. *Contrary to what one might expect, sample surveys can be more reliable in the results obtained than population surveys.* In part this is due to the fact that the more respondents surveyed, the greater the opportunity there is for human and mechanical error in obtaining, coding, and analyzing information. But it is also due to the fact that modern scientific sampling procedures give the surveyor tools for determining the accuracy of results obtained in a sample survey.[4]

Slonim notes that the advantages of a sample survey over a population survey are that the administrator can "cut costs, reduce manpower requirements, gather vital information more quickly, obtain data that could not possibly be available otherwise, obtain more comprehensive data, and actually increase the accuracy of his figures in some instances [1966, p. 3]." These are indeed impressive reasons to learn the requirements of sampling and to avoid population surveys.

Since a sample is a mini-representation of the population it should reflect the population characteristics as closely as possible. This "reflection" is referred to as the representativeness of the sample and is achieved through a process of random selection.

**Representativeness.** The objective of a sample survey is to make *inferences* (draw conclusions) about the population from a sample of that population. Therefore the sample must be *representative* of the defined population. If it is not, the conclusions drawn from the survey will be biased in favor of those characteristics overrepresented and will not, therefore, be a true picture. Representative samples, in short, are those which include the same characteristics, in approximately the same proportion, as those found in the total population.

The Institute for Social Research at the University of Michigan (1969) provides a good example of a representative and a nonrepresentative sample. The Institute notes that observing two teenagers and drawing conclusions about teenagers in general is a nonrepresentative sampling procedure and thus is fraught with many possible errors of misinterpretation. No two persons can possibly possess all the characteristics, let alone possess them in the same proportion, that are found in a population such as "teenagers in general." On the other hand, as the Institute notes, "tasting a spoonful of soup to see how the whole pot is seasoned" may well be an appropriate sampling approach. Assuming that the soup has just been stirred, it is a fair assumption that a spoonful will be

---

[4]The interested reader may want to read Slonim (1966) for a fuller and quite readable understanding of these points concerning the reliability of sample surveys.

representative of the contents of the entire bowl of soup. If the process of observing different pairs of teenagers is followed several times, the information derived will probably vary, whereas several tastes of the bowl of soup will probably lead to the same taste results.

Checking for representativeness is a relatively easy matter *if* the administrator knows the relevant characteristics to be found in the population and the proportions in which they occur. If he has this information, he merely has to check the sample selected against the population to see if these characteristics appear in comparable proportions. For example, if one relevant characteristic is sex and he knows the frequency of male-female occurrence in the population, it is not difficult to check the survey respondent list to see if the male-female ratio is close to that found in the population. (This is tested further in Chapter 10.)

Other population characteristics such as age, race, income, and number of children in the household are not as easy to ascertain as male-female ratio. Therefore it is incumbent upon the administrator to collect and update information about the characteristics he might be interested in exploring regarding the school district population. This is an ongoing task.

Even with all of these precautions, there will inevitably be times when there is insufficient knowledge about the occurrence of relevant characteristics in the population. When some population characteristics are not well known, one cannot precisely know if the sample selected is really representative. However, by applying random selection in drawing samples it is possible to increase the probability of representativeness.[5]

**Random Selection.** To achieve randomness all individuals, subgroups, aggregates, or items in a defined population must have an equal chance of being chosen to participate in the survey.[6] Random selection minimizes the chances that the sample selected will be prejudiced in favor of any particular characteristics found in the population.

*Random selection does not assure that the sample will be representative.* It does assure that human bias does not enter the selection process, thus enhancing *the potential for representativeness.* To avoid human bias the sample respondents should be drawn strictly by chance.

**Tables of Random Numbers: An Approach to Selection by Chance.** To meet the criteria of randomness, a method which assures that respondents are selected by chance should be employed. There are various ways of drawing respondents by chance, ranging from the drawing of names from a hat or fishbowl to the

---

[5] We employ terms such as "randomness" and "random selection" for simplication of vocabulary. These notions are usually subsumed within the concept of "probability" in the literature (cf. Kerlinger, 1973).

[6] Be sure that the list of the population is complete. Otherwise all elements in the population cannot have an equal chance of being selected to participate in the survey.

**Table 6.1**

**Number of Digits Assigned to Names on Population Lists**

| If the total of the population falls between: | Then the following number of digits should be placed beside each member's name: |
|---|---|
| 1 and 9 | 1 (e.g., 1,2....9) |
| 10 and 99 | 2 (e.g., 01,02....99) |
| 100 and 999 | 3 (e.g., 001,002....999) |
| 1,000 and 9,999 | 4 (e.g., 0001,0002....9999) |
| 10,000 and 99,999 | 5 (e.g., 00001,00002....99999) |
| 100,000 and 999,999 | 6 (e.g., 000001,000002....999999) |
| 1,000,000 and 9,999,999 | 7 (e.g., 0000001, 0000002....9999999) |

spinning of a roulette wheel. However, a method which approximates pure chance selection involves the use of a table of random numbers. This method comes closest of all selection methods to the elimination of human bias. Tables of random numbers are developed mechanically. Therefore, there is no order or system introduced into the numbering.

The first step in the process is to assign a number to each member on the population list. Care should be taken that the numbers in front of all names on the population list have an equal amount of digits. This is necessary so that a set number of digits can be drawn from the table of random numbers which will apply to all members of the population. A review of Table 6.1 should help the reader to choose the appropriate number of digits to put before all names on the population list.

With the names on the population list appropriately numbered it is now possible to begin to randomly draw respondents by using a table of random numbers.[7] Before making the first selection the reader should decide whether he will follow the table horizontally, vertically, diagonally, up or down, right or left. After this initial human choice is made, the selector must continue in that direction as he draws numbers.

It might be useful to illustrate the process of using a table of random numbers (Figure 6.1). Let us say that the population numbers 5,536 (a four-digit number) and the desired number of sample respondents is 250. Each name on the population list is assigned a four-digit number (e.g., 0001, 0002, ... to 5,536). The schoolman then turns to the table of random numbers to draw the required

---

[7] An extensive compilation of random numbers tables has been made by the Rand Corporation. These tables, several of which have been included in the present volume, may be a useful acquisition for school districts with large populations. Rand Corporation, *A Million Random Digits with 100,000 Normal Deviates* (New York: Free Press, 1965).

**Figure 6.1**
Illustrative Table of Random Numbers[a]
Row

| | | | | | | | | | | |
|---|---|---|---|---|---|---|---|---|---|---|
| 00000 | 10097 | 32533 | 76520 | 13586 | 34673 | 54876 | 80959 | 09117 | 39292 | 74945 |
| 00001 | 37542 | 04805 | 64894 | 74296 | 24805 | 24037 | 20636 | 10402 | 00822 | 91665 |
| 00002 | 08422 | 68953 | 19645 | 09303 | 23209 | 02560 | 15953 | 34764 | 35080 | 33606 |
| 00003 | 99019 | 02529 | 09376 | 70715 | 38311 | 31165 | 88676 | 74397 | 04436 | 27659 |
| 00004 | 12807 | 99970 | 80157 | 36147 | 64032 | 36653 | 98951 | 16877 | 12171 | 76833 |
| 00005 | 66065 | 74717 | 34072 | 76850 | 36697 | 36170 | 65813 | 39885 | 11199 | 29170 |
| 00006 | 31060 | 10805 | 45571 | 82406 | 35303 | 42614 | 86799 | 07439 | 23403 | 09732 |
| 00007 | 85269 | 77602 | 02051 | 65692 | 68665 | 74818 | 73053 | 85247 | 18623 | 88579 |
| 00008 | 63573 | 32135 | 05325 | 47048 | 90553 | 57548 | 28468 | 28709 | 83491 | 25624 |
| 00009 | 73796 | 45753 | 03529 | 64778 | 35808 | 34282 | 60935 | 20344 | 35273 | 88435 |
| 00010 | 98520 | 17767 | 14905 | 68607 | 22109 | 40558 | 60970 | 93433 | 50500 | 73998 |
| 00011 | 11805 | 05431 | 39808 | 27732 | 50725 | 68248 | 29405 | 24201 | 52775 | 67851 |
| 00012 | 83452 | 99634 | 06288 | 98083 | 13746 | 70078 | 18475 | 40610 | 68711 | 77817 |
| 00013 | 88685 | 40200 | 86507 | 58401 | 36766 | 67951 | 90364 | 76493 | 29609 | 11062 |
| 00014 | 99594 | 67348 | 87517 | 64969 | 91826 | 08928 | 93785 | 61368 | 23478 | 34113 |
| 00015 | 65481 | 17674 | 17468 | 50950 | 58047 | 76974 | 73039 | 57186 | 40218 | 16544 |
| 00016 | 80124 | 35635 | 17727 | 08015 | 45318 | 22374 | 21115 | 78253 | 14385 | 53763 |
| 00017 | 74350 | 99817 | 77402 | 77214 | 43236 | 00210 | 45521 | 64237 | 96286 | 02655 |
| 00018 | 69916 | 26803 | 66252 | 29148 | 36936 | 87203 | 76621 | 13990 | 94400 | 56418 |
| 00019 | 09893 | 20505 | 14225 | 68514 | 46427 | 56788 | 96297 | 78822 | 54382 | 14598 |
| 00020 | 91499 | 14523 | 68479 | 27686 | 46162 | 83554 | 94750 | 89923 | 37089 | 20048 |
| 00021 | 80336 | 94598 | 26940 | 36858 | 70297 | 34135 | 53140 | 33340 | 42050 | 82341 |
| 00022 | 44104 | 81949 | 85157 | 47954 | 32979 | 26575 | 57600 | 40881 | 22222 | 06413 |
| 00023 | 12550 | 73742 | 11100 | 02040 | 12860 | 74697 | 96644 | 89439 | 28707 | 25815 |
| 00024 | 63606 | 49329 | 16505 | 34484 | 40219 | 52563 | 43651 | 77082 | 07207 | 31790 |
| 00025 | 61196 | 90446 | 26457 | 47774 | 51924 | 33729 | 65394 | 59593 | 42582 | 60527 |
| 00026 | 15474 | 45266 | 95270 | 79953 | 59367 | 83848 | 82396 | 10118 | 33211 | 59466 |
| 00027 | 94557 | 28573 | 67897 | 54387 | 54622 | 44431 | 91190 | 42592 | 92927 | 45973 |
| 00028 | 42481 | 16213 | 97344 | 08721 | 16868 | 48767 | 03071 | 12059 | 25701 | 46670 |
| 00029 | 23523 | 78317 | 73208 | 89837 | 68935 | 91416 | 26252 | 29663 | 05522 | 82562 |
| 00030 | 04493 | 52494 | 75246 | 33824 | 45862 | 51025 | 61962 | 79335 | 65337 | 12472 |
| 00031 | 00549 | 97654 | 64051 | 88159 | 96119 | 63896 | 54692 | 82391 | 23287 | 29529 |
| 00032 | 35963 | 15307 | 26898 | 09354 | 33351 | 35462 | 77974 | 50024 | 90103 | 39333 |
| 00033 | 59808 | 08391 | 45427 | 26842 | 83609 | 49700 | 13021 | 24892 | 78565 | 20106 |
| 00034 | 46058 | 85236 | 01390 | 92286 | 77281 | 44077 | 93910 | 83647 | 70617 | 42941 |
| 00035 | 32179 | 00597 | 87379 | 25241 | 05567 | 07007 | 86743 | 17157 | 85394 | 11838 |
| 00036 | 69234 | 61406 | 20117 | 45204 | 15956 | 60000 | 18743 | 92423 | 97118 | 96338 |
| 00037 | 19565 | 41430 | 01758 | 75379 | 40419 | 21585 | 66674 | 36806 | 84962 | 85207 |
| 00038 | 45155 | 14938 | 19476 | 07246 | 43667 | 94543 | 59047 | 90033 | 20826 | 69541 |
| 00039 | 94864 | 31994 | 36168 | 10851 | 34888 | 81553 | 01540 | 35456 | 05014 | 51176 |
| 00040 | 98086 | 24826 | 45240 | 28404 | 44999 | 08896 | 39094 | 73407 | 35441 | 31880 |
| 00041 | 33185 | 16232 | 41941 | 50949 | 89435 | 48581 | 88695 | 41994 | 37548 | 73043 |
| 00042 | 80951 | 00406 | 96382 | 70774 | 20151 | 23387 | 25016 | 25298 | 94624 | 61171 |
| 00043 | 79752 | 49140 | 71961 | 28296 | 69861 | 02591 | 74852 | 20539 | 00387 | 59579 |
| 00044 | 18633 | 32537 | 98145 | 06571 | 31010 | 24674 | 05455 | 61427 | 77938 | 91936 |
| 00045 | 74029 | 43902 | 77557 | 32270 | 97790 | 17119 | 52527 | 58021 | 80814 | 51748 |
| 00046 | 54178 | 45611 | 80993 | 37143 | 05335 | 12969 | 56127 | 19255 | 36040 | 90324 |
| 00047 | 11664 | 49883 | 52079 | 84827 | 59381 | 71539 | 09973 | 33440 | 88461 | 23356 |
| 00048 | 48324 | 77928 | 31249 | 64710 | 02295 | 36870 | 32307 | 57546 | 15020 | 09994 |
| 00049 | 69074 | 94138 | 87637 | 91976 | 35584 | 04401 | 10518 | 21615 | 01848 | 76938 |

[a]Source: Rand Corporation, *A Million Random Digits With 100,000 Normal Deviates*, New York: Free Press, 1965. By permission.

250 respondent numbers. (It is possible that duplicate numbers will be drawn, although not very likely. If this occurs the duplicate numbers should be discarded and not be counted toward the total of 250 numbers to be drawn. Numbers next to names on the population list will have to be checked off as the drawing proceeds to catch those duplicate numbers if they occur.)

Begin the draw by letting the pencil fall where it would on the table of random numbers (Figure 6.1). If we had decided to proceed horizontally (and back horizontally down the page when we run out of numbers on a row) and our pencil had landed on row 00021, twenty columns before the end of the row, the first number selected would be 5314. The person with that number would be drawn for the sample. Continuing horizontally to the end of the row, the next four numbers would be 0333, 4042, 0508 and 2341. All of these numbers correspond with numbers next to individuals on the population list, so four more persons would be drawn for the sample. Continue, as predetermined, down the page and back horizontally. Thus, on row 00022, the first number, going from right to left, is 3146. The second and third numbers are 0222 and 2218. Persons assigned these numbers would be added to the sample. The next number is 8040. This number is greater than any of the numbers assigned to persons on the population list. Therefore it must be discarded. The next number, 0675, matches that next to a name on the population list. The following number, 5756, is too large and cannot be used. This process would be continued until the desired 250 numbers which correspond to numbers on our population list are selected. If we were unable to draw the entire 250 numbers going through the table the first time, we would then turn to a second table of random numbers to continue the draw.[8]

Human bias can be eliminated if the schoolman follows the foregoing procedure of drawing numbers. Remember, after deciding the path to follow in the table, remain faithful to that decision and do not arbitrarily change directions. Do not lift the pencil and start at some other point on the table. Finally, continue the draw sequentially until the desired number of respondents is selected.

Tables of random numbers can be employed as selection vehicles for virtually any random selection system. Therefore the reader is encouraged to use the tables whenever possible to minimize human bias in sample selection.

### VARIETIES OF RANDOM SAMPLES

There are a number of variations on random sampling which could be used to select respondents who, as a group, represent the population. Four of the most frequently employed are presented below: *simple random sampling,*

---

[8]The table of random numbers exhibited in Figure 6.1 and three others are provided for readers who must draw large samples. These can be found in Appendix B.

*stratified random sampling, systematic sampling,* and *cluster sampling.*[9] Because the choice of the system used depends heavily upon the purposes of the survey and the resources available to carry it out, the advantages ("pluses") and disadvantages ("minuses") of the systems are presented, as well as a description of the process required in using them.

**Simple Random Sampling.** Simple random sampling is the system upon which all other random selection systems are based. Thus "an understanding of any of the refined variations presupposes an understanding of simple random sampling [Ackoff, 1953, p. 92]." Simple random sampling is the easiest of the systems to use because it requires no refined regrouping of the population before sample respondents are selected. Such regroupings are required in stratified and cluster sampling and sometimes necessary in systematic sampling.

Simple random sampling requires only that one assign numbers, consecutively, to members on a population list. With this numbered population list in hand, the sample respondents are drawn by using the table of random numbers process discussed above. When the desired amount of numbers which correspond to numbers on the population list are drawn, the selection process is complete.

*Pluses and Minuses.* The major plus of simple random sampling is that the administrator does not have to know characteristics of the population to be able to select respondents. There will be occasions when this will be the case. For example, the study may require comparisons between races in the community. In a highly mobile community such up-to-date information may be difficult to maintain. *If* all members of the community are included on the population list, the probability is that a sample which approximately represents the community's racial composition will be drawn. Another plus of simple random sampling is that resources do not have to be consumed in initially sub-grouping the population (which, as the reader will note, is often the case in other random sampling procedures).

On the minus side, when the administrator *does* have substantial information about relevant characteristics found in the population, simple random selection does not permit him to take advantage of such knowledge. When he possesses such information, the schoolman might choose to employ one of the refinements of simple random sampling noted below.

**Stratified Random Sampling.** It may be suspected that specific characteristics found in the population, such as age, sex, race, income, parent status, and

---

[9]The reader who would like to explore alternatives to the random selection systems described here will find annotated references in Appendix D. A good first source might be Russell L. Ackoff, *The Design of Social Research* (Chicago: University of Chicago Press, 1953). See especially Chapter IV, "The Practical Research Design: Sampling," pp. 83–131.

frequency of voting, significantly affect the way different people react to given school issues. If the administrator thinks this might be true, he will want to guarantee that such characteristics appear in the sample drawn so that he can see if such suspicions are accurate. For example, he may have reason to believe that younger adults are more supportive of school financial needs than older adults. If so, he would want to be certain that younger and older age groups (his best guess would lead him to develop age group categories) are well represented in the sample to be drawn. Similarly, he may want to know if there are perceptual differences concerning school fiscal support between those who vote and those who do not vote in bond referendums. If so, he would want to be sure both of these citizen groups are represented in the sample.

To be sure that these groups are adequately represented in the sample the schoolman might use stratified random selection. The primary requirement is that he be able to determine the frequency of occurrence of relevant characteristics in the population. He would begin the process by dividing the population into *strata* based upon the relevant characteristic he wants included. For example, the last example given above would require him to divide the adult population into two strata: voters and nonvoters. Once the population is divided into the appropriate strata he would go about the sample selection in the same manner as that described in the simple random sample selection, drawing the desired number of respondents from each of the sublists.

There are two variations of stratification: *proportional* and *weighted* stratified random sampling. Which is more appropriate depends on the needs of the surveyor. Proportional stratified random sampling permits the administrator to make inferences from the results obtained in the survey directly to the population. This is possible because the number of respondents in each stratum in the sample is proportional to the number of such members found in the population. For example, if the characteristic of interest is voter activity and 25 percent of the adult population can be classified as voters,[10] then the voter stratum would contain 25 percent of the sample respondents and the nonvoter stratum would contain 75 percent of the sample respondents.

In the second approach, weighted stratified random sampling, specific strata are purposefully overrepresented in the sample. This may be appropriate if certain strata are not well represented in the population but, for reasons beyond size, are decisive characteristics of the population. For example, continuing with the example of the school bond referendum, voters may constitute only 10 percent of the adult population. However, their willingness to exercise their franchise makes them important to school fiscal decision-making well beyond what their numbers might indicate. In this case it might be relevant to overrepresent this stratum in the sample, giving it as much as a five to one

---

[10] A list of voters could be established by checking the poll book of the latest school district election or bond referendum if such a record is maintained.

weighting advantage over the nonvoter stratum, (i.e., the sample would be composed of 150 voters and 150 nonvoters in a 300 respondent survey sample). This would assure that sufficient numbers of those who have chosen to influence school fiscal matters will be selected to respond to the survey. If the sample size was 300 and the voter stratum were proportionately represented, this would result in only 30 voters being included in the survey. This is probably insufficient given the potency of the stratum.

When strata are weighted as in the preceding example, mathematical treatment will be required before inferences can be made about the population. To illustrate, we selected 50 percent of the sample from the voter group and 50 percent from the nonvoter group, when in actuality the voter group represents only 10 percent of the population and the nonvoter group represents 90 percent of the population. While weighting the voters so heavily can give the schoolman more insights into this relevant group, he should bring this stratum back into proportion when making statements about the total population. The voter group responses would have to be adjusted mathematically so that it became only 10 percent of the sample responses *if* it is relevant to make statements concerning the posture of the entire population.

*Pluses and Minuses.* On the plus side, stratified random sampling provides assurance that characteristics which are particularly important to the needs of the survey will be represented in the sample drawn. The administrator knows that desired comparisons of strata will be possible when the coded information is ready for analysis. Weighted sampling permits such comparisons even when a critical characteristic is not well represented in the population.

On the minus side, the administrator must have accurate and detailed information about the characteristics found in the population before he can stratify. In many instances this detailed information is not available. Even when it exists, making it available in the form needed is often a costly and time-consuming process. Finally, when weighted stratified sampling is used, the information obtained must be treated to make it proportional before inferences can be made about the population.

**Systematic Sampling.** Systematic sampling is very much like simple random sampling. The difference lies in the fact that all members of the population have an equal chance of being selected *at all stages* of simple random sampling, whereas in systematic sampling, after an initial random choice is made respondents are picked at regular intervals and only certain members of the population have a chance to be drawn for the sample. However, systematic sampling may be appropriate if specific conditions are met. Further, systematic sampling is easier to employ and less time-consuming than simple random sampling. Following are three instances when systematic sampling might be used.

In the first instance the schoolman may want to systematically select respondents from a population list. When the arrangement of the list does not bias selection of respondents (i.e., favor one population characteristic over others), this may be an appropriate approach. For example, if the population list is alphabetized and the characteristic of interest is age variation in the population as it may affect individuals' responses to a school issue. It is reasonable to assume that members of the population will be randomly dispersed by age throughout an alphabetized list. In this instance, if the population totaled 2,000 members and the desired sample size is 100, all that is required is that every twentieth person on the list be selected. To avoid human bias the administrator begins by randomly drawing a four-digit number from the table of random numbers. When a four-digit number which matches one found on the population list is drawn, all that need be done from that point is to select persons at every twentieth interval from the first drawn number. For example, if 0731 is drawn from the table, that becomes the number of the first person to be selected for the survey. The next person will be the one who is listed next to the number 0751 on the population list. The administrator continues to draw (0771, 0791, 0811, etc.) until he has been completely through the population list and has selected the required 100 sample respondents. Think of the population list as a cylinder; i.e., keep going round and round the list until the required number of respondents are selected.

In the second instance the administrator may want to conduct a door-to-door survey. *If* he is sure that there is a dispersal of household income, race, age, and so on, fairly evenly throughout the community, systematic sampling may be used. If this is the case he will not have to secure a population list and go through the lengthy process of organizing a sample according to geographic areas, as he would have to do in a simple random sample. All that he would have to do is randomly select the first household and then proceed by an interval established as described until the required number of households were surveyed.

In the third instance, the population from which the sample is to be drawn may not be on a formal list, but on a large deck of computer cards. The transfer of the names from computer cards to a population list is time-consuming and expensive. If he is certain that the cards are randomly arranged as concerns the characteristics being explored, the schoolman can draw the sample directly from the deck, using a ruler. The process is quite simple. If the deck is 20 inches in length and the desired sample is 80 of the individuals represented in that deck, all that is necessary is that a ruler be laid across the top of the deck and a respondent be drawn at every ¼-inch interval (20 ÷ ¼ = 80) (Slonim, 1966).

*Pluses and Minuses.* On the plus side, systematic samples are quite easily drawn. The cost and time associated with this selection system are minimal. In many instances this sampling system will be adequate.

On the minus side, one cannot be sure that the sample selected will be representative of the population because all members of the population *do not* have an equal chance of being selected *after* the initial random draw is made. After 07351 was drawn from the population list example given above, only every twentieth person could possibly be selected to participate in the survey. Similarly, the households between established intervals could not be selected, nor could persons whose computer card listing did not fall at the ¼-inch interval on the ruler.

The biggest problem with systematic sampling is that any bias in the population arrangement will result in a bias in the sample. If, for example, the population list noted was ordered by age of members rather than alphabetically, the sample selected might well be biased. Say the population list was composed of a series of subgroups of ten members, each in a descending age arrangement. If intervals of ten were to be used in the sample selection, respondents would always be chosen from the same age strata. If the households in the community were not evenly dispersed (and they rarely are) systematic selection might also result in a biased sample. Similarly, the computer card deck may have been so ordered that the sample selected would not be truly representative of the population.

As a general rule, the schoolman should avoid using systematic sampling when he suspects that there are biases in the way the population is ordered. If he has reason to believe that there is no such bias, systematic sampling may be appropriate.

**Cluster Sampling.**[11]   There will virtually always be a map available which shows the housing units in the community, block by block. Such a map might be used as the basis of sample selection, in substitution for a population list.

Cluster sampling entails several steps. The community must first be subdivided into appropriate clusters. These clusters could be, for example, voting wards, school attendance areas, or defined neighborhoods. The factors which prompted the survey will dictate the definition of a cluster. Once clusters are established, these in turn will have to be mapped in detail to illustrate the individual residential blocks within each cluster. Each block would then be mapped to show each dwelling unit, as a designated number. Finally, if it is relevant to achieve a mix in types of respondents (e.g., male-female or old-young), the person to respond to the survey in each particular dwelling would have to be determined.

An example of this process is illustrated in Figure 6.2. In this case the appropriate clusters are defined as school attendance areas. After the borders of the attendance areas are drawn, each attendance area is next subdivided into blocks. Finally each block in every attendance area is mapped out according to the dwelling units on it. If certain sample characteristics are desired, the

[11] Area sampling is a term often used interchangeably with cluster sampling.

102    Getting the Information

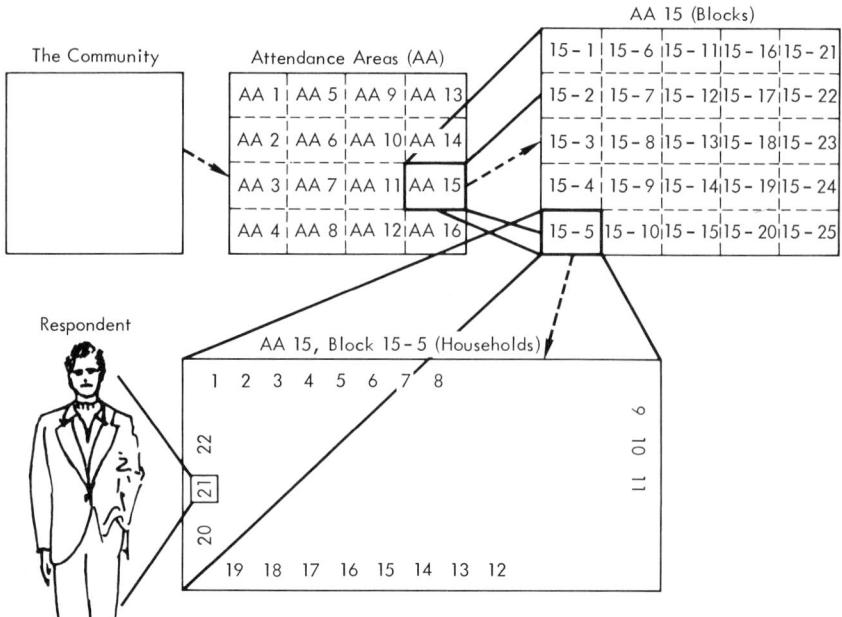

**Figure 6.2**

An illustrated cluster sampling process.

specification of an individual respondent within a selected dwelling unit is then made.

Cluster sampling might be used when there is no list available which accurately portrays the total population and a map of the community may be the only alternative available for drawing a random sample of respondents. For example, using Figure 6.2 as an illustration, let us say that the desired sample size is 160 and each of the 16 attendance areas is of about equal size in population.[12] Then it would be necessary to draw ten respondents from each of the attendance areas. The first task would be to randomly select ten blocks from each attendance area. Next it would be necessary to select a dwelling unit on each of these blocks. An easy method would be to provide instructions which were uniform for fieldworkers who would make the survey, such as "Stand on the Northwest corner of the block and count to the twenty-first dwelling unit." If the unit selected was a multiple dwelling unit, instructions for choosing the residence within it would have to be provided. Similarly, if it is important to vary respondents by given characteristics such as sex or age, then the fieldworker would have to have instructions for achieving this mix. This may be as simple as "Try

[12]If the clusters selected were not about equal in population, then it would be necessary to compute the number of respondents to select from each by estimating the proportion of the population which is in each cluster.

to get a fifty-fifty mix in men and women responding to the instrument" or as complex as a chart specifying the order of respondents (e.g., first respondent should be male, second respondent, female, third respondent, male. . . . ).[13]

Cluster sampling might also be used when a community is so geographically widespread that is is felt to be prohibitively expensive in dollars, time and manpower to sample respondents across the entire district. In this instance, it is a simple matter to randomly draw clusters and then limit block, household, and respondent selection to those clusters drawn.

In either district-wide cluster sampling or limited cluster sampling it must be remembered that the equal chance principle is violated in the same manner that it is violated in systematic selection. In both instances, once the initial random selection is made, not all members of the population have an equal chance of being selected for the survey.

If a cluster sample is chosen, take precautions to assure that the community map used is complete and up-to-date. It is discouraging when a selected cluster turns out to be an open field as a result of urban renewal. It is also discouraging to find that not all members of the population have been given a chance to be selected because a recent housing development does not appear on the map used.

*Pluses and Minuses.* Cluster samples are usually less expensive to obtain than are random samples which require population lists. In addition, it is possible to cut sampling costs in cluster samples by geographically focusing fieldwork. These are pluses of availability and economy.

On the minus side, however, the schoolman may find that losses in representativeness far outweigh gains in economy. Not all members have equal chances of being selected. Further, clusters tend to be more homogeneous (e.g., in socioeconomic status, race, and ethnic background) than total communities. Thus the sample may not include all relevant characteristics found in the total population. For these reasons it is recommended that the other random sampling approaches already discussed be used unless there is no population list available or it is clearly beyond the means of the school district to survey across the total geographical area of the community.

## what size sample to draw

Determining the size of the sample is a matter of making a series of "best guess" decisions and then living with the results of those decisions. There are three pieces of information that are necessary as a starting point. First, how

---

[13] For a detailed discussion of dwelling unit and respondent selection procedures, see Charles H. Backstrom and Gerald D. Hursh, *Survey Research* (Evanston, Ill.: Northwest University Press, 1963), pp. 43–59.

precise must the results be? That is, how much error can be tolerated? Second, how confident must the schoolman be that the results actually fall within the range of tolerance? That is, how much assurance is needed that the results are as reported? Lastly, how will the information from the questionnaire be reported and analyzed? That is, will the data be handled as percentages, such as the percent of citizens favoring a certain curriculum program, or will it be some type of statistic, such as the average (mean) attitude score of citizens compared with previous years?[14] Since most surveys seem to deal with "percentages," this will be the main consideration for the *quantitative* procedures for determining sample size. Once these quantitative decisions have been made they undergo further revision based upon decisions or judgments of a pragmatic nature. Are the resources available for a sample of this size? What level of cooperation can be expected? What analytic needs have we specified? And are there concomitant purposes for this survey? With this general overview of determining the size of a sample we can now treat the specifics of this decision-sequence.

## *QUANTITATIVE DECISIONS*

**Tolerance of Error.** The amount of error that can occur without undo harm to the study is related to the purposes of that investigation. If the purpose of the survey is to predict an outcome, *and* the knowing of that outcome is crucial, *and* it appears to be an issue that may be very closely contested, *then* there would be little tolerance for error. The results might have to be very precise. On the other hand, if the study is to explore reasons for something that has occurred, *and* if some fluctuation in the responses would still permit the analysis desired, *then* a relatively larger error-figure oculd be accepted. Usually these error-figures are expressed as a number of percentage points within which the results might vary. Thus, if the schoolman wants to know the outcomes of a bond referendum that may be fairly close, he might only be able to tolerate an error of 1 or 2 percentage points. The results that the sample provides would be accurate *plus or minus* 2 percentage points (if he had specified 2 percent as his tolerance of error). In the Table of Sample Sizes (Table 6.2), the level of tolerated error is listed on the left side of the table.

**Confidence.** Tolerance is only a part of the selection, for the schoolman must specify how *confident* he must be that the results do indeed fall within the percentage points specified. Is it necessary for him to be *very confident* or could

---

[14]None of the information required for determining sample size refers to the size of the population. It is sometimes assumed that the sample should be a certain percentage of the population, but that assumption lacks verification. The procedures detailed in this section *do not* require knowledge of the size of the population.

**Table 6.2**

Sample Sizes for Two Levels of Confidence with Varying Degrees of Tolerance (Assuming "Uncertainty" for the Percentage of Occurrence)[a]

| Tolerance of Error in Percent (+ or −) | 95 times in 100 | 99 times in 100 |
|---|---|---|
| 0.5 | 38,400 | 66,000 |
| .7 | 19,592 | 33,673 |
| 1.0 | 9,600 | 16,500 |
| 1.5 | 4,267 | 7,333 |
| 2.0 | 2,400 | 4,125 |
| 2.5 | 1,536 | 2,640 |
| 3.0 | 1,067 | 1,833 |
| 3.5 | 784 | 1,347 |
| 4.0 | 600 | 1,031 |
| 4.5 | 474 | 815 |
| 5.0 | 384 | 660 |
| 6.0 | 267 | 458 |
| 7.0 | 196 | 337 |
| 8.0 | 150 | 258 |
| 9.0 | 119 | 204 |
| 10.0 | 96 | 165 |
| 15.0 | 45 | 74 |

[a]There are tables available (cf. Parten, 1950, Chap. IV) which will indicate *lower* sample sizes *if* it is known what the likely occurrence of the key responses is likely to be. In school surveys the distribution of such key responses is rarely known. Even when it is, there are usually multiple facets of information with different distributions expected. For these reasons we recommend that these more conservative sample sizes (which are based on a position of "uncertainty") be employed.

Abridged and adapted from Table 5 in *Surveys, Polls, and Samples* by Mildred B. Parten (Harper & Row, 1950, page 317) by permission.

he be satisfied with being just *reasonably confident*? These italicized words are general, descriptive-type expressions and can be translated into probability terms for greater understanding. By *very confident* it is meant that 99 times out of 100 the results will be within the limits specified by the "tolerated error." Thus, 99 times out of 100 the results would be accurate plus or minus five percentage points (if he had specified 5 percent as his level of tolerated error *and* 99 in 100 as his confidence level). As will be seen shortly when we examine the Table of Sample Sizes, if the schoolman can be satisfied with a lower level of confidence (what we termed "reasonably confident"), then he will be able to employ a smaller sample. The lower level is confidence 95 times out of a 100 that the results fall within the limits specified. Table 6.2 depicts both levels of confidence and is useful for comparing the effects of these levels of confidence on sample size.

**Percentages and Sample Size.** The tables can now be considered as a first indicator of sample size. Table 6.2 is used for either very high confidence (99 times in 100) or reasonably high confidence (95 times in 100), *and* when the information will be in the form of percentages. If, for example, the administrator's concern is whether or not the campaign to "get out the vote" is successful, he might ask a sample of the community if they will be voting. With a level of confidence of 99 in 100 he can enter Table 6.2 to examine sample sizes. Under the column headed by "99 times in 100" he will find sample sizes for various levels of tolerance. Suppose he is reasonably sure that 70 percent are likely to vote. He might then adopt a fairly high tolerance of error, perhaps as much as 15 percentage points. For that tolerance limit (± 15 percent) he finds a sample size of 74 would be sufficient.

Table 6.2 also reports sample sizes when the level of confidence is that 95 times in 100 the results will fall in the tolerance limits selected. To illustrate we will use the same example. By reducing his level of confidence to 95 in 100, the sample size needed to predict the voter turnout would only have to be 45. Under the column headed by "95 times in 100," the figure 45 is given for a tolerance of error level of 15 percentage points. This is a small enough sample to allow the administrator to take two or three such readings in the community to trace the effects of the campaign.

The two examples given above employed fairly large levels of tolerance (± 15 percent). Selecting those tolerance levels helped to reduce considerably the numbers needed in the sample. More often than not, though, the schoolman will be working with narrower bands of tolerance. He will need to know if the results are accurate within 2, 3, 4, or 5 percentage points. For example, if it is necessary to predict the outcome of an election of board members, where the likely percentage of votes is unknown, *but* there is need for accuracy (i.e., a low tolerance for error) of no more than 3 percentage points, then the table will indicate that a sample size of 1,067 is necessary to achieve confidence in the outcome 95 times in 100. To increase that confidence to 99 to 100 increases the sample size to 1,833; an increase of almost 800 cases. This may help the schoolman to decide whether or not increased confidence is worth the increased costs of those extra respondents.

**Statistical Measures and Sample Size.** If the information that the questionnaire will provide is some type of statistic such as the average income or average score on an attitude instrument, then a different procedure for determining sample size is necessary. The computations for such procedures are not difficult but require certain skills and concepts that would require lengthy discussion. We recommend identifying someone within the school system who might have this background (a high school mathematics teacher, economics teacher, or director of research), or going outside the system to a nearby college or university.[15]

Whether working with percentages or statistical measures we would raise one caution: in computing the size of a sample it is better to err toward conservatism. That is, a sample that is a bit large is better than one too small. Note, too, that the tables and computations are only starting points for determination of sample size. These initial decisions may help the administrator as he considers some of the pragmatic judgments he may have to make before deciding on a final sample size. As he considers some of the judgmental-type decisions considered below, he may find it necessary to either lower his level of confidence, reduce his tolerance of error, or decide on other procedures for implementing the survey. These *qualitative-type* decisions are considered next.

## QUALITATIVE DECISIONS

**Resource and Implementation Decisions.** The resources available in terms of time, manpower, and, money may limit the size of the sample. If results must be obtained and analyzed quickly, then it may not be feasible to conduct a large-scale survey. Likewise, if the dollar and manpower resources are severely limited then it will also be necessary to limit the sample.

The procedure for implementing the survey will have implications for size. Interviews are costly, time-consuming to conduct, and equally time-consuming to analyze. Questionnaires which are hand delivered are also somewhat costly and time-consuming. Telephone surveys bypass travel time requirements and mail surveys reduce time and personnel costs to a minimum. The purposes of the survey will dictate the choice of the field method which, in turn, will set limits on the size of the sample that can be feasibly surveyed. If the sample size must be restricted for some of the preceding reasons, be certain that the commensurate changes in "tolerance of error" and "level of confidence" can be accepted. Reductions in size of sample always reduce accuracy.

---

[15]Whoever you contact will need this type of information:
1. What level of confidence do you want? (95 in 100 or 99 in 100)
2. What error will you tolerate? This is specified in terms of the object being measured: if the measure is "average spending of teenagers in dollars," the error tolerance is ± so many dollars; if the measure is "intelligence," the tolerance is ± so many IQ points.
3. What is your estimate of the standard deviation of that measure in your population (your community)? If you are using a published or standardized instrument then standard deviations are usually provided. If you do not have such information you will have to make a best guess in collaboration with the consultant.

With these three pieces of information the sample size can be computed (cf. Parten, 1950; or Mouly, 1963).

**Cooperation Decisions.** How cooperative are your respondents? Some respondents will not want to participate while others may simply not be available to take part. If this type of attrition is expected to be fairly high, then the size of the sample should be increased commensurately. Past surveys and general knowledge of the population might serve as predictors of attrition rate. It should also be noted that certain field methods reduce attrition while others may promote it. Interviews and questionnaires which are hand delivered will usually result in high completion rates while mail and telephone surveys will lead to lower completions and returns.

**Analytic-Mode Decisions.** The procedures that will be employed for analyzing the information may require minimum numbers for computation. If such procedures seem necessary they may require enlarging the sample size (see Chapter 10). It may also be that a number of categorizations of the data have been planned. Will the sample size permit the sub-analyses desired? For example, if it is necessary to compare the responses of "parents, under 30, with more than three children" with some other category, will there be sufficient numbers to allow a reasonable estimate in that category? If the sample size were only 74 or 45 as in our earlier examples, it is highly unlikely that anything more than a simple dichotomous categorization (e.g., voters-nonvoters) would be possible.

Decisions related to analysis also emerge in terms of response categories for questions. The more possible choices for answering a question, the more dispersed will be the sample respondents. Dichotomous choices (e.g., true-false, yes-no) limit the choices of sample respondents and thus provide large groups for comparisons. If many response choices are desired for questions, the size of the sample may have to be increased.

**Concomitant Purpose Decisions.** If there are purposes *other than* the survey-information-purpose, then those adjacent needs may necessitate a different decision relative to the size of the sample. It may be that the survey is also used as a public relations or a dissemination device. If that were the case then a sample considerably larger than otherwise necessary might be drawn. Sometimes surveys are useful means for introducing an idea or practice to a relatively large segment of the adult members of the community. If the expense is justifiable to the district then by all means employ the larger sample. Once again, larger samples provide greater accuracy.

The decisions about sample size should probably be made by the chief school officer together with the staff person who will be handling the technical conduct of the survey. This is a key decision area since the opportunity for concomitant outcomes should not be overlooked.

## summary

The contents of the chapter centered upon ways of finding the right people to respond to the right questions. Initially a decision must be made between a purposeful selection or a random selection of respondents. Purposeful selection, the deliberate selection of specific respondents, might be used when there is little information available and it is necessary to run a pilot study or when only key respondents in an issue possess required information. How purposefully selected respondents are chosen and how many are surveyed is dependent upon the needs of the survey.

Random selection requires that the population first be clearly identified and that a sample of this population then be chosen by chance. Relevant characteristics of the population concerning the needs of the survey should be known so that checks can be made on the sample selected to see if it is representative of the population. A table of random numbers may be used to be sure that the sample selected will be free of human bias.

There are variations of random sampling systems which can be used to select the sample. Four such variations were presented: simple random sampling, stratified random sampling, systematic sampling, and cluster sampling. The pluses and minuses associated with each were summarized to help the administrator decide which system is appropriate for his survey needs.

Finally, considerations concerning size of sample were presented. These include the precision of results required; the confidence needed that the results will actually be precise; the way the information will be reported and analyzed; and, finally, a series of pragmatic considerations.

On the basis of the information presented in the past two chapters the reader should be able to construct a survey instrument and select the sample of respondents who will provide information upon which he can make inferences concerning the population. Now the task is to actually collect the information required. This process, usually referred to as the "fieldwork" stage of survey research, is the focus of the next chapter.

## references

ACKOFF, RUSSELL L., *The Design of Social Research.* Chicago: University of Chicago Press, 1953.

BACHRACH, PETER, and MORTON S. BARATZ, "Decisions and Nondecisions: An Analytical Framework," *American Political Science Review,* No. 57 (Sept. 1963), 632–42.

DAHL, ROBERT A., *Who Governs.* New Haven, Conn.: Yale University Press, 1961.

HUNTER, FLOYD, *Community Power Structure*. Chapel Hill, N.C.: University of North Carolina Press, 1953.

Institute for Social Research, *Interviewer's Manual*. Ann Arbor: University of Michigan, May 1969.

KERLINGER, FRED N., *Foundations of Behavioral Research* (2nd. ed.). New York: Holt, Rinehart & Winston, 1973.

MOULY, GEORGE J., *The Science of Educational Research*. New York: American Book, 1963.

PARTEN, MILDRED, *Surveys, Polls, and Samples*. New York: Harper & Row, 1950.

POLSBY, NELSON W., *Community Power and Political Theory*. New Haven, Conn.: Yale University Press, 1963.

SLONIM, MORRIS JAMES, *Sampling*. New York: Simon & Shuster, 1966.

# Asking
# in the Right Manner

*seven*

Fieldwork, the activities related to contacting and obtaining responses from people in the sample, is the next stage in the survey process. Once the questionnaire or interview schedule has been pretested and the sample drawn, the fieldwork can begin. Some preplanning can take place after the choice of instrumentation has been made and an estimate of sample size has been obtained. However, the major portion of fieldwork planning must await the final instrumentation and drawing of the sample. If the district contracts with a commercial survey organization or university survey center to operate the study, school officials will undoubtedly be called on to assist in these planning activities. If the district is operating its own study, officials should be alert to the need for obtaining expert assistance in those aspects of preparations beyond their capabilities.

The chapter focuses on the means of achieving optimum results for both questionnaire and interview approaches to surveying. There are basic preparations which have to be made regardless of method, including sample verification, estimates of personnel needs, scheduling, cost considerations, and arranging for a central location to house telephones and staff. Special preparations, particularly in the training of personnel, are dependent upon the nature of the instrumentation to be used.

Self-administering questionnaires, those constructed with instructions for completion by the respondent included within the instrument, can be distributed by mail or in person by fieldworkers. Minimal staff training is needed, but timing of the distribution and follow-up contacts with respondents is critical for obtaining maximum results.

Interviews, on the other hand, require a well-trained fieldwork staff to make personal contacts with respondents to obtain the desired information. Knowledge of interview processes and techniques is essential for success. These basic differences between questionnaires and interviews should be kept in mind when reading the following sections.

## objectives in fieldwork

There are three objectives in fieldwork. First, maximum effort should be made to obtain a 100 percent usable return from the sample. Second, there should be a minimum of negative residue left in the community; that is, fieldwork should be conducted in a manner which does not upset or antagonize respondents. Third, fieldwork should be carried out with economic expenditure of time and money. Accomplishing each objective requires planning.

Gaining a maximum response from the sample means that each individual chosen should be contacted and encouraged to respond. Second and third contacts may be needed in order to reach people who were not at home when the first call was made or who fail to return the completed questionnaire within a few days. It is important to make these follow-up contacts since it has been found that those who respond only after several contacts can differ significantly in occupations, age ranges, and opinions from those reached in the initial contact (Hennessey, 1965, pp. 75-76). In planning the fieldwork, time and scheduling allowances should be made for follow-ups.

Conducting the survey without leaving negative residue in the community means that the fieldwork staff must conduct itself with tact and courtesy. People have to feel that the surveyors are sincere in asking for opinions and that their responses will be kept confidential. Inquiries about the survey should be answered politely. Appointments with respondents must be kept. Poor performance can create resistance and anger in the community before the survey is completed. Moreover, the next survey may be met with open hostility from the start. The time to highlight the elements of good human relations for the survey staff is during the training period.

Keeping expenditures of time and money to a minimum can only be done through careful planning of the fieldwork. The choice of methods directly influences the basic costs: it costs more to have people contact people than it does to make contacts by mail. Once the choice has been made, however, costs can be controlled by developing estimates of personnel needs, recruiting capable people appropriate for the tasks, and having district personnel operate the training program. Preparing a time schedule, including contact time, follow-up, and reviewing travel requirements will also aid in economizing on time and money. The use of volunteer help and school staff members, as well as operating the survey from a school office, whenever feasible, will reduce costs. However, compromises which cut into the obtaining of quality results are false economies.

## basic preparation

Planning fieldwork takes time and attention to detail. While each survey is different and the nature of the instrumentation will vary, several preparatory tasks can be started after the sample has been drawn and the pretest of the instrument has been made. These are verification and organization of the sample, estimates of personnel needs, scheduling the fieldwork, and arranging for a central location from which to operate the survey.

### VERIFICATION AND ORGANIZATION OF THE SAMPLE

Before actual fieldwork begins, that is, before interviewers begin to call on respondents or questionnaires are distributed, the sample should be verified and organized. These two steps help assure that the right respondents will be contacted.

Verification means making sure that the people selected for the sample are at the addresses or locations listed for them. Several methods are used for verifying, including observation, checks on returned mailed announcements, and telephone calls.

Observation is easily done but provides checks on only the grossest indicators. For example, driving through the several areas to be surveyed can identify a block that has been vacated in anticipation of an urban renewal project; spot-checking on addresses will reveal inaccuracies and idiosyncrasies in house numbers. At vacation times, keen observers can often judge whether or not people are away.

The return of mailed announcements of the survey provides another means of checking the sample. If such a mailing is made prior to the survey, proper timing will aid in verification through letters returned by the post office. Inaccurately addressed letters and letters to deceased persons will come back. By marking "do not forward" on the envelopes, persons who have moved since the sample list was compiled will also be identified.

The telephone check is the most effective verification method but requires careful handling and timing in order to avoid biasing responses to the survey before it starts. Using a small percent of the sample, randomly selected, a systematic series of telephone calls can be made to ascertain correctness of name, sex, address, and other information. The inquiry should be written out so that the same message is given in each call. Errors in the sample list can be corrected using the results of these calls.

The checks may reveal the need for substitutions in the sample. The substitute respondents should be selected by the same process used in drawing the original list. In a stratified sample, care should be taken to insure that the substitute respondent has the same characteristics as the person being replaced.

When this work is completed, the sample is ready to be organized for fieldwork. This is an important step for avoiding several pitfalls which lead to biased survey results. First, it helps to insure complete coverage of the sample. Second, it increases the likelihood that the time schedule will be maintained. Third, it reduces decisions on the part of fieldworkers, thus enhancing the consistency of results.

A simple system of control cards, prepared in advance, is the basic organizing tool. Figure 7.1 shows an illustrative sample control card.

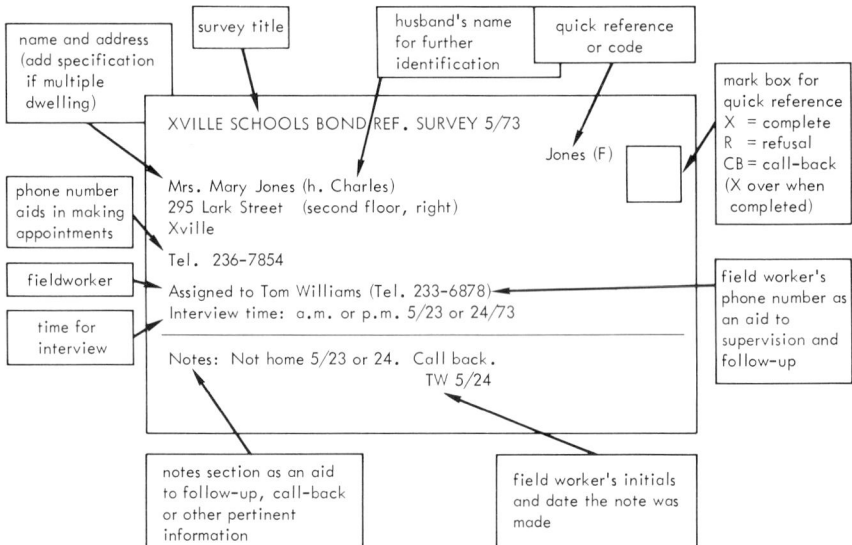

**Figure 7.1**
Illustrative sample control card.

A 5" × 8" index card is large enough to display the needed information and to keep it from being lost. A duplicate set for distribution to fieldworkers is desirable while the master set is retained by the survey office at a central location. Although the illustration is for an interview situation, control cards for questionnaires would contain similar information about respondents. The lower portion of the card might be used to record follow-up measures and the dates on which they were taken.

Giving each respondent or questionnaire a code number may be desirable for quick identification and reference. The code number should be put on the control card if it is assigned to an individual. Codes can be as simple as serially numbering each person or instrument. They can also be complex with each digit or other symbol representing a characteristic; e.g., sex, age, neighborhood, or other information. Where computer processing is used, such markings are an aid to batching and preliminary categorizing of respondents. If codes are printed on the instrument, be sure to tell respondents that the numbers they see are for use in handling data and not for later identification of individuals.

With a card for each respondent, rapid checks on the progress of the survey are easy to make. Marking the box indicates when the individual has been interviewed and a few simple calculations will yield the proportion of the sample completed or the number of call-backs to be made at any point in the field operation. The system also reduces the chances of missing any respondents.

The cards also reduce mechanical problems. They are easily batched by locations, sex of respondents, interview time, or interviewer. Substitute respondents can be put in and the other respondents removed without rearranging the entire list. Interviewer load can also be shifted with ease by a telephone call or two. At the end of the fieldwork, the cards become a record of the activity which will aid data interpretation and help in planning future surveys.

*PERSONNEL NEEDS*

Estimates of personnel needs should be made as early as possible in order to plan recruitment and training of the fieldwork staff. Here, the nature of the instrumentation and the method of administration bears heavily on the type of people recruited and the amount of training which will be needed. The size of the survey sample and geographic spread, as well as the length of time planned for fieldwork, influence the number of fieldworkers and clerical staff needed.

In general, the nucleus of the fieldwork staff should consist of those people who have been involved in planning and devising the survey. Their thorough knowledge of its purposes and development lends continuity as well as direction to the fieldwork. Additional personnel should be recruited on the basis of their aptitudes and experience in survey work and their availability. These conditions argue for a paid staff and against the use of volunteer help. In many communities there are people available who have had at least some exposure to survey work either through college courses in social and behavioral sciences, education, or social welfare. Other people have had fieldwork experience in taking the federal census or as part-time reporters for major polling organizations such as Gallup or Harris. While training is still required for the specific task, it is easier to build on previous knowledge or experience.

Volunteers, relatively inexperienced as they may be, should not be ruled out as potential fieldworkers. If sufficient training and supervision can be provided, it may be advantageous to use people who know the community extremely well or who have special knowledge of and entrée to the population being surveyed.

The coordination and supervision of field activities should be put in the hands of a study coordinator. The person designated might be the director of school-community relations or another administrator familiar with the community who has been closely involved with the development of the study. Insofar as is possible, he should be freed from his regular duties during the fieldwork portion of the survey. All planning and changes in plans, scheduling, work assignments, and problems are his responsibility. He should also supervise the training of staff and, in most cases, supervise the people in the field.

The clerical staff might be drawn totally from school offices. Clerks will be needed to collate materials, type up assignments, answer telephones, and see that completed instruments are sorted for preliminary analysis. One clerk should be put in charge of the control cards, making sure that the completion or follow-up of each respondent is noted as it is received.

*SCHEDULING FIELDWORK*

In scheduling survey work, the basic rule is to get in and out of the field as quickly as possible. This is necessary for two reasons. First, people's opinions and attitudes change as events occur to change their perceptions. In order to keep the effects of changing conditions to a minimum, the time span between the first and last respondents contacted should be kept to a minimum. Second, it is highly desirable to avoid contamination of the sample which can occur if people who were surveyed earlier have an opportunity to talk about their interview or their responses with other persons who might be surveyed later. Therefore, all time sequences in fieldwork are arranged around the activities associated with reaching respondents in the shortest possible time span. The sequences of events to be discussed are plotted on a time line in Figure 7.2.

The activities include any announcements of the survey, the contacts with respondents, as well as follow-ups or call-backs where necessary. If it is decided to make a general public announcement of the impending survey by means of newspaper stories, notices in the school newsletter, or radio and television spots, this should be done just a few days before the first contacts are made. This also applies to individual letters to prospective respondents informing them that they have been selected to participate in the survey. Short notice serves a dual purpose: it keeps down speculation, rumors, and possible resistance; but more than that, the announcement is fresh in the respondent's mind when he receives the questionnaire or the interviewer comes to his door. Follow-up or call-back activities might be scheduled to begin immediately after the initial contacts have been made. The tentative percent of second notices or contacts to expect can be judged from the pretest. It is difficult to say how many further attempts might have to be made to reach any one respondent. In some situations, such as key participant studies, there is literally no end to attempts. With general population respondents, it may be uneconomical to go beyond three additional contacts.

The training of personnel should be scheduled so that it is completed before contacts with respondents begin. For clerical staff, training may consist

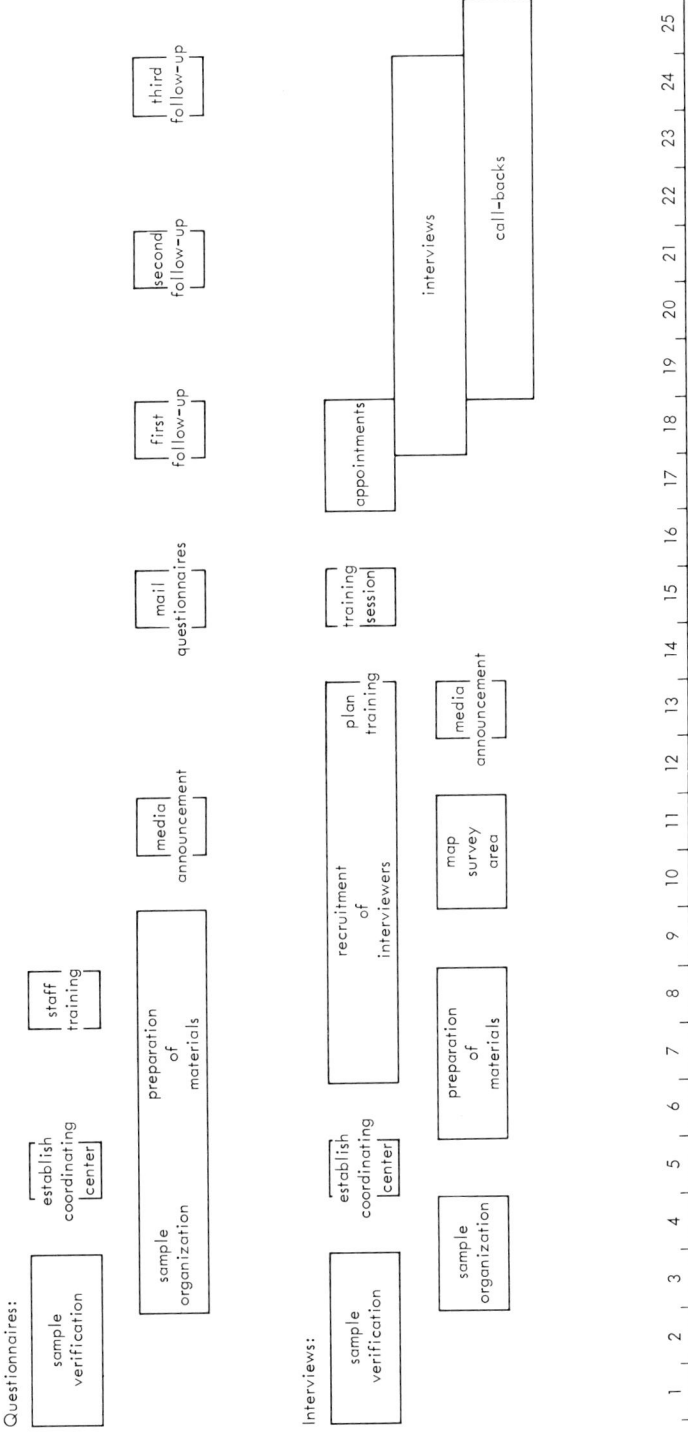

**Figure 7.2**
Illustrative fieldwork time schedules for questionnaires and interviews.

of learning how to read and mark control cards, what questions to anticipate from the community, and becoming familiar with survey materials. The coordinator can give this training in about an hour. If fieldworkers are to be utilized, training sessions should be planned so they may learn the general plan of the study, how to introduce themselves, what questions respondents might raise and how to use the control cards. How much training is necessary depends on the nature of the instrumentation, the experience of people recruited, and the amount of record-keeping expected of them.

Training sessions of one or two hours should provide fieldworkers with sufficient background. Written training guides should be provided along with examples of survey materials. There should be time to practice techniques and for questions and answers. The coordinator may lead the session, utilizing such materials as the National Opinion Research Center training manuals or materials developed by the makers of the instrument. Occasionally, trainers may have to be hired due to the complexity of the instrument or with a large staff to train. People with this experience can be found on college and university campuses and in private polling or market research organizations. Their fees can range from $50 to $150 or more per day.

## COORDINATING CENTER FOR FIELDWORK

A central location or office for coordinating all fieldwork is essential. The purpose is to keep the fieldwork moving in a systematic coordinated fashion and to handle any problems which may arise. Through use of fieldworkers' reports or the flow of completed questionnaires, the timing and sequencing of the survey are monitored and adjustments made as needed. The center also provides a locus for handling citizens' questions or complaints about the survey.

## COSTS

Sound planning includes financial planning and, as with any other school endeavor, a budget for fieldwork should be drawn up after a review of the cost factors involved.

Some indications of fieldwork costs have already been given. Before going further, it seems well to summarize the cost factors which need to be considered in planning. Table 7.1 lists several considerations for office space, equipment and supplies, and personnel costs. In the following sections there will be additional discussion of costs with reference to this list.

Having examined some of the basic preparations for fieldwork, the discussion turns to the application of these activities for questionnaire and interview methods. Special preparations for use with each type of instrumentation are also included.

Table 7.1

Cost Factors to Consider in Fieldwork

| Factor | Considerations |
| --- | --- |
| Office space for coordinating center | Usually no cost, as an office or room in a school building can be utilized. |
| Equipment and supplies | Usually school typewriters, copiers, envelopes, paper, and pencils can be made available. If commercial printing of instruments is desirable, this will be an added cost. |
| Clerical staff | Usually, school personnel can be temporarily assigned if plans are made in advance. Additional clerks, if needed, should be compensated at the prevailing wage rates. Unpaid volunteers may be used for some unskilled tasks. |
| Communications | Generally, routine communications costs will not exceed the school's usual expenses for such items. However, announcements, questionnaire mailings, and follow-up mailings or telephone calls may require additional funds. It is recommended that announcements and questionnaires be sent by first-class mail. Media announcements via newspaper, radio, and television can usually be made without cost as news stories or public service announcements. |
| Fieldworkers Recruitment and training | Recruiting can be done by telephone, letter, or newspaper ad. If trainers need to be hired, the cost will range between $50 and $150 per trainer. If fieldworkers are hired, they should be paid for the time taken in training. |
| Compensation | Fieldworkers are usually paid by the hour. Where the fieldwork consists of dropping off and picking up instruments, pay would be the prevailing rate for canvassers employed by business firms. Experienced interviewers can command between $5 and $10 per hour. Volunteers may be used in either instance, but additional training will be needed and greater workloads may fall on the coordinating center staff. These costs in time and effort should be compared to the money costs of achieving high quality results. |
| Travel | Fieldworkers, paid or volunteer, should be reimbursed for the use of their own automobiles in conducting the survey. The rate should be the prevailing per mile rate used by the school system. Reimbursement for meals may also be necessary, depending on the working hours set for the survey. |
| Special requirements | Maps, overnight accommodations for trainers, cost of training manuals, and overtime pay allowance for clerks or others may be necessary. |

## fieldwork for questionnaires

Survey instruments which are self-administering can be mailed to respondents or left with them with instructions for completion and return. Such questionnaires can be used when the surveyor believes he will get a satisfactory set of responses even though there is no opportunity to probe respondents. Costs are low as the need for highly trained, highly skilled personnel is virtually eliminated. Questionnaires also have an advantage in that they may be filled out more or less at the respondent's convenience. There is, however, an increased risk of obtaining less than a desirable number of responses; responses will be received from people who have the motivation to complete and return the instrument. The numerical problem can be overcome by increasing the size of the sample. Announcements and cover letters may aid motivation.

There are several methods of distributing self-administered questionnaires. Each has its advantages and disadvantages which are largely measured in terms of the usable response. But, in general, the greater the expenditure of time and money, the greater the usable return.

*MAIL-OUT AND RETURN METHOD*

Utilizing this method requires that each respondent in the sample receive a self-administering questionnaire by mail with a pre-addressed, stamped envelope for its return. Most materials can be prepared in advance and sent out according to the survey schedule. Mailing costs are low compared to the costs of interviews and even hand delivering. The cost per questionnaire rises with each follow-up card or letter, but so does the usable response. The average rate of return for the questionnaire alone is somewhere between 65 and 75 percent. A follow-up card or letter will increase that return by another 10 or 15 percent. (See Sax, 1968, p. 216.)

Motivating respondents by the use of announcements, cover letters, follow-up cards, letters, or telephone calls is a major factor. An announcement mailed to each respondent a few days prior to the day set for mailing the questionnaires will alert each to the fact that he is to receive the questionnaire. In the cover letter, mailed with the instrument, the purpose of the survey is explained and the respondent is urged to complete the questionnaire and send it back. Assurance about the confidentiality of answers is also stressed. Follow-up cards or letters, either sent blind, that is, to all respondents whether or not they have returned the instrument, or just to those who have failed to respond within a given amount of time (if the questionnaires have been coded), remind the individual that he has received the questionnaire and that his response is wanted. The initial follow-up letter may be followed by second and third follow-up letters (perhaps including another copy of the instrument) or even a telephone call as a final urging to complete the questionnaire. This bombardment of communications all takes place within ten to fifteen days, giving the respondent a sense of urgency about completing the questionnaire.

Personnel needs for mail-out and return surveys can become fairly heavy. While highly skilled personnel are not needed, people are required to prepare materials, sift through the sample control cards, marking them for completion or follow-up and then seeing to it that the letters are posted or the telephone calls are made. Most people can be trained for these tasks in an hour or so. The number of people needed will, of course, depend on the size of the sample and the number of follow-ups planned.

As indicated, the actual costs of mailing are relatively low and most personnel can be hired at the prevailing wage scale for clerical help. There is no real problem in using volunteer help as long as a sufficient time commitment is made and all tasks are adequately staffed.

*DROP OFF-PICK UP METHOD*

In the drop off-pick up method each respondent in the sample is called on personally by a fieldworker and given a self-administering questionnaire to complete in time for the fieldworker to pick it up by appointment, usually the next day. The method has the advantage of personal contact at relatively low cost as fieldworkers do not need to be as highly trained as they do for interviewing. A dozen respondents can be visited in just a few hours and the factor of personal contact can increase the response rate considerably over the mail-out. With one or two call-backs, response rates of 75 to 90 percent are not uncommon in the authors' experience. The disadvantage is that there are two trips to each respondent by a fieldworker.

The motivational problem is, in part, handled by the fieldworker at the respondent's door. Announcements through the media are helpful in alerting people to the fact that the survey is being conducted. There should still be a cover letter on the questionnaire clearly indicating the purpose and value of the investigation and the name of the sponsoring organization. Fieldworkers should plan at least two call-backs if the respondent has not completed the questionnaire at the time of the pick up appointment. If the respondent still has not completed the questionnaire, a mail-back option can be used by leaving a pre-addressed, stamped envelope with the respondent asking him to mail it in when he has completed it. The mail-back option can be followed up with a postcard reminder a few days later.

The number of fieldworkers needed for this method is not too difficult to estimate. The time required to deliver and pickup the self-administered instruments can be ascertained from the pretest. This time is multiplied by the number of respondents in the sample and then divided by the total number of hours available for the survey. The result is the number of workers needed. For example, if drop off and pick up for each respondent requires an hour of time and a sample of 200 is to be contacted over a five-day period (one day = eight hours), then five full-time workers would be needed to accomplish this task. Obviously, a shorter working time or a larger sample will increase the number of fieldworkers needed to make the contacts. Additional time should be allowed for travel in the field and for record-keeping on the part of fieldworkers. It is probably best to err on the side of saturation by having a few more fieldworkers than the arithmetic calls for.

The training of fieldworkers for the drop off-pick up method is minimal. Even those people without previous experience can learn a standard introduction to use at the door, how to handle respondents' queries, and how to make the pickup appointment in just a few hours' time. Training can be conducted by district personnel a few days before contact work begins. The standard introduction and other instructions, including how to use the control cards and where to get help, should be printed and a copy given to each worker. Some familiarization or orientation to the community should be part of the training program. In the training session, time should be allowed not only for reviewing instructions and practicing the techniques but also for questions from the fieldworkers. For this reason it is recommended that the training sessions be held with all fieldworkers attending the same session.

The assignments for fieldworkers should be concentrated geographically to reduce travel time and expense. Each worker might well plan his own route through the community, randomizing his calls by time of day and evening. Thus, he improves the chances of finding respondents at home by compensating for people's various shopping habits, work shifts, and other scheduled activities. There are advantages to having the same worker complete his portion of the sample. He can keep track of his own call-backs and plan his time. With a readable map, this is easily done.

Making maps of the survey area serves two purposes: indicating respondent locations and planning travel routes. Using a fairly detailed map of the community and the sample control cards it should be possible to mark the residence of each person in the sample. This will give a rough check on the geographic distribution of respondents as well as indications for assignment loads to fieldworkers. Obviously, it makes good sense to have a fieldworker cover as small a geographic area as possible in obtaining his designated respondents. This maximizes contact time and minimizes travel time. Each fieldworker should be provided with a map of the survey area he is to cover. It is preferred that the map be a copy of his section of the larger map. The master map, of course, should be posted in the coordinating center.

It should be noted that if the sampling is being done by the cluster method and selection of dwelling units within the blocks has been left to the interviewer or fieldworker, the maps for this use must be highly detailed and up-to-date. (See Chapter 6). On each map the blocks to be sampled must be clearly indicated for the fieldworker and the directions for selecting the household or households from a designated block must be spelled out on the map. If the interviewer or fieldworker is also to select the person from within the dwelling unit to be interviewed, directions to this effect must be given at the same time. Finally, the fieldworker must be instructed to mark the dwelling unit selected on his map and return it to the coordinating center when he has completed his fieldwork.

The greatest costs of the drop off-pick up method are for personnel.

Fieldworkers should be engaged for the length of the survey, plus a training period, and will probably be paid the prevailing wage scale in the area for canvassers employed by business firms. Then too, there is the cost of transportation with each fieldworker being compensated at the prevailing per mile rate for use of his automobile plus reimbursement for meals during the time he is in the field. Unpaid volunteer workers can be used but it might be difficult to obtain people who will commit sufficient time for carrying out assignments. This might result in the need for constant consolidation and reassignment of workers for call-backs by the coordinating staff. Volunteers should be reimbursed for their transportation costs.

*OTHER METHODS FOR ADMINISTERING QUESTIONNAIRES*

Occasionally it may be possible to reach specified populations or stratified samples by other means. If, for example, the population is all persons attending parent-teacher association meetings in the district for a given month, it could be arranged to have a person on hand at each of the meetings to administer the questionnaire to the group present. Parents who consult with school guidance counselors or who come in for conferences with teachers might be asked to complete questionnaires about their meetings. The instructions can be handed to respondents at the end of the meeting session.

Several methods are to be discouraged, however. These include sending instruments home with youngsters and printing questionnaires in the school newsletter. These procedures almost always violate scientific sampling techniques. In addition, bias results from unstandardized motivational techniques of introduction and follow-up. Use of youngsters as messengers is especially bad as it can be perceived as undue pressure on parents to respond.

## interviews

The face-to-face interview is an intense, highly flexible means of obtaining information from respondents. It can be applied to many different kinds of problems, from gathering opinions and attitudes to ascertaining knowledge that people have about any particular topic. It is flexible in that a skilled interviewer can apply several strategies to motivate respondents, gain their confidence, and elicit the responses that are needed. This is particularly true in the unstructured interview where the interviewer has great freedom to ask questions and probe further in seeking the information needed. It is also true, to some extent, in the structured interview because the interviewer can repeat questions on the spot and use the probes included in the schedules. When information about attitudes and opinions is being sought, the interview is probably the best way of obtaining that data. When this information is sought from key participants or samples of community influentials, the interview is the only method which serves adequately.

The interview also has its disadvantages. It takes a great deal of time, requires skilled personnel for the interviewing, and is expensive. Additional problems arise with unstructured interviews in that the collating and coding of responses must be done in order to make the data usable. (See Chapter 8.) Finally, even with structured interviews, there are always variations in interviewers' approaches which introduce possible bias into the results. Some of this can be overcome by intensive interviewer training, but even that will not entirely eliminate the problem.

## HOW TO ARRANGE AND CONDUCT INTERVIEWS

Interviewing of respondents should usually be carried out on an appointment basis. The interviewer should arrange his own appointments, either by letter or preferably by telephone. The appointment should be at the convenience of the respondent. Part of making it convenient for him is to inform him of the time commitment necessary to complete the interview. This initiation is the first opportunity to motivate the respondent. Therefore, the message should contain the purpose of the survey, the importance of his responses, and the identification of the survey's sponsor.

Interviewers should always be on time for their appointments and should utilize the first few minutes of the appointment to gain rapport with the respondent. The interviewer introduces himself by name and affiliation as well as by reiterating the purpose of the survey. After this introduction, he should answer any questions which the respondent may have about the survey, the impending interview, or the interviewer himself. At this point, it is well to assure the respondent again that his answers will be kept strictly confidential.

Once rapport has been gained and the respondent is ready, the interviewer goes on with the interview schedule, asking each question and utilizing rephrasing and probes only where indicated. The skillful interviewer maintains a neutral tone of voice when reading questions to respondents. A change in voice which emphasizes a certain word or phrase may be interpreted by the respondent as a clue to the "desired" response. With the structured interview, that is, one where the questions are to be asked only as they are written, the interviewer reads each question exactly. If rephrasing is permitted according to the interview schedule, the rephrasing should not lead the respondent to a specific answer, but rather it should be a restatement of the question in different words. Rephrasing is necessary when a respondent either asks for a repeat of the question or hesitates to answer. However, interviewers should not be too quick to rephrase when a respondent hesitates; he may be simply thinking through his answer.

In more unstructured interviews, that is, where the information being sought requires some explanation or elaboration on the part of the respondent, probe questions are very often included in the interview schedule. These are written in parentheses below the question for the guidance of the interviewer. In this situation, the question is asked as it is written and the respondent is given time to respond. If the answer does not contain sufficient information to satisfy the question, the interviewer uses the probe statement. In gathering opinions, probe questions such as "How did you come to think that way?" or "Would you explain that notion?" or "Why is that?" are usually part of the schedule. Probes should be stated in the same neutral tone of voice as the question and the respondent should have sufficient time to think through his answer. The interviewer should not be put off by responses such as "I don't know" or "I've never thought about that." These may simply be stalling responses on the part of the respondent while he is thinking through the question. Restating the probe will usually bring an answer.

Occasionally, respondents will reply to questions by asking the interviewer his opinion or what other people in the survey have said. However, under no circumstances should an interviewer share his attitudes with the respondent. Any interjection of the interviewer's opinions will lead to a biased answer by the respondent rather than to his views of the situation. Such questions by a respondent can be turned aside by the interviewer's restressing the importance of the respondent's opinions, as opposed to the interviewer's opinions or the opinions of others.

Interviewers must be good listeners! Carefully listening to the responses is the only way of determining whether or not an answer has been completed or if rephrasing or a probe is necessary. In addition, the answer helps the interviewer phrase his further questions and probes, using the ideas and even some of the words which the respondent has used. This not only aids communication between interviewer and respondent, but also helps the person being interviewed feel that his responses are worthwhile.

The interview must be carefully paced. Respondents have only a limited amount of time to spend with the interviewer and the interviewer will want to ask all of the questions within that time span. The pacing of the interview is, therefore, quite important, and the interviewer should maintain control of the interview and keep the respondent from wandering as he answers questions. If the interviewer listens carefully and has a thorough knowledge of the general direction of the questioning, he is in a good position to control the pace of the interview. This control should not be obtrusive since respondents who feel pushed or perceive that shorter answers seem desirable will soon begin to lose interest in the interview. Once rapport between interviewer and respondent breaks down, the interview, for all practical purposes, is over. On the other hand, a well-paced interview yields maximum information. If the person being interviewed believes he is being listened to, he will usually answer fully and forthrightly, taking up the pace set by the interviewer.

In completing the schedule, the interviewer should be sure to ask all questions. These include the personal items, demographic data, about the respondent. Since this information is necessary for the classification of respondents in the development of appropriate subgroups for handling data, it is very essential that these questions be included.

Note-taking is an essential part of interviewing. It should be done as unobtrusively as possible so that the respondent is not distracted. Notes should be taken as the respondent talks so that gaps are not created in the interview response. The answers should be recorded as fully as possible and in the respondent's own words. When interviewers use their own words, these have to be interpreted later and the interpretation may not be the same as the respondent's answer. To aid in this situation, interviewers should be trained to use a fairly standard form for their notes. Abbreviations should be those in standard, common usage and abbreviations for special words frequently used in a particular study should be standardized for all interviewers. These notes should be fleshed out as soon as possible after the interview, preferably before the next interview. By getting at his notes quickly, the interviewer can recall key words used by the respondent and other phrases or clues to his thinking. It is also a good idea to make the writing as neat as possible so that others may read what the interviewer has written down without difficulty.

In interviewing, some call-backs will usually be necessary. Some respondents will not be at home or will not be able to keep appointments. Thus, another appointment will be necessary. Occasionally, an interview may have to be stopped in the middle due to another commitment of the respondent or an emergency situation. In these instances, the interviewer will have to return to complete the interview. The reestablishment of rapport for the call-back is essential before picking up with questions from the schedule. On these call-backs, it is useful for the interviewer to summarize some of the questions asked during the first meeting and then go on to the questions still to be answered.

In addition to his notes, the interviewer has other record-keeping chores. The control cards (Figure 7.1) which identify respondents should be marked as soon as the appointment is obtained. This will establish a schedule for the interviewer to follow. If the interview is concluded, the card should be marked as a completion. If a call-back is necessary, that should be marked on the card and another appointment made. By keeping the control cards up to date, the interviewer knows the exact status of his assignment. If cluster sampling is used, the interviewer should mark the residence where the interview was taken and indicate, either on a control card or on the map itself, completion or call-back, as well as the sex of the respondent, or other information about the individual requested by the survey coordinator.

In assigning interviewers for fieldwork, it is usually best to permit the interviewer wide latitude in arranging his own schedule. The time span for the actual contact work is based on the length of time needed for each respondent as determined from the pretest of the instrument. Added to that, if not already determined from the pretest, should be time for traveling and record-keeping on the part of fieldworkers. There should also be a time allowance for call-backs and later completions. These time factors, multiplied by the number of people in the sample and divided by the number of working days for field activity, will indicate the number of interviewers needed. In completing his assignment, the interviewer will do best to randomize his appointments or interviews. This means that he will have morning, afternoon, as well as evening appointments, avoiding the biases introduced by a consistant appointment time. It will also help overcome the biases introduced by the fact that men usually work away from home during the day, while housewives are available for interviews in the morning hours or afternoon. By randomizing his appointments, the interviewer improves his opportunities of finding males at home during the day.

## *PERSONNEL NEEDS AND TRAINING*

The selection and training of interviewers is critical. While there is no ideal type of person to be recruited, there are some guidelines, in terms of interviewer characteristics, which can help. It is important to note, however, that the characteristics of respondents also bear on the quality of the interview obtained, as the interviewer interacts with the respondent during the interview. (See Richardson, 1965, pp. 305-37.)

Generally, college graduates obtain somewhat better interviews than non-college-trained people. Those who majored in the social and behavioral sciences are somewhat more accurate in their interview recording than those who majored in physical sciences or business. Persons between 26 and 50 years of age seem to obtain higher quality interviews than either younger or older people, and young people seem to establish a better interview relationship with middle-age respondents. Finally, female interviewers seem to get more responses from respondents than do their male counterparts (Sax, 1968, pp. 212-13). It has also been observed that overly aggressive people and people who like to talk do not make very good interviewers. As noted above, the interviewer must be a good listener and not a person who wants to engage in discussion or exchange opinions with others.

From the perspective of who the potential respondents are, other characteristics of interviewers may become more critical. Responses of blacks, for example, have been found to differ depending on whether the interviewer was black or white. Middle-class interviewers seem to attribute greater conservatism to working-class respondents than do working-class interviewers (Sax, 1968, pp. 213-14). Thus it might be that former school dropouts would obtain better interviews from recent dropouts than would college graduates and parents might be the better interviewers of parents. It rests with the survey coordinator to examine these considerations in recruiting fieldworkers.

Experience in interviewing is, of course, a major factor in the quality of interview obtained. Whenever possible, the schoolman should try to recruit individuals who have had experience interviewing, either through college courses or through employment by one of the national polling organizations or even a government census-taking agency. It would be well for him to maintain a list of qualified interviewers who can be contacted when a survey is being planned. This list would eventually include people trained by the school and experienced through school surveys of the community.

The training of interviewers for a particular survey is necessary whether they have had experience or not. The training can be carried out by school personnel familiar with the purposes and development of the survey, or trainers can be hired from polling organizations or possibly, the field service unit at a local college. The training session should be carefully planned and take place two or three days before the interviewers make their first contacts with respondents.

Training sessions for interviewers usually include the following elements. First, there is a general introduction to the survey and its purposes. This can be spelled out by the study coordinator and others who helped develop the design. The instrumentation is gone over carefully so that all interviewers understand the nature of each question and the information it is designed to elicit. These reviews help the interviewer understand what he is to listen for. In going over the instrument, permissible rephrasings and probes are discussed and interviewers become familiar with the ways of obtaining full data. Second, the various questions and inquiries which respondents may have about the survey or their part in it should be reviewed. A number of these topics will be gleaned from the pretest information and passed on to the interviewers as things to be anticipated. Third, the record-keeping necessary on the part of interviewers, the marking of control cards, note-taking, and the writing of protocols or reports of their interviews should be covered. Standardization of this record-keeping is important and all interviewers should be familiar with the forms and the data wanted by the study coordinator. Fourth, some orientation or familiarization with the community should be presented. The director of school-community relations might well prepare a brief statement giving the socioeconomic characteristics of the population, identifying neighborhoods, and giving a brief account of the current status of school-community relations. This information will aid interviewers in handling themselves with respondents. Fifth, there should be time for questions and answers so that the concerns of interviewers can be aired. Finally, there should be time to practice the interview. Fieldworkers can be paired off to practice going through the schedule with each other and check each other's techniques. The survey coordinator might well observe some of these practice sessions and give pointers to interviewers who seem to be having difficulty.

A thorough training session can take two or three hours of intensive work. It is preferable that all interviewers in the survey be trained at the same time; if the number does not exceed twenty, they can probably be trained all at one session. This will not only eliminate the expense of added training sessions, but will expose all interviewers to the same explanations and discussions. The session will be even more productive if the instructions for the survey are written out and used as a guide for the training session.

The last point concerning interviewers is remuneration. If the school district obtains experienced interviewers for its survey work, it should be prepared to pay the prevailing hourly wage for such people. Depending on the part of the country and the experience of the interviewer, this may run as high as $10 per hour. In addition, interviewers are usually reimbursed at the prevailing rate per mile for the use of their automobile. Using unpaid volunteers can reduce costs considerably, but may be false economy in that the incidence of poor and inaccurate interviews will increase. This can be offset in some measure by the training program and increased supervision of interviewers as they carry out the contact work.

## *INTERVIEWS BY TELEPHONE*

In some limited instances it may be possible to interview by telephone. The major difficulty with this technique is that all potential respondents may not have telephones and those people who do not may be quite different from those who do. This will bias the results. Another problem is motivation. It may not be convenient for the respondent to take the call or he may be unable to listen well due to distractions which the interviewer does not know about. Finally, the interview schedule must be fairly well structured and brief in order for the interviewer to maintain control of the interview. Instructions to respondents need to be simple and the questions uninvolved to prevent the respondent from losing interest. Clues to loss of rapport are limited to voice inflections and poor response content. Refusal or termination of the interview can be accomplished by just hanging up the receiver. However, if the survey is limited to a small sample and there are relatively few questions to be asked, the telephone interview may be sufficient.

Each interviewer will need to have a written copy of the standard introduction to be used, a set of the questions to be asked, and control cards for the respondents to be called. As with other interviews, the calls should be randomized by time of day. The answers to questions and probes need to be recorded and written up as soon as the call is completed. If the respondent is not at home or finds it inconvenient to complete the interview, a call-back should be arranged and the control card so marked.

Interviewers will need to be selected and trained with some care. Some experience in telephone canvassing and a pleasant telephone voice are desirable. In training, the standard introduction should be learned as well as some of the techniques used in the in-person interview.

## summary

Several approaches for survey fieldwork have been presented as ways of achieving maximum results economically. The major advantages and disadvantages of these fieldwork approaches have been brought together in Table 7.2. While the choice of instrumentation, made earlier in the designing of the survey, dictates the basic approach to be used, considerations of personnel needs, scheduling, and costs can vary. Careful planning of the fieldwork was stressed, and guides for doing this planning were detailed for effective coverage of the sample, recruiting and training fieldworkers, scheduling field activities, and developing cost estimates.

Table 7.2

**Advantages and Disadvantages of Several Fieldwork Approaches**

| Approach | Advantages | Disadvantages |
|---|---|---|
| Mailed questionnaire | Can reach large samples at relatively low cost | Difficult to achieve 100 percent response |
| | Personnel need not be highly trained | No personal contacts |
| | All materials can be prepared in advance and distributed according to schedule | Cover letter and follow-up provide the only motivation |
| | | Requires carefully written instructions to respondents |
| Drop off-pick up questionnaire | Personal contacts aid motivation | May require a large number of fieldworkers |
| | High response can be achieved within a few days | Travel time and expenses may run high |
| | Personnel need only minimal training | Requires carefully written instructions to respondents |
| | Personnel costs are relatively low | |
| | Most materials can be prepared in advance | |
| | Little record-keeping by fieldworkers | |
| Group administered questionnaire | Low cost | Very limited use |
| | Few staff needed | Must be used with the population |
| | | Restricted by availability of respondents in groups |

Table 7.2 (continued)

Advantages and Disadvantages of Several Fieldwork Approached

| Approach | Advantages | Disadvantages |
|---|---|---|
| Interview | Personal contacts to motivate respondents | Requires highly trained fieldworkers |
| | High response can usually be attained | Costs for fieldworkers and training are high |
| | Provides opportunity to probe respondents to gain extensive data | Travel expense and contact time can be high |
| | Smaller sample can be used | Usually requires a good deal of respondent's time |
| | | Substantial record-keeping by fieldworkers is necessary |
| Telephone interview | Few staff needed | Very limited use |
| | No travel costs | Easily biased by the vagaries of telephone subscriptions and services |
| | | Difficult to motivate respondents |

In discussing the specific approaches to using questionnaires and interviews, these topics were further elaborated. The advantages and disadvantages of methods, summarized in Table 7.2, were presented. The procedures to follow for motivating respondents, completing the instrument, and recording the results were outlined.

references

GORDON, RAYMOND, *Interviewing: Strategy, Techniques and Tactics.* Chicago: Dorsey, 1969.
HENNESSY, BERNARD C., *Public Opinion.* Belmont, Calif.: Wadsworth, 1965.
RICHARDSON, STEPHEN A., BARBARA SNELL DOHRENWEND, and DAVID KLEIN, *Interviewing: Its Forms and Functions.* New York: Basic Books, 1965.
SAX, GILBERT, *Empirical Foundations of Educational Research.* Englewood Cliffs, N.J.: Prentice-Hall, 1968

# THE PROCESS OF ANALYSIS

# PART THREE

The analytic process is not a complicated or foreboding task. It is simply a set of procedures for arranging data so as to uncover trends, differences, or associations. It is a process of separating a whole into its major components for examination, internal comparison, and for comparisons with the whole. This is not to say that highly sophisticated and complicated procedures do not exist or are not employed. The emphasis in this book, though, is on basic approaches, since it is our belief that such techniques can yield sufficiently useful information to aid the schoolman in decision-making and problem resolution.

Analysis probably begins with the very first procedures in this book, that is, with problem specification. However, for practical purposes the process of analysis in the forthcoming discussion will be restricted to the period between the collection of documents or the return of questionnaires and interviews and the interpretation of that information. Essentially the process flows from the collecting and coding of information, to the arrangement and description of the results, to statistical analysis for interpretation, and finally to the reporting of the interpretations.

Most of the detailed procedures in the previous section (Part II) were directed to the survey coordinator and the personnel conducting the survey. In this section it is the analysis team that we will be addressing. As a member of that team the superintendent may want initial involvement to help evolve the approaches that will best answer the questions or problems which initiated the survey. The detail of this section, however, is primarily for the working members of that analysis team.

In Chapter 8 we describe techniques for collecting, scoring, coding, and storing the questionnaires and documents. Both structured and unstructured data are considered although the general approach emphasized is to translate as much as possible the unstructured information into a quantifiable, structured format.

Chapter 9 treats that phase of analysis which is paramount in importance, the arrangement or ordering of data so that they may be most easily examined. It is here that the schoolman wants primary involvement. Visual examination of ordered data is not only a legitimate form of analysis, but is perhaps one of the most useful forms to be pursued.

Interpretation through statistical procedures is treated in Chapter 10. While mention is made of a number of statistical approaches, the bulk of the chapter is devoted to a single statistical test, *chi-square.* This one statistic is an analytic tool that has wide applicability. There is sufficient detail in the chapter so that the analysis team can learn and apply the technique. Finally, a most important discussion of the meaning of "significance" and particularly *political* or *practical significance* concludes this section.

# Collecting
# and Coding Data

*eight*

The analytic phase of understanding the community is a combination of frustrations and rewards. From its very beginning, with long and almost intolerable waiting for the data to be returned, there are anxious moments. In fact, however, this can be an exciting and rewarding period if the process is controlled so that patterns and interpretations may emerge with relative ease. In this chapter we will concentrate on procedures for accumulating, coding, and making initial arrangements; for ordering data so that the later steps in analysis may follow without undo complications. The emphasis throughout the chapter as well as the two following chapters will be on "hand analysis." This is not to imply that mechanical aids such as computers should not be employed, but rather that hand analysis procedures (1) are relatively easy to conduct, and (2) will likely aid understanding of interpreted data. At the end of the chapter we will discuss computers in the analysis process with some brief comments as to when they may or may not be appropriate.

There is one more aside we should note before discussing "collecting" and "coding" procedures. The *object* of these procedures, that is *data,* should first be clarified. While the term was introduced earlier, it is so central to this section on analysis that we want to review its meanings again.

### data: the object of analysis

The term *data* is bandied about as though there were no doubt that all know what it means in its entirety. Actually everyone probably does have at least an intuitive grasp of the concept. When the term is used without a qualifier it refers to any "facts" whether real or perceived that are conveyed to the observer. Certain data are easily counted, measured, or quantified as, for example, the voters in a district, the persons attending adult education classes, broken windows, or readers of the school newsletter. Such data we refer to as *structured,* since they may be grouped or arranged into some identifiable patterns.

All data that do not fit the *structured* category we classify as *unstructured.* Usually the data in this category are more "qualitative" than "quantitative." That is, the information conveyed is of an individual judgmental nature as, for example, the "goodness" of a system, the more "influential" persons in a community, the "aesthetic qualities" of a school building, or "preferences" for one curriculum over another. It is extremely difficult to interpret this type of data and to work with it in its original form. Whenever possible, we would urge that *unstructured data be transformed into structured data.* If this can be done, then all of the procedures or techniques for interpreting structured data can be applied to the unstructured data. Since the techniques for analyzing structured and unstructured data differ at times, each of these types of data will be treated separately after the general discussion of procedures for collecting and coding the data.

## collecting and coding

Regardless of which type of data are being collected, the first stage is to accumulate the data in some fashion that will facilitate their examination and eventual interpretation. As raw data are accumulated they must be stored until sufficient returns arrive for preliminary examinations. If a logical classification scheme can be determined, then the returning documents or survey instruments can be placed in file folders within that classification scheme. To clarify, rather than waiting until all of the returns have been received, steps should be taken to establish some necessary divisions of the information and to log the documents or questionnaires in those categories as each comes in. If, for example, the locations of the responses are important, then establish as many file folders as there are locations and insert the response sheets in the appropriate folders as they arrive. Something as simple as this permits a type of scanning of the returns that would have been extremely difficult otherwise.

In all likelihood the classification scheme for logging the responses will derive from the problem that first generated the survey. In particular, after specifying the problem certain elements were probably identified as the "most likely factors associated with the deviation." The breakdown of those elements would likely be the category labels for the file folder.

As each returned questionnaire is filed a second process may also be underway, that is, recording the returns so as to provide a check on the "goodness" or "representativeness" of the sample. If some type of random sample has been made (as suggested in Chapter 6), then the extent to which the actual sample is representative of the population can be ascertained. This can be done in as simple or as complex a manner as desired, but our preference is to use the simpler techniques. One such approach is to select one or two demographic variables that are known about the population, such as the distributions of males and females, or the proportions of families with no children, one child, two children, and so on, and compare these with the sample. This assumes of course that the appropriate demographic questions were asked in the survey. As the returns come in, a tally sheet is started with the appropriate categories listed. Table 8.1 shows such a tally sheet partially completed. In the first column are listed the categories that were previously selected; the second column lists the proportions *known* for that community; while the third column provides space to tally the appropriate response category as the questionnaire is received and filed.

**Table 8.1**

**Tally Sheet for "Goodness" of Sample**

| Category | Population Percentage | Sample Tally | Sample Frequency[a] | Sample Percent[a] |
|---|---|---|---|---|
| Family No Children | 38.6 | ||||  ||||  ||||  ||||  /// | | |
| Family One Child | 32.7 | ||||  ||||  ||||  ||||  ||||  ||||  / | | |
| Family Two Children | 18.4 | ||||  ||||  // | | |
| Family Three Children | 8.2 | ||||  / | | |
| Family Four Plus Children | 2.1 | // | | |
| | | Totals | | |

[a]These categories cannot be completed until all of the returns have been tallied.

Once all of the questionnaires have been filed and so recorded, the table can be inspected to see to what extent the sample conforms to the population, at least on that one variable or characteristic. If the proportions are approximately equal then there is greater belief that the sample is reasonably representative. If there is need to go to a second step of sophistication, a simple statistical technique (chi-square) can be applied to determine whether or not the sample differs from the known distributions of the population. This approach will be treated in Chapter 10. If it should happen that the distributions are *not* representative, then there are some alternative actions that can be pursued. One such action is to seek more returns, particularly from the deficient segments of the population. A second course of action would be to increase the sample by sending out more questionnaires or conducting more interviews with a second random sample (a type of sequential sampling, Simon, 1969, p. 234). This type of sampling procedure may be economical but will not assure that the proportions will change. A third approach is to live with the sample returns and *weight* them for the bias. Any of these approaches increases the possibility of bias and produces additional problems for the survey. In the long run, the best approach may be to analyze the data with the realization that the results may be biased but noting the direction and size of the bias. With these few cautions regarding sample bias in mind, we turn now to the collecting and coding phase for structured and unstructured data.

*STRUCTURED DATA*

As the questionnaires containing structured data are returned they need to be examined for representativeness (as indicated above) and missing data. Missing data may require some decisions on the part of the investigator. If the data missing are in the demographic area, then the rest of the information may be meaningless. On the other hand, the return envelope may provide at least one piece of demographic information—the general location of the sender—which would facilitate limited use of that response. If the data that are missing are in the body of the questionnaire, then a separate decision as to its usability will have to be made. Normally such missing data will be classified as "blank" or "no response." If most of such substantive data are omitted the questionnaire should probably be discarded.

Since questionnaires are usually spread out over a number of pages, with multiple categories of information, it is desirable to transpose the information and place it on a single page, or even a single column of a page.[1] Figure 8.1 shows a sample page "summary sheet." Each of the major categories that have been selected is highlighted and described. The numbers across the top (1, 2, and 3) refer to the number *assigned* to the questionnaire. Each questionnaire recorded is assigned such a number so that it may be matched with the appropriate column of the summary sheet as necessary. Each summary sheet would have room for ten sets of responses so that higher numbers could be added, in order, to the top column. That is, when the eleventh questionnaire is recorded a *one* is written in front of the "1" already on the summary sheet (*11*) and 11 is written on that questionnaire.

[1] If computers or needlesort processes (discussed briefly later) are used, the transposing would be to computer cards or sort cards.

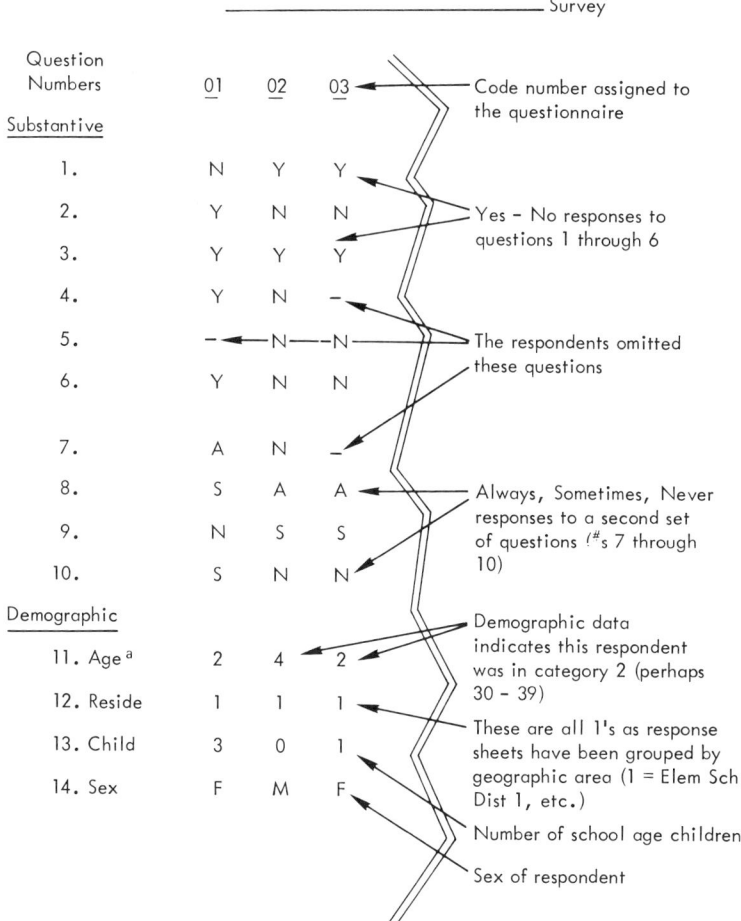

**Figure 8.1**

Summary Sheet 1

[a]These categories (Age, etc.) are for illustration only. The actual demographic categories will be determined according to the purposes of the survey.

Three question formats are depicted in the figure: questions 1 through 6 indicate responses to questions asking for a *yes* or *no* response; questions 7 through 10 indicate responses for an *always, sometimes,* or *never* type question; questions 11 through 14 are for demographic data.

An example of a *yes-no* question might be:

1. Have you ever served on a school board?
   ____ yes     ____ no

The second format of questions might have been of this nature:

7. Do you attend school board meetings?
   \_\_\_\_ always    \_\_\_\_ sometimes    \_\_\_\_ never

These are samples of a variety of question formats that were treated in Chapter 5. Almost any of those formats could be transformed so that the responses can be listed in abbreviated form.

A more complicated questionnaire might involve some sort of scoring, as with an attitude scale (cf. Chapter 5). In that case the scale score could be listed for each question and a space provided for a total score should that also be appropriate. The purpose of the "summary sheet" is to place the most relevant data in a single place to aid inspection and examination.

### UNSTRUCTURED DATA

Since data that are structured or quantified are reasonably easy to work with, whenever possible the qualitative, unstructured-type data should be so transformed. The transformation process in this case involves categorizing the data so that they can be compared, contrasted, and perhaps counted. The categories should have been decided upon before the data were collected since our general assumption is that all of the techniques we employ are purposeful. In most cases, a problem has generated the processes and the categories should directly relate to clarifying or answering that problem. On the other hand, we have also mentioned the need for a continuous monitoring of the community in which case the data may be generated without specific problem categories in mind. In either case, though, the general approach with this type of data is to gradually immerse one's self into that data to familiarize and ascertain a feeling for the types of responses occurring. This leads to categories for quantifying and counting. The process of categorizing the qualitative or unstructured data is called *content analysis*.

**Content Analysis.** Content analysis has grown from a technique for abstracting information from military broadcasts and communications to a method of analyzing any form of unstructured data.[2] Holsti (1969) defines content analysis as the application of scientific methods to documentary evidence. It requires *objectivity* in a *systematic* fashion leading to *generality* and is essentially a cyclical process of categorization or classification. The unstructured information, whether open-ended interview questions, newspapers, speeches, or observations of behaviors, is read and reread until logical groupings appear. These initial test categories (groupings) are recorded and employed as the material is again

---

[2]Some excellent discussions and examples of content analysis are found in Berelson, 1952; North, Holsti, Zaninovich, and Zinnes, 1963; Holsti, 1969; and Fox, 1969, Chap. 22.

reviewed. The survey director may want to make frequent checks with the superintendent to see if the emerging categories are appropriate. If the categories seem sufficient and useful for generating insights relative to the initiating problem, the cycling stops and the statements within each category are analyzed. If, on the other hand, there is still information that does not fall into the initial categories then additional groupings are generated and the cycle of reading, categorizing, and checking continues. Some examples may help to clarify this approach.

*Example 1:* Assume that the administration needs to get a reading from the public about a proposed junior high school. Also, we will assume that there are no indications about community feelings so that an open-ended interview approach is employed. Once the notes from the interviews are typed and available, they need to be scanned to generate some useful or relevant categories. In order to keep track of the notes and to be able to retrieve the original statements for comparisons and contrasts, they must first be assigned a designation or code number.

The simplest format for coding might be to take one or two pieces of demographic information and combine those with a number. Thus, if the interview included the number of school-age children in the family as well as the geographic location of the home, those two descriptors could be combined to help identify the particular interview. Some examples might be: 3n (i.e., 3 children and living in the north part of the community); or ∅se (i.e., no children in the family and their location is in the southeast sector of the community). Since there may be more than one interview with each code descriptor (that is, more than one family with three children located in the north sector [3n]), as the interviews are returned a number could be added to the code. There would then be a 3n—1 and a 3n—2. To keep track of the added numbers, a sheet listing numbers from 0 to 100 may be prepared. This sheet can be attached to the box or file folders where the interviews will be stored. As each interview is ready for filing, it should be assigned the next number of the sheet and that number then crossed off.[3]

A coding process of this nature not only permits quick access to the original interviews, but also facilitates early identification of the representativeness of the sample as described earlier. It is relatively easy to make a frequency count of the responses for the two designators used above (number of children and geographic location) and to compare the counts with known proportions of the population.

At this point the typed and coded interviews can be scanned for categories. A list of potentially useful topics or phrases are abstracted from a

---

[3]The combination of demographic descriptors and numbers may seem complicated but it should help to reduce the possibility of duplicate code numbers being assigned to different interviews.

**Table 8.2**

**Topic List from Interview Sample**

Purpose: To ascertain "feelings" about proposed junior high school.

| "Topic Statement" | "Feeling" | Assigned Code |
|---|---|---|
| Aesthetically inferior—not needed | – | 0se–5 |
| Too dangerous to walk to it | – | 3se–9 |
| Cost of constructing | 0 | 2n–27 |
| When ready to use? | 0 | 2nw–13 |
| Reflection of community—needed | + | 1w–2 |
| Who will name it? | 0 | 0w–6 |
| Why junior high school?—Cost | 0/– | 1s–22 |
| It's about time; needed | + | 3sw–18 |
| Cost outrageous | – | 0w–15 |
| Is it most accessible? It's needed | –/+ | 4e–32 |
| When ready? Why brick? Does community want it? | 0/– | 2s–29 |

- a selected phrase that seems to capture the interview
- judged feeling: + = positive, 0 = neutral, – = negative
- number of school age children
- location of respondent
- assigned number

small sample of the interviews. For each, the appropriate code is noted so that the total interview might be recovered as necessary. In this case, though, the simple *content* categories may not be sufficient for the purposes of the administration. The schoolman may want to know what the public *feels* about the proposed school. To get at the "feelings" of the respondents it may be sufficient to determine if the interview responses were generally positive (+), neutral (0), or negative (–) about the proposed school. *If* that feeling can be ascertained from the statements made, then the appropriate symbol might also be noted on the form recording these test categories (see Table 8.2). In this way there is greater potential for generating the categories that would allow for the analysis of trends, associations, and differences.

We will consider Table 8.2 further in the next chapter when some procedures for arranging information are discussed. At that time the symbols used for designating "feeling" (+ 0 –) will be depicted so as to aid the analysis and interpretation of this type of data.

*Example 2:* In this example the problem is to find out what issues concern the community. In particular the schoolman wants to know which issues in this area are being placed before people and the issues which they are speaking out on. One approach that might give him at least a start in this pursuit would be an analysis of the local newspapers. He might ask his assistant to look at a random sample of about 20 newspapers from the past six months to a year. In each of the papers his staff man might peruse the "Letters to the Editor," the editorial pages, and perhaps the first two or three pages of the paper. In his reading of the "letters," he would be looking for topics that the public is speaking out on, to try to develop some categories for these issues. He would approach the editorial pages in the same fashion, trying to classify the topics of editorials dealing with the schools. The first two or three pages of the paper would be read to ascertain what topics, either in the local schools or education in general, the news media have selected to emphasize as important. His reading of these sections would suggest to him some appropriate topics or categories for grouping and counting. One suggested technique for generating these categories is to list a word or phrase which captures the topic that is found. If a word can help recall a topic then that will be sufficient; if more than a word is necessary a phrase, clause, or sentence should be developed. The category designation (whether word or phrase) must be sufficiently explicit so that it does not distort the intent of the original topic. Specifying categories is difficult and comes only from practice. It is part of the cyclical process described earlier, generating test categories.

To recover the original information it is suggested that the date of the paper, the page, and the section be recorded after the statement. Table 8.3 illustrates an example of generated topics from a small sample of newspapers. If the list is long enough to generate categories for all of the topics, then a topic form would be developed and tried on a larger sample of papers. If the list is not sufficiently definitive, then more papers are sampled for topics. The topics listed in Table 8.3 may suggest some categories but are probably not sufficient for generating categories that would cover all topics. One category, for example, might be "Protests," which would include strikes, boycotts, protests, walkouts, and the like. Another emerging category might be in the area of budgets or funding, to include such topics as school aid, program cuts, and wages. A third possible category may be specified as "New Programs," or perhaps "Controversial Topics in the Schools." Whatever the categories generated are, they should be related to the initial problem or concern, in this case finding out the concerns of the public and news media.

The list of topics in the illustrations is too small for making any generalizations about the community or their concerns. With a longer list the topics might be grouped within categories as to "editorials," "letters," or "news." Within each of the classifications there might be a further ordering by the dates of the reports. These arrangements might aid some interpretive estimates by the schoolman and his assistant. They might ascertain community concerns (letters) in contrast to the bias of the paper (editorials) as well as the reported flow of events or problems (news items). It might be interesting, for

**Table 8.3**

**Topic List from Newspaper Sample**

Purpose: To discover concerns about education of community and news media.

| Topic | Page or Section | Date |
|---|---|---|
| Teacher Right to Strike Repealed | 3 | 4/15/73 |
| AFT Threatens Strike | 1 | 5/4/73 |
| Latest Campus Craze—Study | editor | 12/5/72 |
| Striking Teachers Try New Tactic | 2 | 12/9/72 |
| School Lunch Program Cut | 1 | 10/7/72 |
| Central High Wins | 1 | 11/27/72 |
| Defends Teaching by Commercial Firms | letter | 11/27/72 |
| Increase Driver Education | letter | 11/17/72 |
| Budget Cuts May Reduce School Aid | editor | 9/17/72 |
| Students Boycott School 6 | 2 | 1/11/73 |
| Parents Protest Teacher Dismissal | 3 | 6/2/73 |
| Defends Sex Education Program | letter | 10/3/72 |
| Sex Ed: School—No; Home—Yes! | editor | 10/8/72 |
| Tigers Win Again | 1 | 11/30/72 |
| School 6 Teachers Want Control Restored | 2 | 1/13/73 |
| Education Resumes at School 6 | 3 | 1/15/73 |

example, to assess the importance of sports in this community (front page news items) in comparison with the importance of teacher-personnel problems (page 2 or 3 news items). Whether or not that contrast is real or only apparent would necessitate a much larger sample of papers. Nevertheless, this process may help to clarify the classification, coding, and analysis of such data.

Before concluding this chapter with some discussion of the role of computers in analysis, we should remind the schoolman that a *key* should be developed and filed at the same time that codes are devised. The *key* is simply the long-hand description of each symbol or code that is being employed in the survey. It is disheartening and frustrating to return to data and not be able to remember the codes that were so laboriously devised. If the intent of this chapter is to reduce frustration, then certainly a "code-key" is a necessary item.

## computers in analysis

As was stated earlier, our emphasis on "hand analysis" is not meant to detract from the role that computers might play in analysis. Computers can be tremendous aids *if* they are employed in a rational and controlled manner. When is it appropriate to pursue the analysis of data through the use of computers? Unfortunately there are no definite answers to this question, only some general guidelines. Assuming that "hand analysis" has developed a feeling for the process and a confidence in the outcomes, then computer assistance is relevant where: (1) surveys are frequently repeated; *and* (2) there are reasonably large numbers of cases involved (perhaps samples of 150 or larger); and (3) there are many repetitive statistical operations necessary for data interpretation. Thus, if the administration needs some type of reading of the community's attitudes every year, then a computer approach would be quite sensible.

If the computer approach seems appropriate, then what is needed? First and foremost, of course, is access to a computer. The *hardware* (the computer and companion machines) may be available on a cooperative basis from a neighboring institution of higher learning: university, college, or community college. If not there, then computer time might be purchased from a local business or industry. However, such time is usually quite expensive and sometimes difficult to acquire. Another possibility is through shared services at the intermediate district level (county, or even across county lines). The last two possibilities are to purchase a computer (probably a used one from a nearby industry) or to lease a machine from the manufacturer. Both of these alternatives are also expensive propositions but, depending upon the volume of work, may be appropriate expenses to undertake. The hardware is less than half of what is needed. To accompany the machines there are a multitude of programs that are necessary (usually referred to as "software"). Many programs are available from computer companies or from libraries of programs at nearby universities. Where programs are not available, they must be written for the particular machine to be used.

To write programs requires skilled personnel. Such personnel are necessary for the operation of any size of computer setup. In fact, since the development of questionnaries, coding, and data preparation would differ considerably from the procedures we have detailed, if the computer is employed then the personnel resources must also be employed early in the survey process. Perhaps the one rule that might be offered for computer use is to *involve the computer resource persons (programmers) as soon as possible in the survey process.* At the very *latest,* such resource persons should be involved in the structuring of the questionnaire and all steps that follow.

We would strongly recommend that the schoolman give serious thought to securing consultant help from a university survey research center when a decision to computerize seems necessary. Such centers have skilled personnel, techniques, and equipment for all phases of surveys. Using their services may, in fact, cost less than having the district secure its own equipment and conduct large-scale repetitive surveys.[4]

We still contend, however, that experiencing a survey from beginning to end has benefits that may not occur from contracting for such services. In particular, when the district plans and conducts the survey, personnel develop an understanding of the applicability and limitations of surveys which they can

---

[4] For further understanding of computers and their applications, see Boroko, 1962.

put to use when contracting for survey services. More important, the involvement of local personnel in the survey is likely to increase the acceptance and implementation of the recommendations that emerge. It is this latter reason that leads us to recommending some additional possibilities that still include the substantial involvement of the school system personnel in all major phases of the survey.

## INTERMEDIARY RESOURCES

There are in-between approaches that are available for those who may want to employ some level of technology but lack the physical and human resources necessary for computers. For sorting information there is a needlesort process which involves only three pieces of equipment: cards, a punch, and a long needle. Essentially the system involves punching notches along the edge of a card. Each card contains one questionnaire. If the need were to find all persons who were under 25 years of age, then the needle would be inserted in the hole corresponding to that question on the deck of cards. Since only those under 25 would have a notch punched in that place, those cards would fall out when the needle and deck are lifted. These types of sorts would be performed for all of the frequencies desired.

For computational assistance there are small desk-size computers which can handle complicated procedures and multiple analyses with comparative ease. Many of these desk computers can be tailored to the individual needs of the user; that is, certain keys may be replaced with statistical functions "built into" the machine. The Monroe desk computers, for example, can perform chi-squares, correlations, difference of means tests, means, standard deviations, and many other analytical procedures with no more effort than using an adding machine. Such machines sell for a few thousand dollars or may be leased for a fraction of this cost with the rental applied to the purchase of the machine. If such an aid is available then many hundreds of cases may be handled with a direct saving in time and dollars. We would strongly recommend that desk computers be examined if the school system sees the value of repeated surveys. For understanding the community, its needs and desires, these technological aids are dollars well invested.

## summary

A very central part of understanding community is abstracting meaning from the data. This process of analysis involves an understanding of data, coding, storing, and scoring of information as a beginning step. The raw information, whether it is structured data (counts or numbers) or unstructured data (qualitative or unordered data), must be categorized and ordered to maximize understanding. Whenever possible, unstructured data should be transformed to the structured format. This transformation then permits all of the techniques for structured data to be applied.

We have recommended that "hand analysis" be pursued since it builds a familiarity and understanding. Once confidence has been achieved, then aids such as needlesorts, desk computers, or standard computers may be pursued. In general, such technology is restricted to extensive surveys that are to be repeated with fair regularity. These aids, though, are also useful where analysis requires many repeated *statistical* operations with large numbers of cases.

In the next chapter the analysis process that centers on the arrangement and description of data is discussed. This descriptive process enhances the opportunity for uncovering trends, differences, and associations in the developing picture of the community.

## references

BERELSON, BERNARD, *Content Analysis in Communications Research.* New York: Free Press, 1952.

BOROKO, HAROLD, ed., *Computer Applications in the Behavioral Sciences.* Englewood Cliffs, N.J.: Prentice-Hall, 1962.

FOX, DAVID J., *The Research Process in Education.* New York: Holt, Rinehart & Winston, 1969.

HOLSTI, OLE R., *Content Analysis for the Social Sciences and Humanities.* Reading, Mass.: Addison-Wesley, 1969.

NORTH, ROBERT C., OLE R. HOLSTI, M. GEORGE ZANINOVICH, and DINA A. ZINNES, *Content Analysis.* Evanston, Ill.: Northwestern University Press, 1963.

SIMON, JULIAN L., *Basic Research Methods in Social Science.* New York: Random House, 1969.

# Arranging and Describing Data

*nine*

The goal of analysis is to ascertain patterns or trends. There is no better way to do this than to visualize the information. The construction of *pictures* is essentially the process of arranging and describing data. For the professional statistician graphic representation of data is frequently a starting point; for those less familiar with the techniques involved it is often overlooked or avoided. The rationale for this step rests squarely on the frailties of human beings: we are limited by our perceptual abilities. There is far greater likelihood that we will be able to uncover patterns or associations from a visual picture than from a set of unordered numbers or written statements. In this chapter we will cover some general techniques for depicting structured data, and then present some special approaches for picturing unstructured data.

## approaches for depicting structured data

The techniques described below are most appropriate for structured data. This is due to one of the special characteristics of such data; it is quantifiable and can be counted and ordered. Once again we stress the importance of transforming unstructured data so that these approaches may be applied. Four simple approaches–histograms, line graphs, scattergrams, and descriptive statistics—will be highlighted since they are probably sufficient for the types of problems or information that the schoolman will pursue.

*HISTOGRAM*

The histogram or bar graph is simply a frequency chart giving a visual picture of the relative strength, degree, or occurrence of each category. In its most familiar form it is a bar graph as seen in Figures 2.8, 2.9, and 2.10 in Chapter 2. Construction of such charts requires the identification of categories and a count of occurrences within that category (cf. Walker and Lev, 1958; Games and Klare, 1967; Glass and Stanley, 1970).

In Chapter 8 (Figure 8.1 and Table 8.2) there were examples of structured and unstructured data arrangements. As long as they allowed some form of frequency or count, they could be graphed. For example, if the information that was initiated in Figure 8.1 were completed, there might be a desire to graph the frequency of *yes* and *no* responses for the first six questions, comparing these occurrences between families with children and families without children residing in Elementary School District 1. Such a graph might have looked like that in Figure 9.1; *apparently* the graph depicts a more intensive "positive" response among the families with children.

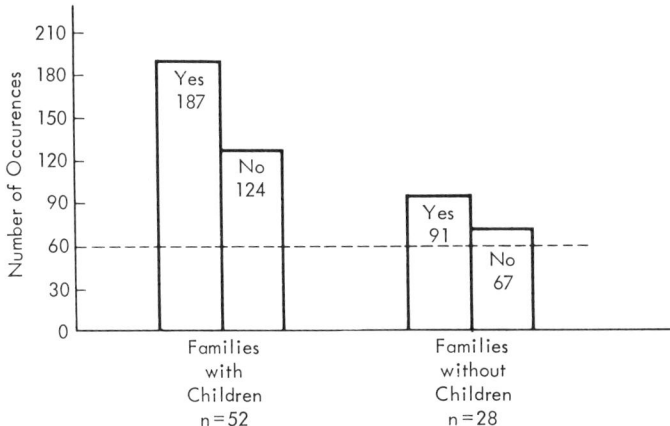

**Figure 9.1**

Bar graph depicting "Yes-No" responses for families with and without children in E.S.D. 1 (using frequencies).

A second example could be generated from the unstructured data collected and depicted in Table 8.2. In this example there might be a need to compare the positive (+), neutral (0), and negative (−) "feelings" for families with and without children. In this case the graph would appear something like that in Figure 9.2. Here the result seems to be that families with children are more *positively* disposed toward their school than childless families.

150    The Process of Analysis

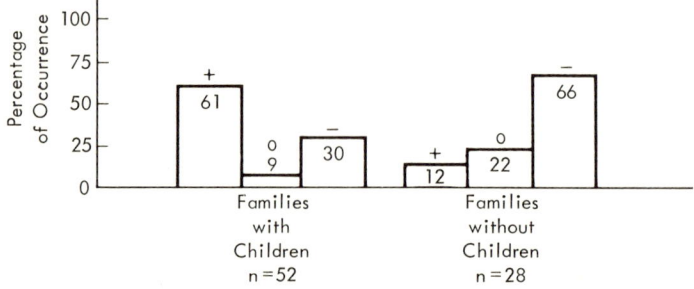

**Figure 9.2**
Bar graph depicting positive, neutral, and negative feelings for families with and without children in E.S.D. 1 (using percentages).

The bar graph or histogram is sometimes useful, but it can lead to gross errors if certain cautions are not taken. The purpose of arranging the data in this form is to help the viewer to ascertain differences and similarities, not to confuse the analytic process. At the very least, the following three points should be considered:

1. Be sure that the categories are clear and distinct.
   Figure 9.1 (in contrast to Figure 9.2) demonstrates a confused categorization for it indicates an $n$ of 52 yet depicts some 187 positive responses. It happens that this is accurate, for each family had six questions to which it was responding thus affording a total possibility of 312 yes and no responses that could be counted. Nevertheless, the way that it is drawn confuses rather than aids in analysis.
2. Be sure to start a bar graph at zero.
   For example, turn to Figure 9.1 and place a piece of paper or your hand over the graph *below* the dotted line. This would give you some idea of what the lengths of the bars would look like if we had used 60 as the base line for the graph. In that event the analysis might be that the "yes" responses were, for each category, about double the "no" responses. A quick check of the actual responses shows this to be a false impression.
3. Be sure to indicate whether you are using raw data (frequency counts) or percentages.
   While either may be used and may be useful, some false impressions can be fostered when using frequency counts where the groups are not of equal size. Figure 9.1 might be interpreted as showing a "stronger" favorable count among the families with children. In actuality, the percentages of yes-no responses for the two categories are exactly the same; 60 percent showing "yes" votes and 40 percent "no" votes. Figure 9.2 utilizes percentages and thus depicts the relative strengths of feelings for the two categories; that is, there is a substantially greater positive feeling among those families with children.

## LINE GRAPH

The line graph is primarily an aid for assessing a state or condition over time and, from that assessment, making predictions for future times. This is frequently referred to as the process of *trend analysis*. Simon (1969, p. 357) cautions about this type of analysis and highlights a necessary condition if it is pursued:

> The important point is that the past is never a guarantee of the future, and prediction should never be a mechanical extrapolation. Merely drawing a graph with time on one axis and on the other some variable that shows an apparent consistency in movement is a very dangerous basis for predicting that the next time period will follow the same apparent movement. The safer basis for extrapolation of an observed trend into the future is an *understanding* of the various forces that underlie the process. Gaining such an understanding is more a matter of saturation in the situation than of scientific technique.

Each of the examples in Chapter 2 depicted a trend over time, but each also demonstrated a need for understanding factors associated with the apparent trends. In general, there are three considerations for any line graph and the analysis of trends. First, there is a need to select the clearest possible *indicators* for the trend variable. Examples of indicators might be tax rates, changes in assessed valuations, attendance figures, voter turnout, employment, or any identifiable, countable measure. The second consideration is the *time* variable. What is the most appropriate time measure and interval? For data on rapidly recurring events, several months of monitoring may be sufficient. Other events occurring only once a year may not reveal any pattern or flow unless at least a five-to-ten-year record is maintained. Finally, the most appropriate related factors must be identified and recorded. What factors are related and which are most important? This is what Simon (1969) was referring to when he noted that gaining the type of *understanding* that enables the researcher to identify relevant forces is more a matter of saturation than science. As with "content analysis," described in the previous chapter, ascertaining these types of factors is a process of immersing one's self in the totality of the situation.

The following example may demonstrate some of the approaches for analyzing trends as well as the dangers involved. The director of adult education was concerned about the budget allocations for his program so he accumulated data on enrollments. The data he generated were then depicted on a Trend Analysis Sheet (Figure 9.3). Across the top of the sheet are figures showing the school district population and the enrollments in adult education. The enrollment figures for each year are graphed below that data. On the vertical axis he listed enrollments in increasing units or intervals of 25 persons (from 2,000 to 2,025, etc.). Along the horizontal axis are the years for each of the enrollment figures, which is the time dimension selected. Below the graph there is room for *relevant* factors to be listed and identified against the plots on the graph. For example, the director noted that there was a fire in the home economics section of the junior high school in 1972. It appears that he has associated that fire with the decreased enrollment for that one year.

When the total picture is viewed, *as the director perceived it,* it appears that there is an increasing trend in enrollments and that projections might be for further increases. If he followed his analysis he might argue for an increase in budget and prepare for additional personnel to staff the adult education program.

**Figure 9.3**

Trend Analysis Sheet: Adult Education Enrollment Analysis.

|  | 1969 | 1970 | 1971 | 1972 | 1973 | 1974 | 1975 |
|---|---|---|---|---|---|---|---|
| District Enrollment | 30,000 | 30,600 | 31,518 | 32,148 | 32,791 | 33,447 |  |
| Adult Ed Enrollment | 2,000 | 2,030 | 2,051 | 2,048 | 2,073 | 2,095 |  |

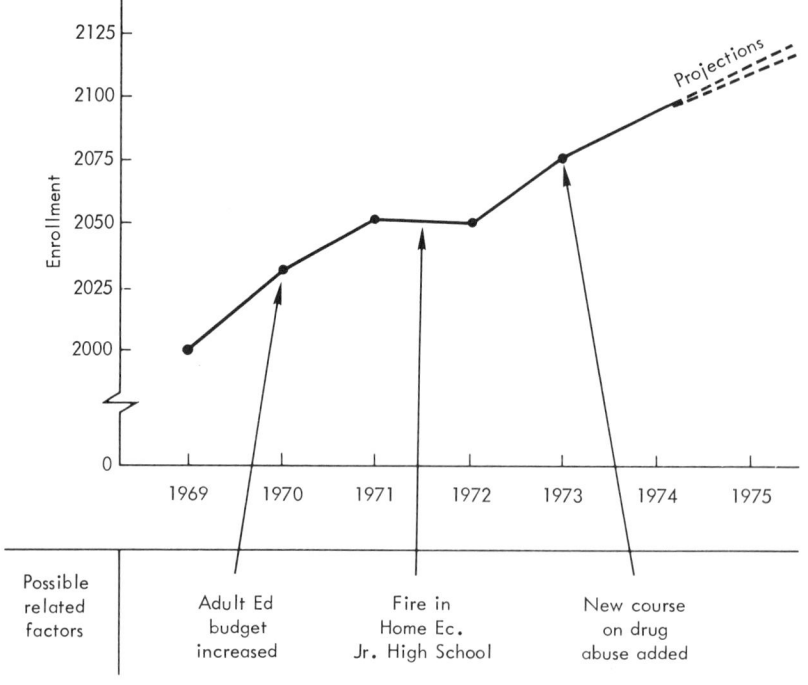

Unfortunately, he may not have selected the most appropriate *indicator* for viewing the adult education program. He neglected to include the changes in school district population as a possible relevant factor for consideration. If he wanted to see to what extent the program was meeting the needs of the district, or at least what portion of the district was attending adult education classes, he might have used as an indicator the *percentage of district population* enrolled in adult education. Thus, for 1969 there were 30,000 adults in the district, of which 2,000 were attending adult classes. The percentage, then, would be 2,000/30,000 or approximately 6.6 percent. In that year 6.6 percent of the school district was attending adult education classes. Using this percentage as an *indicator* on the vertical axis, the line graph would appear like that in Figure 9.4. In this view, with the relevant factors identified as the increases in district population, the analysis might be that this program may soon have to be modified. Now the question might be, at what point does the percentage enrolled become critical for ascertaining support of the program?

**Figure 9.4**

Trend Analysis Sheet: Adult Education Enrollment Analysis 2.

|  | 1969 | 1970 | 1971 | 1972 | 1973 | 1974 | 1975 |
|---|---|---|---|---|---|---|---|
| District Enrollment | 30,000 | 30,600 | 31,518 | 32,148 | 32,791 | 33,447 |  |
| Adult Ed Enrollment | 2,000 | 2,030 | 2,051 | 2,048 | 2,073 | 2,095 |  |
| Adult Ed as Percent of District | 6.6 | 6.6 | 6.5 | 6.3 | 6.3 | 6.2 |  |

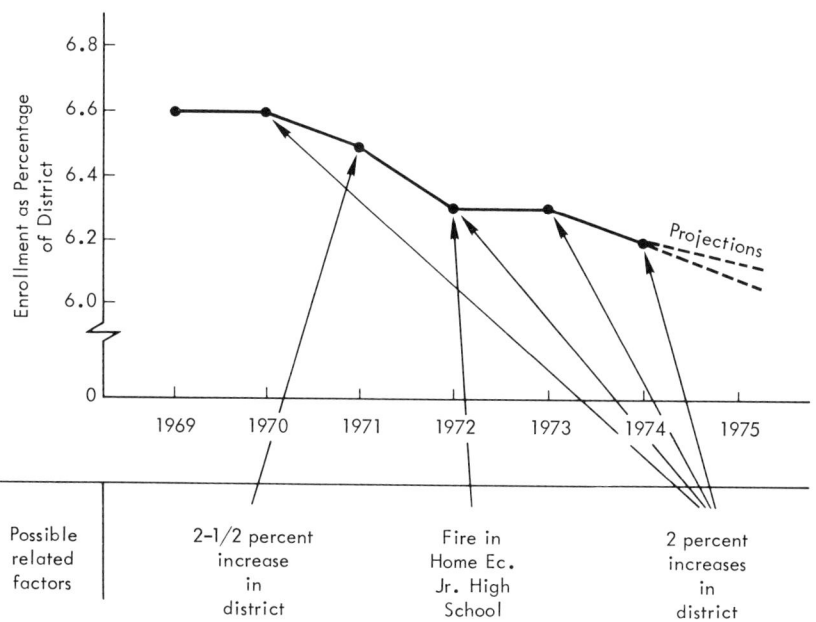

The main point from the example is that line graphs and the analysis of trends may be useful, but require considerable attention both in construction and in analysis. Furthermore, projections from past history may not always be clear-cut or straight-line changes. Aside from the suggestions given above and those in the next section on *scattergrams,* ascertaining curvilinear changes requires a reasonably sophisticated knowledge of mathematics.[1]

## SCATTERGRAM

A useful yet often overlooked technique for describing data is the scattergram. A scattergram, or scatter diagram, is essentially a pictorial representation of paired observations (Games and Klare, 1967, Part D). In other words, it requires two variables that are logically related; e.g., the attitudes of parents toward "open space classes" *and* the length of time that those parents have been residents of the community; or, citizen support of the school system *and* the amount of involvement those citizens have experienced. In each case two observations have been recorded about the same person or subject.

The latter example of citizen support and involvement might prove useful to demonstrate the value of the scattergram. Given that the administrator wants to determine whether or not the program of community involvement was associated with the willingness of the community to support the schools, a survey instrument was developed for each of the variables, a sample selected, the instruments administered and returned. After scoring and coding the instruments each respondent would have two scores recorded: (1) a score indicating the present level of involvement, and (2) a score indicating his present feelings toward the school system (ranging from negative to positive). The scattergram would be constructed by plotting the two scores as a single point for each respondent. In Figure 9.5 the scores of the following seven respondents are plotted:

| Respondent | Involvement Score | Support Score |
|---|---|---|
| A | 4 | 1.5 |
| B | 5 | 4.0 |
| C | 8 | 3.5 |
| D | 6 | 3.0 |
| E | 1 | 3.2 |
| F | 3 | 2.0 |
| G | 4 | 2.0 |

[1] For introductory understandings see Bross, 1953; Bursk and Chapman, 1963; and Glass and Stanley, 1970. More advanced sources are Dyckman, Smidt, and McAdams, 1969; or Clelland, deCani, Brown, Bursk, and Murray, 1966.

Arranging and Describing Data    155

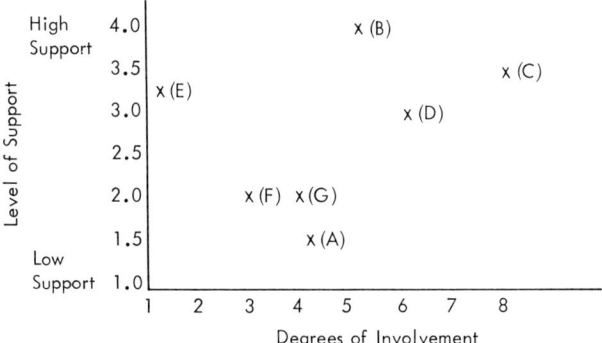

**Figure 9.5**
Involvement-support scores plotted for seven respondents.

Respondent C was highly involved in the schools (as defined in the instrument) and was also quite highly supportive of the school system. Respondent E, on the other hand, was hardly involved at all, yet was also quite positive in his support for the system. The last respondent, G, was neither highly involved nor highly supportive. But a picture does not emerge with so few plots as seven; a substantial number are necessary. Figures 9.6, 9.7, 9.8, and 9.9 depict some of the alternative scattergrams that might have occurred from a survey in a single district. The first one (Figure 9.6) depicts almost a perfect random distribution of the plotted points. There is no apparent relationship between the two variables. While this may be immediately disheartening, the administrator must not conclude that involvement is totally unrelated to the level of support, at least not yet. It may be there is a time lag for support to be generated so that he may want a follow-up survey conducted at a later date with a sample drawn from that same population.

The second scattergram (Figure 9.7) is the one that the administrator would probably find most encouraging. In this case there is a high positive association between the two variables. That is, as the variable of involvement increases, so too the variable of support increases. Notice that it is not a perfect straight-line relationship but a scattering of the plots with the trend running from lower left to upper right in direction. While this is positive evidence supporting the school involvement program, any conclusions should be carefully weighed. The time lag mentioned for the first case might also be operative here, only in this instance time might reduce the effects noted. Again a follow-up survey would be helpful.

In contrast to the two previous cases, the third scattergram (Figure 9.8) is extremely discouraging. Exactly the opposite of what was anticipated is

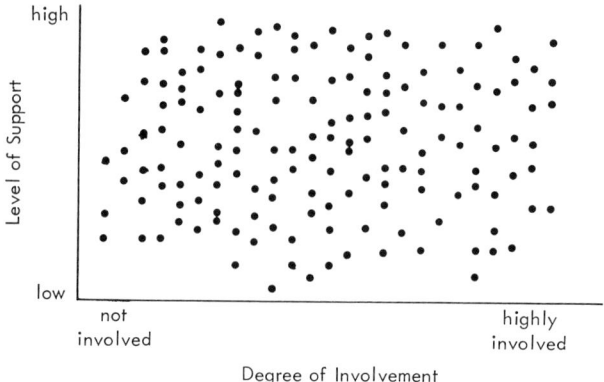

**Figure 9.6**
Scattergram 1: No Relationship.

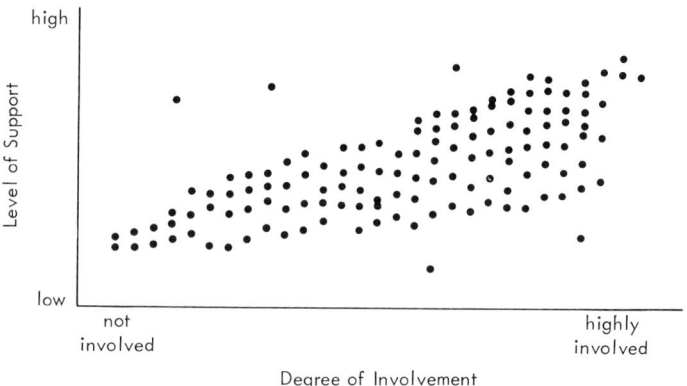

**Figure 9.7**
Scattergram 2: Positive Relationship.

observed. This picture shows an inverse or negative relationship. As participation or involvement increases there is a decrease in the support for the school. How to explain such an occurrence is part of the interpretative process. One possibility might be that as citizens become more involved in the school they also increase in their knowledge of what the school is doing, and, perhaps, that increased knowledge discourages support rather than encourages it. Perhaps additional information that had been included in the survey could be tapped to shed light on the relationship found. Thus, if there were some measure of "knowledge of the school" included, the preceding speculation could be immediately tested. If not, perhaps a follow-up approach might be tried.

The last example (Figure 9.9) is the most complex and perhaps interesting.

Arranging and Describing Data    *157*

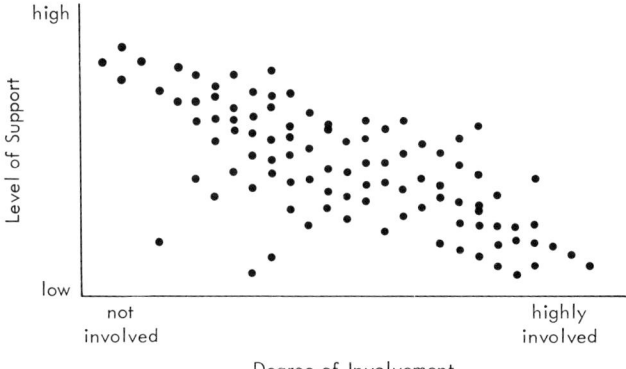

**Figure 9.8**
Scattergram 3: Negative Relationship.

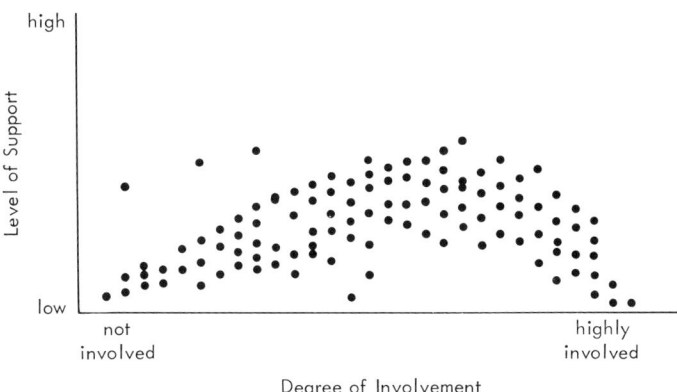

**Figure 9.9**
Scattergram 4: Curved Relationship.

What is depicted here is that support for the schools increases as involvement increases *but* after a certain level of involvement continued increases are matched with *decreasing* support. While there are competing possibilities for explaining this curved relationship, the important point is that it may not have been discovered at all if the scattergram had not been constructed. One of the statistical techniques of association (probably a simple correlation) would have indicated a fairly high level of relationship, but the administrator could be in trouble if he had only relied on that type of technique. In fact, this is the crux of the present chapter: to picture the data *before* applying statistical techniques of analysis.

**Density Map.** Before leaving the scattergram one additional technique for picturing data should be mentioned. We consider this technique, the *density map*, a subset or special type of scattergram. Generally, this is the recording of observations (as positive support by +, neutral by 0, and negative by -) in the appropriate sections of a map of the area of concern. To demonstrate, if the interview data collected and depicted in Table 8.2 (Chapter 8) were to be pictured in a density map, it might look like the map presented in Figure 9.10. In each of the geographic sections the +s, -s and 0s have been drawn dependent upon the *feeling* the interviewer ascertained from his conversation with the respondent. The picture seems to indicate a predominant number of negative feelings (-s) in the west and southeast sectors of the community, while the southwest and southern sections seem to be most positive in their reaction to the school.

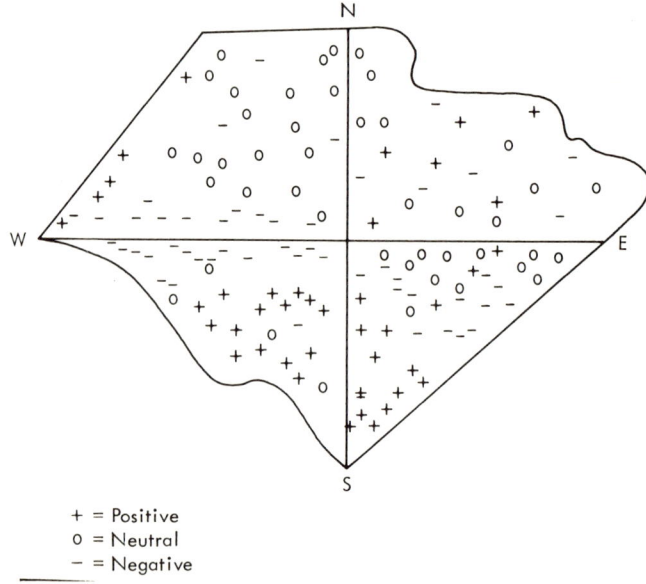

+ = Positive
0 = Neutral
- = Negative

**Figure 9.10**

Density map depicting positive, neutral, and negative feelings toward a proposed junior high school.

While many administrators may prefer to see an actual map or outline of a map for this density mapping, we have found that the topological equivalent of the district map is more flexible and more accurate for use. A "topologically"[2]

[2]Topology, or "rubber-sheet geometry," allows for distortions of surfaces so long as their basic characteristics remain the same. The circle has merely *smoothed* out the jogs and curves in its equivalent map. In all other ways, the characteristics have not been changed.

equivalent map for that portrayed in Figure 9.10 is the simple circle drawn in Figure 9.11. The major value of the circle map is that the geographic areas can be drawn in as sectors and can be given an area proportionate to the population that actually resides in that sector. Thus, while location-wise or physically all of the sectors are equal, as drawn in Figure 9.11 about 25 percent of the population of the district resides in each of the south and southwest sectors. When the "feelings" are plotted in the proportionate mapping, a somewhat different picture may then emerge. Figure 9.12 shows one such density mapping with proportionate sectors. It indicates a sufficient support for the new school but highlights dissent in certain sectors of the community.

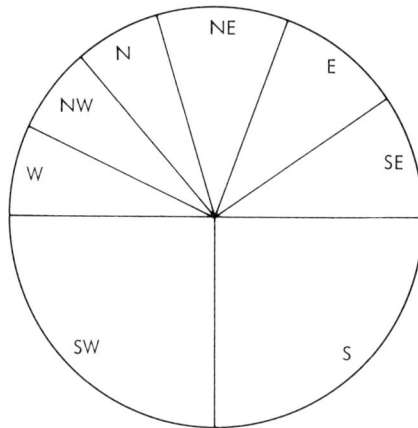

**Figure 9.11**
Topological equivalent map.

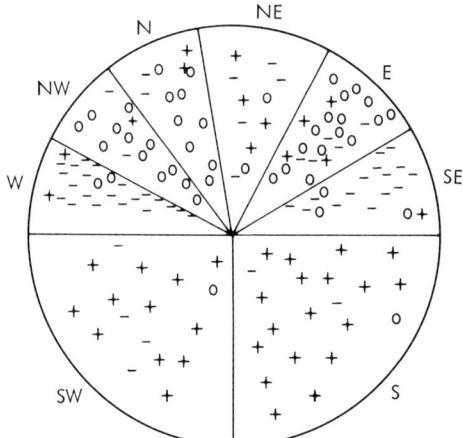

**Figure 9.12**
Proportionate density map of feelings toward proposed junior high school.

All of the preceding techniques have relied on visual presentation. There are other forms of description that may also be appropriate for structured data, in particular, descriptive techniques employing mathematics and statistics.

*DESCRIPTIVE STATISTICS*

All of the mathematical techniques such as the mean, median, mode, and the range[3] are appropriate for structured data. Each of these techniques helps to describe the data and facilitates examination for the purpose of analysis (cf. Games and Klare, 1967; and Koenker, 1971). There are times when one or two of these techniques may be more appropriate than others, or when some may hide or distort data (Huff, 1954). The general caution is not to rely on one technique, but to try a number of them when it seems appropriate. Each can be helpful under certain conditions. A summary sheet similar to that used to log the individual responses (Figure 8.1) is also a helpful tool for collecting together these general statistical descriptors. These may also be graphed and diagrammed to picture the generalized responses. The recommendation is not to restrict the analysis to a single technique or approach, but to broaden it as much as possible to facilitate refinement of the interpretive picture.

## depicting unstructured data

If the unstructured data do not lend themselves to categorization, then they must be depicted from the unordered state. The process of arranging and describing unstructured data is as much an art as it is a science. Sometimes the key step in this process is to physically locate the apparently similar transcripts or items together so that they can be read and reread as a unit. Earlier, in Table 8.3 (Chapter 8), we described a newspaper analysis; an attempt to discover concerns about education as such concerns were given news space. The process we suggested was one of describing the article in a sentence or phrase and indicating where it was located in the newspaper. Perhaps the most sensible follow-up would be to group the articles by section and date and read through them again. In essence the purpose here is to develop a written and documented description, akin to a "scenario" or descriptive passage. We can only underscore that working with unstructured data is difficult, time-consuming, and demands great patience. The investigator must use every tool at his disposal but in the end it is his own mind-set and analytic insights that will provide the interpretive results sought.

Not to dispute the preceding paragraph, but indeed to underscore it again,

[3]*Mean* is the arithmetic average. *Median* is the middle score in a distribution. *Mode* is the most frequently occurring score. *Range* is the difference between the lowest and highest scores in the distribution.

the investigator might gather together as many of the staff associated with the project as possible and include them in this stage of analysis. While he may have to rely on his own judgments later, the feelings, opinions, beliefs, and interpretations of the staff could be tremendous aids in the development of the descriptive scenario. This is particularly evident when the staff have been involved in conducting interviews or making transcripts. The visual clues or cues that may not have been transmitted in the report or questionnaire must have a vehicle for entering the analysis. The group conference is one such vehicle.

## summary

Since it is difficult to abstract meaning from unordered information, data are arranged and described to form visual pictures. This process is an essential step in the analysis of information. Without it, there is too high a probability of overlooking the patterns and associations within the community.

While there are techniques that may be used with either structured or unstructured data, whenever possible qualitative information should be transformed to resemble the quantitative format. Techniques that assist in describing and arranging structured data include histograms or bar graphs, line graphs for trend analysis, and scattergrams. A special type of scattergram is the density map.

Descriptive statistics are appropriate for quantitative data and are recommended to the interpreter for use. Data should be described and arranged in a number of ways so that the opportunity for interpretive messages to emerge is facilitated.

Information that does not lend itself to reasonable transformation must be utilized in its basic form. To aid in understanding such information the grouping and study of the data is the one main technique. A mind that is readied through reading and study may be prepared to cope with the major task of describing the picture that the unstructured data can bring forth.

The third and final stage of analysis is carried through in the next chapter. The transformed data needs interpretation for final understanding. Selected statistical tools for the building of that understanding form the central thread of the chapter.

## references

BROSS, IRWIN D. J., *Design for Decision.* New York: The Free Press, Collier-Macmillan Canada, Ltd., 1953.

BURSK, EDWARD C. and JOHN F. CHAPMAN, eds., *New Decision-Making Tools for Managers.* Cambridge, Mass.: Harvard University Press, 1963.

CLELLAND, RICHARD C., JOHN S. DeCANI, FRANCIS E. BROWN, J. PARKER BURSK, and DONALD S. MURRAY, *Basic Statistics with Business Applications.* New York: John Wiley, 1966.

DYCKMAN, T. R., S. SMIDT, and A. K. McADAMS, *Management Decision Making Under Uncertainty.* London: Macmillan, 1969.

GAMES, PAUL A., and GEORGE R. KLARE, *Elementary Statistics.* New York: McGraw-Hill, 1967.

GLASS, GENE V., and JULIAN C. STANLEY, *Statistical Methods in Education and Psychology.* Englewood Cliffs, N.J.: Prentice-Hall, 1970.

HUFF, DARRELL, *How To Lie With Statistics.* New York: Norton, 1954.

KOENKER, ROBERT H., *Simplified Statistics.* Totowa, N.J.: Littlefield, Adams and Company, 1971.

SIMON, JULIAN L., *Basic Research Methods in Social Science.* New York: Random House, 1969.

# Interpretation
# and Statistical Analysis

*ten*

The steps in the process of analysis are not as discrete or sequential as have been described. They are cyclical or at least overlapping but have been separated mainly for ease in discussion and treatment. Much of what was described in the previous chapter went beyond coding and arranging of the data and involved interpretation as well. Here, though, that phase of the process, the interpretive, will be treated in some detail. We will especially focus on a single statistical test, the chi-square test. While other statistical tests will be mentioned, this one will be treated in detail. Chi-square has tremendous versatility and is simple to compute. Learning its applications will greatly enhance the administrator's capabilities for interpreting data and ascertaining the fine points of his community.

## interpreting

The capstone of the cumulative parts of this book is in the *explaining* of why or how certain discrepancies or deviations occurred. This process of *explaining* is essentially what we mean by interpretation. However, it is not a simple singular event, but rather a sequential set of recurring processes. Kaplan (1964) argues that the behavioral sciences are concerned with a double process of interpretation. "The behavioral scientist must first . . . construe what conduct a particular piece of behavior represents; and then he must search for the meaning of the interpreted action, its interconnections with other actions or circumstances [Kaplan, 1964, p. 34]." From our perspective this process is akin to the development of a picture. After light-sensitive paper has been exposed to a negative that paper is placed in a developer. As the paper rests in the solution an image begins to emerge. This treatment of the paper in the developer is the first level of interpretation. If the paper is removed too quickly the image is weak, the detail missing, and it may be difficult to discern what the image is. On the other hand, leaving the paper in too long clouds the paper, darkens and bleeds the lines so that the image is stark and perhaps unrecognizable. Within limits a certain time in the developer will produce a clear, sharp picture which will enable the viewer to recognize the image. This is our first level of interpretation, that is, arranging the data and working with the data long enough to produce a sharp clear picture of the acts or events but not so long that we become overloaded with data and thus confused.

The second level is in viewing the picture to ascertain its meaning. In art this is an examination of the object-representation for affective and cognitive understanding. So too in the understanding of community data; if the picture that the data produces is clear, then the administrator must work with that picture to understand the interrelations of the elements, to sense the meaning and implications for actions or decisions. But to attempt the advanced level of interpretation without first having produced a clear picture is to suffer certain failure.

Handling differences or associations will vary according to the type of data that is being treated. Those data which are structured will require some understanding of statistical tools and some elaborative discussion. For ease in handling, then, we will treat the unstructured data first and follow those approaches with the statistical tools for structured data.

## *UNSTRUCTURED DATA*

Ascertaining associations with unstructured data is basically a process of cross-checking of information as available and generating new information when it is not at hand. As the documents or interview reports are read, questions as to whether or not certain events or occurrences are associated may be raised. These questions are then focal points for the rereading of the additional information. Thus, for example, if one respondent indicates that a particular community member's speeches precipitated incidents in the neighborhood, then other interviews are read to see if they may also mention this. If not, then an additional probe of other respondents may be necessary. So too with differences in the perception of the respondents: What contrasts the respondents in respect to their differences? Does the demographic information highlight relevant contrasts? Are there other respondents who could aid in explaining the differences? Frequently a type of sequential interviewing aids in uncovering

**Interpretation and Statistical Analysis** *165*

answers to questions that the information from the previous respondents raised. In essence these approaches are validity checks on respondent perceptions which reduce the possibility of erroneous interpretations. Sequential interviewing also shifts the burden of explaining the differences or associations from the investigator alone, to a shared position between investigator and the future respondents.

Beyond these few suggestions for working with unstructured data there are the procedures described in Chapter 8 for transforming such data to a structured format. The transformed data lend themselves to many graphic and statistical approaches that are relatively easy to apply and understand. However, in either case there is still the necessity for making sense of data either as they are, or transformed. Only through a total immersion of the investigator in the data, its background, and the problem that gave rise to the study will that level of interpreting be achieved.

*STRUCTURED DATA*

When interpreting structured data the most frequent concerns are whether certain variables are related or whether they differ from one another. The "concerns" are, in essence, *hypotheses* that the administrator wants to test. The processes we described in Chapter 2 for specifying a problem were, in fact, procedures that lead to the statement of testable hypotheses, although stated in question form. Are there, for example, significantly more negative votes cast by citizens without children than by citizens with children in the schools? Or, is there a relationship between the number of Scandinavian families moving into the community and requests for certain changes in curriculums? The administrator should have at least one statistical tool at his command for examining such associations and differences; for testing the hypotheses that he has generated. We feel that familiarity with the chi-square test[1] will provide the administrator with that necessary decision-making tool. This statistical test will be described in the next few pages with examples and computation procedures. It is a test that is simple to compute by hand or machine, requires few assumptions or criteria for use, yet is an extremely versatile tool for analysis.

We still emphasize, though, that the visual techniques described in the previous chapter be a first order of priority. For example, the scattergrams give a reasonable estimation of relationship. When there is doubt about the relationships it is useful to compute the degree of relation or the correlation of the variables. While the chi-square statistic could be useful even here, the most generally employed approach is the Pearson Product Moment Correlation designated by a small letter "r." If this test is not familiar to the schoolman then he should seek the aid of a statistician in his system or from an outside source.

This is also our recommendation relative to computing the difference of means referred to as the "t test." Again this is a very helpful technique for

[1]The symbol for chi-square is the Greek letter *Chi* with the raised number *two* $\chi^2$.

determining whether or not two groups differ from one another on some measure.[2] In this case, though, the chi-square statistic will be a simple and useful substitute so that it would not be necessary to seek a consultant. This is our primary aim, to provide the schoolman with a sufficient background of knowledge and techniques so that he may pursue, in its entirety, the analysis of his community. To achieve that goal, we will devote most of the remaining pages in this chapter to chi-square.

### an introduction to chi-square

From a technical point of view chi-square is a statistical test used to determine if a sample distribution differs significantly from an assumed or expected distribution. The test is used with data in the form of simple counts or frequencies such as the numbers of voters versus nonvoters; the preferences of parents compared with couples without children; or distribution of "pro" and "con" residents in district A versus district B versus district C and so on. If the data are not in the form of counts or frequencies (e.g., achievement scores, ages, etc.) they can be transformed. This process is one of establishing sensible categories or intervals, as those scoring between 60 and 65, or persons between 20 and 25 years of age, and then counting the numbers falling in those categories.

The question we attempt to answer through the chi-square test is whether the frequencies observed in the sample differ from some hypothetical or assumed distribution. To clarify this further, assume that a survey of 180 persons was conducted and the respondents indicated their feeling about establishing a sex education program with 100 favoring such a program and 80 indicating opposition. Is that difference of 20 persons a significant difference? That is, would it be likely that the total population of the community from which the sample were drawn would be weighted towards establishing a sex education program?[3] To answer that question the chi-square test might be computed.

The four general steps that comprise the computation rule for chi-square are:

---

[2]Both $r$ (correlation) and $t$ (difference of means) are well described in such sources as Koenker, 1971; Popham, 1967; Games and Klare, 1967; and Glass and Stanley, 1970. All of these are appropriate for basic background and coverage, but the Koenker source is especially good for quick reference and computation procedures.

[3]Note that even if that difference were significant, there is still a *political consideration* as to the decision of whether or not to institute the program. This survey is only a single piece of information that may aid the administrator in making his decisions. This is discussed further toward the end of this chapter.

1. From each set of observed frequencies ($f_o$) subtract that set's particular expected frequencies ($f_e$):

$$(f_o - f_e)$$

2. Square the result:

$$(f_o - f_e)^2$$

3. Divide that result by the frequencies expected for that set:

$$\frac{(f_o - f_e)^2}{f_e}$$

4. Sum the results of each of those final computations: (the symbol for "sum" is $\Sigma$)

$$\chi^2 = \Sigma \left[ \frac{(f_o - f_e)^2}{f_e} \right]$$

In our example there are two sets of observed frequencies, those *in favor* (100), and those *opposed* (80). What are the *expected* frequencies? This number is derived from an assumption of "indifference." By "indifferent" is meant the community as a whole does not lean toward any particular position. Thus, if the community were perfectly *indifferent* about this question, then they would be divided exactly in half, 50 percent in favor and 50 percent opposed. Since the total sample is 180, half of that number (50 percent × 180) would be the expected frequency for each of the two sets of observed frequencies. A summary of this information is depicted in Table 10.1)

Table 10.1

Observed and Expected Frequencies for Sample Favoring and Opposing Sex Education Program

|  | In Favor Of | Opposed To | Total |
|---|---|---|---|
| Frequency Observed | 100 | 80 | 180 |
| Frequency Expected | 90 | 90 | 180 |

The chi-square test can now be computed following the computation schedule detailed above:

Step 1: $(f_o - f_e)$   $100 - 90 = 10$ and $80 - 90 = -10$

Step 2: $(f_o - f_e)^2$   $10^2 = 100$   $-10^2 = 100$

Step 3: $\dfrac{(f_o - f_e)^2}{f_e}$   $\dfrac{100}{90} = 1.11$ and $\dfrac{100}{90} = 1.11$

Step 4: $\Sigma \left[ \dfrac{(f_o - f_e)^2}{f_e} \right]$   $1.11 + 1.11 = 2.22$

$\chi^2 = 2.22$

To ascertain some meaning of the value calculated ($\chi^2 = 2.22$) we must compare that result against a *known* set of outcomes, that is, a table of chi-square values. In Appendix C we have provided an abridged table of chi-square values for different levels of probability and typical levels of *degrees of freedom*.[4] The probability level that is used is the option of the individual. This is directly associated with the "levels of confidence" which was discussed in Chapter 6. The .05 level means that fewer than 5 times in 100 could the value of chi-square have occurred by chance alone. So too with .01, that is, fewer than 1 time in 100 could the result occur by chance. If the administrator is satisfied with "reasonable certainty," then the .05 level is appropriate. If he needs to be very sure of the outcome then he may select the .01 level of probability.

Thus in our example, if the .05 level is selected, and if the value of $\chi^2$ is *greater than* the recorded value (for the appropriate number of degrees of freedom), then he may conclude that fewer than 5 times out of 100 would a value as large as found have occurred by chance alone. If he is willing to accept such a chance occurrence as much as 10 times out of a 100 cases, then he could use the .10 level of probability. We will return to this type of decision in a later section of this chapter when we discuss the meaning of significance.

In the example given above the value of chi-square was 2.11 with 1 degree of freedom (d.f.). The chi-square table in Appendix C, for 1 degree of freedom, at the .05 level of probability, indicates that the value 3.841 would have to be *surpassed* to have a significant chi-square. Since 2.11 at the .05 level is less than 3.841, we can say that there is no significant difference in the community between those in favor of initiation of a sex education program and those opposed. Thus the superintendent or curriculum director should not assume that

---

[4]The conceptual meaning of *degrees of freedom* is beyond the intent of this book. It is a necessary calculation for interpreting the value of a computed chi-square and is easily determined. The rule is: degrees of freedom = (the number of columns − 1) times (the number of rows − 1). Thus, for our example above (from Table 10.1): 2 − 1) × (2 − 1) = 1 degree of freedom.

the community will support such a program. The decision-maker may need to generate further support if it seems educationally sound to institute such a program.

The example depicts the simplest use of chi-square and demonstrates its ease in calculation as well as its usefulness for interpreting differences within a community. In the next sections we will look at chi-square and a priori expectations; significant differences with more than two groups; chi-square as a test for determining questionnaire item discrimination; and finally its use for determining representativeness of sample responses ("goodness of fit"). The sequence of discussion is designed to build an understanding of this test with its versatility and capabilities.[5]

## CHI-SQUARE AND A PRIORI EXPECTATIONS

In the example given above the expected frequency was based on an assumption that the community preferences would be *indifferent* or *equally distributed*. If there is previous information that would indicate that the community preferences are *not* equally distributed, but in fact have followed a consistent pattern, then *that* pattern should be used as the expected frequency. For example, suppose that in previous years the voters of a small district have repeatedly passed bond referenda with about 55 percent favoring and 45 percent against such proposals. This year the vote was very close. Out of 1,000 casting votes, 510 favored the issue and 490 opposed it. Did this year's voting pattern differ significantly from that of previous years? Referring back to Chapter 2, is this a significant deviation from a previously established pattern?

The a priori expectation for this example is 55 percent of those casting votes (of 1,000) and 45 percent (of 1,000). The necessary information for calculating chi-square is depicted in Table 10.2.

Table 10.2

**Observed and Expected Frequencies for Sample Favoring and Opposing a Bond Referendum**

|  | Favoring Referendum | Opposing Referendum | Total |
|---|---|---|---|
| Frequency Observed | 510 | 490 | 1,000[a] |
| Frequency Expected | 550 | 450 | 1,000[a] |

[a]The observed and expected frequency *totals* must always be equal.

[5]While a number of sources for chi-square have been mentioned, we will follow the notation and general chi-square development of Koenker's (1971) *Simplified Statistics*.

The calculation for chi-square would be exactly as for the earlier example:

$$(f_o - f_e) = 510 - 550 = -40^* \text{ and } 490 - 450 = 40$$

$$(f_o - f_e)^2 = -40^2 = 1600 \text{ and } 40^2 = 1600$$

$$\frac{(f_o - f_e)^2}{f_e} = \frac{1600}{550} = 2.909 \text{ and } \frac{1600}{450} = 3.556$$

$$\chi^2 = \Sigma \left[ \frac{(f_o - f_e)^2}{f_e} \right] = 2.909 + 3.556 = 6.465$$

$$\chi^2 = 6.465$$

degrees of freedom (d.f.) = (columns - 1) × (rows - 1) = (2 - 1) × (2 - 1) = 1

*Since the frequency observed minus the frequency expected $(f_o - f_e)$ is squared, the result is *always positive*. Therefore, there is no need to consider signs when using chi-square; it is always positive.

Once again consulting the chi-square table in Appendix C we find that for 1 degree of freedom at the .05 level of probability the value is 3.841. Since the calculated chi-square of 6.465 exceeds that value, we can conclude that the voting pattern for this year *does* differ significantly from the patterns of previous years. Note though that the calculated value *does not exceed* the table value for .01 probability, (6.635), thus the conclusion may be tempered somewhat. The information is an early warning that the support pattern of his community *may* be shifting and actions *may* be necessary to identify the reasons for the shift. The superintendent must integrate this information with such *political* knowledge as he can muster to decide whether this is the appropriate time for change.

It should be pointed out that the chi-square test using a priori expectations is not restricted to two columns. It is, though, usually employed only with two rows. The previous example might have had three categories or headings for the columns, namely "Those Favoring the Referendum," "Those Opposed," and "Those Voting but Abstaining on That Item." If past balloting had indicated some ratio of those categories (say 50 percent Favoring to 40 percent Opposing to 10 percent Abstaining) then these would determine the expected frequencies. If the voting this year was 490 Favoring, 400 Opposing, and 110 Abstaining, the table to summarize that data and aid in calculation would look like Table 10.3.

**Table 10.3**

Observed and Expected Frequencies for Sample Favoring, Opposing, and Abstaining on Bond Referendum

|  | Favoring Referendum | Opposing Referendum | Abstaining | Total |
|---|---|---|---|---|
| Frequency Observed | 490 | 400 | 110 | 1,000 |
| Frequency Expected | 500 | 400 | 100 | 1,000 |

The calculation of chi-square would parallel the previous calculations except that there would be a different number of degrees of freedom $(3-1) \times (2-1) = 2$ d.f. The calculations would look like this:

$(f_o - f_e) = 490 - 500 = 10 \qquad 400 - 400 = 0 \qquad 110 - 100 = 10$

$(f_o - f_e)^2 = \qquad 10^2 = 100 \qquad 0^2 = 0 \qquad 10^2 = 100$

$\dfrac{(f_o - f_e)^2}{f_e} = \dfrac{100}{500} = .200 \qquad \dfrac{0}{400} = 0 \qquad \dfrac{100}{100} = 1.000$

$$\chi^2 = \Sigma \left[ \dfrac{(f_o - f_e)^2}{f_e} \right] = .200 + 0 + 1.000 = 1.200$$

$$\chi^2 = 1.200 \qquad \text{d.f.} = 2$$

Comparing this value with the table in Appendix C we find that there is *no* significant difference between the observed and expected frequencies. Thus this year's balloting was similar to that observed for previous years. The slight deviations noted were not serious enough to warrant further investigation. We will move on now to some of the other uses of chi-square.

## *CHI-SQUARE AND SIGNIFICANCE AMONG GROUPS*

**Two Groups — Two Categories.** Chi-square is frequently employed when there is a need to determine if two or more groups differ significantly with respect to selected measures. To illustrate, suppose that two districts in the community were sampled proportionate to their population, and asked about their *feelings* concerning a proposed junior high school. After tabulating the

172    The Process of Analysis

results the responses seemed to fall into two categories; those positive toward the proposed structure and those neutral or negative about it. (See Table 8.2 in Chapter 8 for a related summary chart.) In District A there were 76 persons who made positive statements and 44 who made negative or, at best, neutral statements. In District B only 36 persons made positive comments while 28 made negative or at least not positive comments. Is there a significant difference between the two districts in the way they view the proposed school? These figures are charted in Table 10.4. It appears from that table that the districts may differ, for there are 32 more persons (76 - 44 = 32) who view the proposed school favorably in District A while only 4 persons (32 - 28 = 4) in District B separate the two categories. But what does a chi-square test of these figures indicate?

Table 10.4

Observed Frequencies of Persons from Two Districts Making Positive and Negative-Neutral Remarks

|  | Positive Remarks | Negative or Neutral Remarks | Totals |
|---|---|---|---|
| District A | 76 | 44 | 120 |
| District B | 32 | 28 | 60 |
| Total | 108 | 72 | 180 |

The first thing that we notice is that there are no *expected* frequencies provided, nor does there seem to be some a priori set of *expected* frequencies that could be utilized. What needs to be done as a first step is to calculate the *expected* frequencies. That may sound somewhat paradoxical but it is actually quite logical. Given the information that we have it is quite easy to compute these frequencies. Looking at the "Positive" column we find that 108 persons from the two districts made such responses. Altogether there were 180 persons (Total column) who made some kind of comments from the two districts. What percentage, then, made "Positive" comments? 108/180 = 60%. It follows also that the remainder of the comments were made by 40% of the persons interviewed (100% - 60% = 40%). To double check that we see that 72 of the 180 persons made negative or neutral remarks, thus 72/108 = 40%. Now if the two districts do not differ, then we would *expect* that 60% of the positive remarks would be found in *each* of the two districts and likewise 40% of the neutral or negative persons would be found in *each* of the two districts. We would expect, then, that 60% of the 120 persons sampled from District A to have made positive comments (60% $\times$ 120 = 72) so that the *expected frequency* for that cell would be 72. For District B the expected frequency would be 60% $\times$ 60 which is 36. The expected frequencies for the *neutral-negative* cells are computed by multiplying 40% times each of the respective totals for the districts (40% × 120 = 48 and 40% × 60 = 24). These calculations allow us to complete our summary table (Table 10.5) so that chi-square can now be computed.

**Table 10.5**

**Observed and Expected Frequencies of Persons from Two Districts Making Positive and Negative-Neutral Remarks**

|  | Positive Remarks | | Negative or Neutral Remarks | | Totals |
|---|---|---|---|---|---|
|  | observed $f_o$ | expected $f_e$ | observed $f_o$ | expected $f_e$ |  |
| District A | 76 | 72 | 44 | 48 | 120 |
| District B | 32 | 36 | 28 | 24 | 60 |
| Totals | 108 (60 percent) | | 72 (40 percent) | | 180 |

The calculations follow the previous chi-square examples but in this case four cells must be included.

$$(f_o - f_e) = 76 - 72 = 4, 44 - 48 = 4, 32 - 36 = 4 \text{ and } 28 - 24 = 4$$

$$(f_o - f_e)^2 = 4^2 = 16, 4^2 = 16, 4^2 = 16 \text{ and } 4^2 = 16$$

$$\frac{(f_o - f_e)^2}{f_e} = \frac{16}{72} = .222, \frac{16}{48} = .333, \frac{16}{36} = .444, \text{ and } \frac{16}{24} = .667$$

$$\chi^2 = \Sigma \left[ \frac{(f_o - f_e)^2}{f_e} \right] = .222 + .333 + .444 + .667 = 1.666$$

$$\text{degrees of freedom} = (\text{columns} - 1) \times (\text{rows} - 1)$$

$$= (2 - 1) \times (2 - 1) = 1$$

$$\chi^2 = 1.666 \qquad \text{d.f.} = 1$$

As before, the computed chi-square value is compared with the table values in Appendix C. For 1 d.f. at the .05 level of probability our value would have to exceed 3.841 for significance at that level. Since the computed chi-square of 1.666 does *not* exceed that value we must conclude that the differences between the two districts are not significant. Thus, though there are differences in the distributions of remarks between the two districts, those differences are not large enough for us to conclude that they are substantially different. However, the summary table (Table 10.5) might be examined further to see what type of trend it may suggest. Note that for District A the frequency of observed "positive remarks" is greater than what was expected and also that this type of increase is found in the District B "Negative-Neutral" cell. If we put a plus (+) in such cells and a minus (-) in the cells where the observed is less than the expected, we would get a table like that in Table 10.6. Here we see a possible trend from the top left cell to the bottom right cell (the two + cells). This might then be an indicator of an emerging trend, not yet significant, but possibly moving in that direction. If past information were available, it might be consulted; if not, perhaps an additional survey would be needed.

Table 10.6

Chi-Square Summary Table Transformed for Trend Indicators

|  | Positive Remarks | Negative-Neutral Remarks |
|---|---|---|
| District A | + | − |
| District B | − | + |

+ means the observed frequencies *were greater than* expected.
− means the observed frequencies *were less than* expected.

**Questionnaire Item Discrimination.** The chi-square test for significance between or among groups can also be employed to determine whether or not specific questions in a scale (questionnaire) discriminate. That is, if a number of questions are used to determine a person's score (perhaps his attitude or knowledge about something), then chi-square can be used to see if the individual questions are contributing or distracting from the total score. Suppose that one part of a questionnaire was developed to test the level of awareness that citizens have of the school board and its function. The level of awareness was measured by totalling the correct answers to ten questions. Thus, if a person scored high on the test (8, 9, or 10) he demonstrated high awareness, while a low score (0, 1, or 2) indicated low or minimal awareness. Before using that scale with any sizable sample of the community a pilot test was run so that each item could be examined in terms of its "goodness" for determining *awareness*. That process of determining "goodness" is generally satisfied by the chi-square test for item discrimination.

To illustrate this process assume that the "awareness scale" was piloted with sixty persons. After scoring their responses the *highs* (the top 25 percent = 15) were compared with the *lows* (the bottom 25 percent = 15) on each item in that scale. The distributions on Item #1 might have been like that shown in Table 10.7.

**Table 10.7**

Distribution of High and Low Scorers on Item 1

|  | Answered Item Correctly | Answered Item Incorrectly | Total |
|---|---|---|---|
| Top Quarter (25 percent) | 12 | 3 | 15 |
| Bottom Quarter (25 percent) | 5 | 10 | 15 |

A visual inspection of the table will usually indicate whether or not it is necessary to run the chi-square test. If the numbers in the *upper left* and *lower right* cells are *not* greater than the numbers in the other cells, then the item does not discriminate. There is no need to compute chi-square. Tables 10.8 and 10.9 are examples of cases where it is unnecessary to compute chi-square because the items do *not* discriminate. These items must be changed, replaced, or deleted. The logic is that the item is a poor one if it is so ambiguous or misleading that "aware people" tend to answer it incorrectly or those unaware somehow or other find the correct answer. A *perfectly* discriminating item would have *all* of the high scorers give correct answers and *all* of the low scorers answer incorrectly.

**Table 10.8**

Example 1 of Distribution of High and Low Scorers on Item X

|  | Answered Item Correctly | Answered Item Incorrectly | Total |
|---|---|---|---|
| Top Quarter (25 percent) | 4<br>A | 16<br>B | 20 |
| Bottom Quarter (25 percent) | 12<br>C | 8<br>D | 20 |

Note: Since Cell A is less than Cell B, and Cell D is less than Cell C, Item X does *not* discriminate.

**Table 10.9**

Example 2 of Distribution of High and Low Scorers on Item Y

|  | Answered Item Correctly | Answered Item Incorrectly | Total |
|---|---|---|---|
| Top Quarter (25 percent) | 9<br>A | 9<br>B | 18 |
| Bottom Quarter (25 percent) | 9<br>C | 9<br>D | 18 |

Note: Since Cell A is not greater than Cell B, and Cell D is not greater than Cell C, Item Y does *not* discriminate.

While there are at least two ways of computing chi-square in this type of example (cf. Koenker, 1971, on Phi Coefficient), we recommend the process most consistent with that used for the previous examples.

The stages of this process are:

1. Visually inspect to see if the item *can* discriminate. If it *can not,* alter the item or delete it. If it *can* be discriminating, then proceed as follows.
2. Set up a summary table (cf. Table 10.10).
3. Compute *expected* frequencies for each cell.
4. Compute chi-square as

$$\Sigma \left[ \frac{(f_o - f_e)^2}{f_e} \right]$$

**Table 10.10**

**Summary Table Showing Observed and Expected Distributions of High and Low Scorers on Item 1**

|  | Answered Item Correctly | | Answered Item Incorrectly | | Total |
|---|---|---|---|---|---|
|  | $f_o$ | $f_e$ | $f_o$ | $f_e$ |  |
| Top Quarter (25 percent) | 12 | 7.5[b] | 3 | 6.5 | 15 |
| Bottom Quarter (25 percent) | 5 | 7.5 | 10 | 6.5 | 15 |
| Total | 17 (56.7 percent)[a] | | 13 (43.3 percent) | | 30 |

[a]*Reminder 1:* 17/30 = 56.7 percent
[b]*Reminder 2:* 56.7 percent of 15 = 7.5
$\chi^2 = 4.513$    d.f. = 1

If chi-square had been computed exactly as in previous examples the result would be slightly different from the one reported in Table 10.10. This example requires a special correction that is used whenever any cell has less than 20 cases (but only when the degrees of freedom equals 1). To compensate for the instability of chi-square in such cases Yates developed a correction factor called the Yates' Correction (Koenker, 1971). The correction consists of reducing *each* $(f_o - f_e)$ by .5 (five-tenths). Employing Yates' Correction the computation of chi-square for the preceding example (Table 10.10) would be:

$(f_o - f_e) = 12 - 7.5 = 4.5, 3 - 6.5 = 3.5, 5 - 7.5 = 2.5$ and $10 - 6.5 = 3.5$

Yate's Correction:

$(-.5) = 4.5 - .5 = 4.0, 3.5 - .5 = 3.0, 2.5 - .5 = 2.0$ and $3.5 - .5 = 3.0$

$$(f_o - f_e)^2 = 4.0^2 = 16, 3.0^2 = 9, 2.0^2 = 4, 3.0^2 = 9$$

$$\frac{(f_o - f_e)^2}{f_e} = \frac{16}{7.5} = 2.133, \frac{9}{6.5} = 1.385, \frac{4}{7.5} = .533 \text{ and } \frac{3}{6.5} = .462$$

$$\chi^2 = \Sigma \left[ \frac{(f_o - f_e)^2}{f_e} \right] = 2.133 + 1.385 + .533 + .462 = 4.513$$

$$\chi^2 = 4.513 \quad \text{d.f.} = (2 - 1) \times (2 - 1) = 1$$

The conclusion from this calculation of the pretest returns (from the "Table of Chi-Square" in Appendix C) is that Item #1 is one that significantly discriminates between low and high scorers and, as such, should probably be retained in the instrument. While this may seem like a long and tedious process, if the visual inspection is employed as a first step the process is considerably reduced. Frequently it is not necessary to compute all of the item discriminations, the visual inspection may reveal that the item is *obviously* one that distinguishes or discriminates.

**Multiple Groups: Multiple Categories (n × n).** While most of the examples that have been used depict two-by-two comparisons, chi-square is not limited at all by the number of rows or columns that can be employed. The restrictions that *must* be considered, though, are:

1. No cell (either observed or expected frequency) can be empty, that is, zero. If this should occur, the categories must be collapsed or combined to remove the empty cell (see next example).
2. The same person or observation cannot be used in more than one group or category (cf. Games and Klare, 1967; p. 516-17). The chi-square test is employed to see if the groups are independent of one another so that the same person in more than one group would, of necessity, violate that assumption. An example of this error would be trying to compare the political affiliation of voters over a ten-year period with the support or lack of support on school referenda. Whereas the analysis seems to be comparing Democrats, Republicans, and Independents and their support, we may actually have a great number of school supporters who *were* Republicans, *changed* to Democrats, and possibly *later registered*

as Independents. *In each case* they show up as supporters of the schools. It would be very difficult to make any sense out of such a comparison.

An example of where chi-square may be appropriate for understanding a fairly complicated set of results would be the responses according to age of a sample of the community responding to an opinion probe such as: " 'Our schools should institute programmed instruction' (Do you Strongly Agree, Agree, Disagree, or Strongly Disagree?)" The results of the respondent opinions might look like those in Table 10.11. The table indicates that of those between 20 and 30 years of age (row 1), 8 strongly agreed, 12 agreed, 36 disagreed, 26 strongly disagreed, and 12 either had no opinion or left the item blank for some reason. In the second row (those between 31 and 40 years of age) there were *none* who strongly agreed with the item. Since we cannot have empty cells, this table will have to be redrawn with categories *or* groups combined in some alternative logical way. There are two basic options here. The columns headed "Strongly Agree" and "Agree" could be combined to make a group labeled "Agree or Strongly Agree." Or, the two middle age-groups could be combined making the group "31-50."

**Table 10.11**

Distributions by Age in Response to Item X: "Our Schools Should Institute Programmed Instruction"

| Age | Strongly Agree | Agree | Disagree | Strongly Disagree | Blank | Total |
|---|---|---|---|---|---|---|
| 20-30 | 8 | 12 | 36 | 26 | 12 | 94 |
| 31-40 | 0 | 8 | 28 | 25 | 9 | 70 |
| 41-50 | 6 | 6 | 18 | 20 | 10 | 60 |
| over 50 | 22 | 15 | 18 | 14 | 7 | 76 |
| Totals | 36 | 41 | 100 | 85 | 38 | 300 |

Assuming that it is more important to maintain the *strength of agreement* categories distinctly, the middle age-groups have been collapsed to form a new group as depicted in Table 10.12. Note that now all cells have at least five persons included (a necessary minimum for chi-square cells) and the categories or groups seem to be logically formulated.

The expected frequencies are calculated as before. To review this procedure the calculations are shown for the first column (strongly agree). The first step is to calculate what percentage the "Strongly Agree" column total is of the grand total (36/300 = 12 percent). The next step is to use that percentage to compute the expected frequencies for each of the cells under "Strongly Agree." Thus, 12 percent of 94 (the total number of those in the 20 to 30 age group) is

**Interpretation and Statistical Analysis** 179

11.28. That figure becomes the expected frequency for the first cell. Twelve percent of 130 gives the expected frequency for the next group (the 31-50 age group), and 12 percent of 76 provides the last expected frequency for the "strongly agree" category. This same approach is used to compute the other expected frequencies and the chi-square computation is exactly like those from previous examples.

Table 10.12

Observed and Expected Agreements, by Age, with the Statement: "Our Schools Should Institute Programmed Instruction"

| Age Groups | Strongly Agree | | Agree | | Disagree | | Strongly Disagree | | Blank | | Totals |
|---|---|---|---|---|---|---|---|---|---|---|---|
| | $f_o$ | $f_e$ | $f_o$ | $f_e$ | $f_o$ | $f_e$ | $f_o$ | $f_e$ | $f_o$ | $f_e$ | |
| 20-30 | 8 | 11.28 | 12 | 12.88 | 36 | 31.30 | 26 | 26.60 | 12 | 11.84 | 94 |
| 31-50 | 6 | 15.60 | 14 | 17.81 | 46 | 43.29 | 45 | 36.79 | 19 | 16.38 | 130 |
| over 50 | 22 | 9.12 | 15 | 10.41 | 18 | 25.31 | 14 | 21.51 | 7 | 9.68 | 76 |
| Totals | 36 | | 41 | | 100 | | 85 | | 38 | | 300 |
| | (12 percent) | | (13.7 percent) | | (33.3 percent) | | (28.3 percent) | | (12.6 percent) | | |

$36/300 = 12\ PERCENT$    $.12 \times 94 = 11.28$

The computed chi-square value for this example is 36.5682. The degrees of freedom are computed by the rule (rows - 1) times (columns - 1). For this example this is $(3 - 1) \times (5 - 1) = 8$; therefore there are 8 degrees of freedom. Once again the table in Appendix C is entered for d.f. = 8. Under the .05 we see that 15.507 would have to be exceeded for a significant result. Two columns over is 20.090 which would have to be exceeded for a highly significant (.01) result. The computed chi-square value does exceed 20.090, therefore it can be concluded that there is a highly significant difference among the preferences of the groups in our example. But just what or where is that highly significant difference? What does that mean for this example?

Once again a visual inspection is the quickest way to ascertain an answer. By examining the differences between observed and expected frequencies in Table 10.12, we may be able to "see" the significant areas of difference. What this examination reveals is that the younger age-groups (20-30 and 31-50) have *fewer* occurrences than expected in the "Strongly Agree" and "Agree" cells and more than expected in the "Disagree" and "Strongly Disagree" cells. This is exactly the opposite of the "over 50" group where there are *more* "strongly agreeing" and "agreeing" than expected and fewer in the "disagree" categories. This visual inspection indicates differences and a possible trend. As age increases there is an increase in agreement with programmed instruction. It would have been extremely difficult to uncover this possible trend if we had restricted the analysis to simply reporting percentages; it is the comparison of observed frequencies with the expected (that we compute) that facilitates analysis and understanding.

An additional step for ascertaining the association between the two variables is also available by computing a "contingency coefficient" C. The computation of C is very simple:

$$C = \sqrt{\frac{\chi^2}{N + \chi^2}}$$

Thus, for the previous example

$$C = \sqrt{\frac{36.5682}{300 + 36.5682}}$$

which equals .33. Unfortunately C is not directly comparable to the Pearson r[6] but the result still provides some estimate of the association. There is however another statistic that is also simple to compute and does allow for comparison with the more familiar correlation coefficients, namely *Gamma*. *Gamma* requires the data to be ordered or ranked and would be employed if the question was:

> What is the extent and direction of association between *age* and *agreement with this school instituting programmed instruction?*

For this statistic we refer the reader first to Champion (1970; pp. 219-24 and then to Davis (1971).

## CHI-SQUARE AND GOODNESS OF FIT

The last example for chi-square is a test to compare the distribution of a sample against a known distribution for the population. Table 8.1 in Chapter 8 depicted a tally sheet for determining the "goodness" of a sample. That tally sheet is completed in the next table (10.13) and can be used as the basic information for determining if the sample is *representative* of the population. The argument in this type of example is that the sample frequency *should not differ* from the population percentages (which give the expected frequencies).

To compute the expected frequencies the population percentages for each category are multiplied by the total number of the sample. The first category, for example, is "Families with no children" and the population has 38.6 percent such families. The sample size was 350. Therefore, the first expected frequency would be 38.6 percent times 350 which is 135.10. This same procedure is used for each of the remaining categories; multiply the total sample by the population

---

[6] For computation and interpretation of C see Siegel, 1956; pp. 196-202.

## Table 10.13

**Tally Sheet for "Goodness" of Sample**

| Category | Population Percentage | Sample Tally | Sample Frequency | Sample Percent |
|---|---|---|---|---|
| Family No Children | 38.6 | (tally marks) | 130 | 37.1 |
| Family One Child | 32.7 | (tally marks) | 118 | 33.7 |
| Family Two Children | 18.4 | (tally marks) | 66 | 18.9 |
| Family Three Children | 8.2 | (tally marks) | 28 | 8.0 |
| Family Four plus Children | 2.1 | (tally marks) | 8 | 2.3 |
| Totals | | | 350 | 100.0 |

percentage. This information is summarized in Table 10.14 from which the chi-square value is computed.

## Table 10.14

**Observed and Expected Frequencies and Chi-Square Computations for a Test of "Goodness of Fit" of a Sample with a Population**

| Category: No. of Children | Population Percentage | n | $f_e$ (population percent × n) | $f_o$ | $f_o - f_e$ | $(f_o - f_e)^2$ | $\dfrac{(f_o - f_e)^2}{f_e}$ |
|---|---|---|---|---|---|---|---|
| none | 38.6 | 350 | 135.10 | 130 | 5.10 | 26.0100 | .19252 |
| 1 | 32.7 | 350 | 114.45 | 118 | 3.55 | 12.6025 | .11011 |
| 2 | 18.4 | 350 | 64.40 | 66 | 1.60 | 2.5600 | .03975 |
| 3 | 8.2 | 350 | 28.70 | 28 | .70 | .4900 | .01707 |
| 4 | 2.1 | 350 | 7.35 | 8 | .65 | .42250 | .05748 |
| Totals | 100.0 | | 350.00 | 350 | | $\chi^2 =$ | .41694 |

$\chi^2 = .41694$
d.f. $= (r - 1) \times (c - 1) = (5 - 1) \times (2 - 1) = 4$
d.f. $= 4$

The chi-square value of .4169 is now checked for significance in the "Table of Chi-Square" in Appendix C. This time, rather than simply checking under the .05 or .01 levels, the computed figure is compared with all of the values for 4 degrees of freedom. We find that .4169 is just *under* the table value of .429 which is listed for the .98 level of probability. This means that a value of chi-square as large as found in this example could be expected 98 times in 100; that is, there is a slim chance if any that the sample distribution differs from the population distribution *on this characteristic*. The results of this test do not assure that the sample is representative, only that we may have evidence to increase our belief that it is a reasonably representative sample. If this characteristic (number of children in the family) was exceptionally useful for analysis, the chi-square test of "goodness of fit" would have been useful for verifying the representativeness of the sample on that characteristic.

Hopefully, the treatment of chi-square as an analytic tool has been sufficiently elaborate to enable the reader to apply it to problems he may have interest in analyzing. There are many other statistical tests that may also be appropriate and should be employed if they are known or can be utilized with the aid of a resource person. This single tool, though, should be of general benefit since it may be applied under a variety of conditions and for a variety of types of problems.

## how significant is significant?

There is still one important point that must be discussed regardless of the analytic test employed. That is, what is the meaning of *significance?* Throughout this chapter significance has been employed with only partial clarification given to that term. Too often when it is used with statistical tests it takes on a mystical character, a belief that the ultimate has been achieved because two things *differ significantly*. When dealing with samples and statistical tests "significance" usually means *inferred significance*. The results indicate that a difference would be evident in the population. If the two groups being tested differ by even a fraction of a point, and if the statistical test indicates that this is a significant difference, then it may be inferred that such a difference would be evident in the population from which the sample was drawn.

This is directly related to counting two groups that make up the total population and finding that they differ from one another by some amount, perhaps a point or a fraction of a point. If it is the *total* population that has been surveyed then there is a significant difference. No statistical test will provide more information than that — the two groups differ from one another. This might be considered as population significance.

### PRACTICAL-POLITICAL SIGNIFICANCE

The highest level of significance is what we refer to as *practical* or *educational* or *political significance*. By this is meant that the difference found, whether inferred or by population count, is of a large enough magnitude to enable the decision-maker to employ with confidence that difference in his actions. Suppose, for example, the schoolman is trying to determine whether the public relations campaign is having an effect in the community. To do this he is comparing the responses of the community sample against responses from previous surveys. If he finds that there is an increased difference of one percentage point, and this is a significant statistical difference, he must still question whether or not that one point is sufficiently large for some actions to occur. Is a one-point spread of practical or educational significance? Should he act on that information?

The answer to this question brings us to a full cycle, for it is partially addressed in Chapter 2. If a deviation surpasses the tolerance limits that had been established, then by definition it is a deviation that is sufficient to warrant action. It is a political-practical significant deviation. Above and beyond that, though, there are questions of significance related to the *factors associated with such deviations.* It is here that the answer becomes more difficult. How does the schoolman answer questions of significance for this type of finding? By employing a systematic mode of decision-making.[7] By collecting information, analyzing that information, testing it against informed colleagues, then making a selection from the alternatives generated. Surveys, statistics, or other analytic tools are only that, aids or tools. The decisions must still be made by the humans responsible for the process together with those affected by its implementation.

## summary

The final phase of analysis, that involving interpreting for meaning, was the focus of this chapter. Interpretation involves procedures for working with data to produce a clear image of the object being studied. At a second level, interpretation is concerned with abstracting meaning from the picture, ascertaining relationships and differences within the object of study. While there are many approaches for these processes, emphasis was given to descriptive transformations and the single statistical test of chi-square.

The chi-square test was introduced and applied to a variety of problem-types. Its use in simple two-by-two tables was demonstrated, followed by tests of prior assumptions or expectations. Following this was an application with multiple groups and categories with the final application being a test of "goodness of fit" of a sample against a known distribution of a population characteristic. The discussions were deliberately detailed so that the computation and use of chi-square could be maximized for the reader.

We concluded the chapter with a discussion of the multiple meanings of the term "significance." Caution was made that the term not be construed to

[7]For at least one view of a systematic approach to decision-making see Elbing, 1970.

mean more than it does. When used with samples, it means that a difference (or association) could be inferred to exist in the population. When used with populations it means that there is a difference even if that difference is only a fraction of a point. The last use of the term, though, is the most difficult and refers to the sufficiency of difference or association so that decisions might be made.

## references

CHAMPION, DEAN J., *Basic Statistics for Social Research.* San Francisco: Chandler, 1970.
DAVIS, JAMES A., *Elementary Survey Analysis.* Englewood Cliffs, N. J.: Prentice-Hall, 1971.
ELBING, ALVAR O., *Behavioral Decisions in Organizations.* Glenview, Ill.: Scott, Foresman, 1970.
FOX, DAVID J., *The Research Process in Education.* New York: Holt, Rinehart & Winston, 1969.
GAMES, PAUL A. and GEORGE R. KLARE, *Elementary Statistics.* New York: McGraw-Hill, 1967.
GLASS, GENE V., and JULIAN C. STANLEY, *Statistical Methods in Education and Psychology.* Englewood Cliffs, N. J.: Prentice-Hall, 1970.
KAPLAN, ABRAHAM, *The Conduct of Inquiry.* San Francisco: Chandler, 1964.
KOENKER, ROBERT H., *Simplified Statistics.* Totowa, N.J.: Littlefield, Adams and Co., 1971.
POPHAM, W. JAMES, *Educational Statistics.* New York: Harper & Row, 1967.
SIEGEL, SIDNEY, *Nonparametric Statistics for the Behavioral Sciences,* New York: McGraw-Hill, 1956.

## PUTTING IT ALL TOGETHER

# PART FOUR

As a result of the search to clarify a discrepancy the superintendent and his staff will probably find themselves the possessors of an impressive quantity of information. The question now becomes, what should be done with this information? A long-range planning task in which the superintendent will probably want to play a role will be to think ahead to future information needs and develop a means of storing the results obtained. In addition, there is a constant flow of information from other sources which comes across administrators' desks. This information, as well as that which has been developed in the monitoring effort, may prove useful at another time. Chapter 11 presents ways of establishing a *data bank* for information storage and retrieval. The superintendent is encouraged to have his staff establish a data bank *now* so that information (both that which has been developed by the school system and that which is obtained from other sources) can be readily available when the need arises. The step-by-step procedure for development, maintenance, and use of the data bank described in this chapter should be sufficient for administrators to initiate one in their own school districts.

A task in which the superintendent will probably have an immediate interest is the sharing of the results of the search with others: fellow administrators and teachers, school board members, the general community, and possibly educators beyond the confines of the school district. The overriding purpose of the entire project has been to gather information which can help others, particularly policy-makers, to better understand a problem and, hopefully, to provide direction for problem resolution. Therefore the information obtained must be summarized and put into written form. Bringing the results obtained into the policy-making arena is the focus of Chapter 12. Format and composition suggestions explored in this chapter should help the schoolman to write reports which are clear, complete, and interesting. The chapter also serves one additional purpose; that of providing a general summary statement concerning the process of understanding communities.

# Data Storage and Retrieval

*eleven*

The suspected presence of a problem, the observation that something has deviated or changed, raises questions and motivates investigation. This is the usual beginning of data and information collection. However, wise administrators anticipate their needs for data and information out of previous experience, out of knowledge about education and the community. These needs are then projected into possible and alternative futures. For this purpose information sources have to be identified and utilized for what they can supply in advance of problem situations.

The schoolman is literally surrounded by mountains of data and information which may be useful for school-community problem delineation and solution. The school system generates reports of expenditures, attendance, policy decisions, and various operations daily. Every office monitors several school activities and makes records either for its own use or for other users: e.g., teachers, chief school officer, the state education agency. Data and information are also gathered through special studies and surveys of the community. The local governments of the school community, town, city, and county, are also generators of information, compiling numerous records and reports for internal use, other agencies, and public consumption. Private organizations develop information on which to base expansion, services, and publicity. Beyond the community, state and federal governments, major corporations, and specialized service organizations pour out avalanches of information which are of potential use to the school administrator in decision-making.

188     Putting It All Together

The task of the administrator is to identify and gain access to these sources so that information is readily available to him, in its most usable form when needed. The chapter focuses on this task by outlining the steps in establishing and operating a data bank for school-community study. This is followed by the identification of numerous sources of data and information and ways of tapping them.

### anticipating needs

In anticipating information needs, thought must be given to the concepts, ideas, and issues which apply to the area of community understanding. A workable approach to the task is for the administrative staff to ask the questions they would ask if a particular problem were facing them right now. (See Chapter 2.) What data and information would be needed if the district embarked on a facilities planning program? If citizens asked about crime or narcotics usage among high school youngsters, what could the administration tell them? What community organizations provide information and educational counseling about human sexuality for their youth members? What has been the in-migration rate for blacks over the past five years? What educational issues have been examined in newspapers with general circulation in the district during the past 12 months?

The data and information which answer these questions can usually be found and made available through a school-community data bank. The critical starting point is the posing of the questions.

### a school-community data bank

Establishing a community data bank helps the schoolman to deal with the problem of information management in an intelligent and efficient manner. The purpose of a data bank is to have readily retrievable information and data for problem-solving. It provides for receiving, indexing, storing, and retrieving what is needed, eliminating ineffective random searching as well as loss of materials. In short, a data bank helps the administrator to use what he knows.

A data bank has six functions: receiving, converting, indexing, storing, retrieving, and accounting (see Figure 11.1). As items, e.g., reports, tables, charts, abstracts, etc., are received, they are marked as to the originator, dated, and described for indexing. If conversion of data to a more useful form is necessary it is done before indexing. Knowing that there will be several users, items are described by several standard characteristics and entered under the key words of the index. The items are then stored in one form or several, according to their potential uses.

Data Storage and Retrieval    *189*

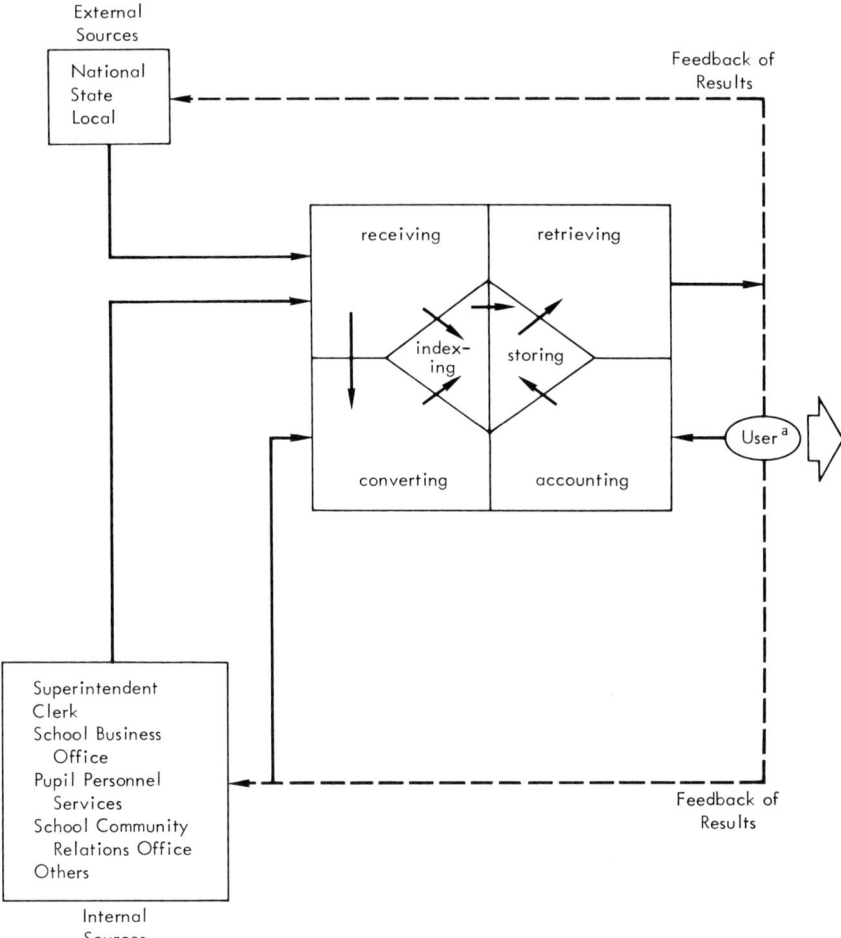

**Figure 11.1**
School-community data bank system.

[a]Probable users would include superintendent, school business official, school-community relations director, principals, staff committees, board committees.

Retrieving is accomplished by describing what is wanted, looking it up in the index, and obtaining the items indicated by the index reference. After use, the item is returned to storage. It should be noted that any results of use, such as summaries and cross tabulations, should be sent to receiving for inclusion in the bank. Accounting means keeping track of items to make sure that what has been taken for use is returned and stored. Each of these functions will be outlined more fully in the sections which follow.

## BASIC CONSIDERATIONS

**Retrieval Levels.** There are several basic considerations in setting up a data bank. The first consideration is retrieval, the efficient location of the data or information wanted. There are three levels of retrieval. In *reference retrieval,* the search will yield a number of items bearing on the topic by titles. The user then uses these references to obtain the items and find answers. In *item retrieval,* the search provides a specific report or other document itself for examination by the user. In *information retrieval,* the search yields the answer to the direct question. The user then examines the answer to see if it satisfies the initiating question. A computer can be programmed to do this as can some manual sorting systems (Holm, 1968, p. 27).

The discussion here focuses on retrieval levels one and two as they are the simplest to set up in a manual system. A data bank, incidentally, does not require electronic data processing or computer capability. However, if the district has machine processing available it should be utilized or the initial design should be such that convertibility can be accomplished in the future.[1]

In districts of between 10,000 and 100,000 population, we believe the data bank conceived here would consist of between 1,000 and 5,000 items with an average of three to five searches per day. As size and complexity of the community increases, the number of items and searches tends to increase. Level of retrieval is, in part, a function of indexing capability and storage capacity. At 1,000 to 2,500 items, direct item retrieval is feasible but if the number is from 2,500 to 5,000 items there should be a reference retrieval system utilizing a manual index. With larger numbers of items or where it is highly desirable to have programmed operations performed on specific data, machine systems are preferred. However, even with machine systems of 50,000 items, 50 percent of the index searches are still typically manual (Holm, p. 268).

**Input-Output Parity.** Another consideration is the parity between input and output. For schoolmen there are regular recurring peak periods of information and data needs: budget presentation, annual meeting, board election. Initially, it would be well to gear up for these peak levels of activity in terms of number of items, rate and frequency of use, i.e.: number of searches per day for a specified period of weeks. Secondly, consideration should be given to the trend data the district might develop for regular use: population figures, tax rates, housing starts. What implications do these have for numbers of items and searches? Finally, there are special uses: data on community organizations, newspapers, industrial planning. Thinking through the types of questions which each of these

---

[1] Regional computer systems, developed through the state education agency, may provide the district with machine capability at the outset. The configurations in Texas and New York, composed of several subsystems, seem to be ideal if participating districts can standardize the types of information to be stored.

raises will soon yield an approximation of data bank size and extent of use, i.e., the input and output.

**Entry Descriptors.** The next considerations are those of entry to the bank for retrieval of data and information. For a community data bank, searches will be conducted for characteristics having to do with populations, organizations, activities, and geography. This means that multiple entry capacity is necessary for adequate searches. To obtain the needed flexibility of entry, items must be described fully. Clues for description come from the kinds of questions which will be posed, that is, the several ways in which the data and information in an item might be requested. For example, district election results might be requested as voting results, referendums, annual meeting, balloting, board elections, or voter turnout. The more descriptors available, the greater the number of questions that can be answered quickly.

However, there is a need to control the descriptors, the vocabulary used for the system. Vocabulary functions as the language link between the originator of the item, the person who stores it, and the several users (Holm, p. 29). For example, the tax roll of the district clerk may be the assessment list of the school business official and the property owners' list to the public relations coordinator. It is essential that cross-references be provided, yet there must be an element of standardization of vocabulary so that items are described with clarity and precision. Careful attention should be given to the vocabulary at the outset in order to avoid indexing problems and confusion.

*INDEXING*

The index is the next consideration: How to group items in the data bank for convenient multiple entry and retrieval. The most usable system for school administrators is an index developed by decision areas which require knowledge about the community, input from the community and output for the community. In other words, the index is made up for retrieving information necessary in developing alternative policies or activities for solving school-community problems and in making choices from among those alternatives. Table 11.1 shows a sample index by decision areas and some of the categories which might be included under each area.

This system of indexing can be further explained by examining one decision area and the categories suggested in that area. For example, annual budget or tax levy voting involves choices for influencing community decision-making. The administrator needs to develop alternative strategies for community participation, designing a campaign, contacting local organizations, and monitoring public opinion. To do so he will need information about previous elections and campaigns, the activities of various local organizations, and voting patterns.

## Table 11.1

**Sample Index Categories for Community Data Bank: By Decision Areas**

### Community Decision-Making

Campaigns
    issues in
    personnel assignments
    publicity

Community study
    methods

Elections for
    board members
    school sites
    tax issues

Influence
    news media
    power structure

Neighborhoods

Organizations
    activities
    name
    publications
    size
    type

Participation
    school sponsored meetings

Population
    change
    characteristics

Public opinion
    editorial opinion
    rumors

Voting patterns
    attendance areas
    neighborhoods

### Community Relations

Alumni

Annual Report

Board policies

Broadcasting
    radio
    television

Community groups, listings
    civic
    home-school
    social
    taxpayers

Newspapers
    editorials
    school issues

School news releases

School publications
    circulation

### Evaluation

Community involvement

Comparisons
    local trends
    neighborhood districts
    national norms

Measurement

Performance goals

Testing program

### Finance

Bond issues
    history

Budget
    codes and classifications
    development
    presentation

State Aid

Taxation
    assessment
    exemptions
    tax base
    tax rates
        county
        school
        town

Tax issue balloting
    voter turnout

Table 11.1 *(continued)*

| Curriculum | |
|---|---|

Academic achievement

Employment needs

Extracurricular

Inputs
   community
      advisory groups
      interest groups
      instructional staff
      professions
      students

Issues in

Level
   elementary
   secondary

Planning

Vocational

Grade levels
   elementary
   secondary

Preparation for higher education

Vocational

Youth

| Students | |
|---|---|

Academic achievement

Community services for
   recreation

Enrollments
   projections
   nonpublic

Participation
   community
   school

Placement

School services for

| Personnel | |
|---|---|

Negotiations

Policies
   state
   local

Staffing
   custodial
   food service
   paraprofessional
   part-time
      class helpers
      consultants
   professional
   secretarial (or civil service)

| Transportation | |
|---|---|

Board policies

Parking

Routes
   streets and roads
   future

Safety

State policies

Statistics

| Goals | |
|---|---|

Adult education

Community expectations

Extracurricular program

| Policy Enunciation | |
|---|---|

Clerk's annual report

Handbooks
   employees
   parents
   students

**Table 11.1** *(continued)*

News releases
School board policy
Superintendent's annual report

### Plant

Community growth
  population
  new housing starts
Community use of facilities
  board policy
  statistics

Condition
Costs
  maintenance
Future needs
Industrial development
Planning
Public housing
Pupil enrollments
Sites
Zoning

This same information will be used in deciding what strategies seem to lead toward achieving the outcome of influencing the community's decision.

The information stored under each decision area is broken down by categories and described, using standard descriptors from the vocabulary developed for the data bank. These are then regrouped by the characteristics which would be sought in making use of that information in the particular decision area. To illustrate, the administrator may want to develop alternatives for influencing community decision-making in working with local organizations. In order to do so, he will need certain information about these organizations such as what kinds of organizations are there? what activities do they engage in? how many members do they have? how many have their own publications? The answers to these questions are characteristics of organizations by which they might be indexed for retrieval. An example of indexing characteristics for organizations is shown in Table 11.2. Other characteristics may be added, depending on the particular ways in which information about organizations might be used (see Sharp, 1965, Chapter 6).

**Table 11.2**

**Sample Indexing Characteristics for Organizations**

| Size | Type | Name |
|---|---|---|
| 10–20 members | alumni | Xville Lions Club |
| 21–50 members | business | VFW Post 792 |
| 51–100 members | civic | West End Taxpayers Assn. |
| 101–150 members | fraternal | Zonta Club |
| | veterans | |

**Table 11.2** *(continued)*

| Activities | Publications |
|---|---|
| birth control advice | bulletins |
| community service | letters to editors |
| tax studies | newsletters |
| youth counseling | slingers |
| voter education | |
| women's rights | |

Once the decision areas, categories, and characteristics have been worked out, the index system is set up for the type of retrieval wanted. For item retrieval, a simple manual index on 3" × 5" cards can be devised and operated for a bank with 1,000–2,500 items. Each card indicates the decision area, the category of information, and the characteristic of the information to be found in the item listed on the card. Sample index cards for item retrieval are shown in Figure 11.2.

Cross-references to other decision areas should be provided on the index cards. This provides for item location in terms of another characteristic yielding different information about the same category. As indicated in Figure 11.2, under community decision-making organizations are listed separately by type and there is descriptive material about each civic organization as one type. The cross-reference to community relations would provide a listing of civic organizations by name, address, and officers' names for the current year.

The item retrieval index has the advantage of giving direct reference to an item containing information on one characteristic. However, additional searches are needed if the user wants information on several characteristics. The index is easily updated by substitution or addition of cards for new data. If an item is removed as obsolete, the cards referring to the item are also removed.

If a reference retrieval system is chosen, the index system is more compact as several items and cross-references are listed on a card for one characteristic. For a data bank of 2,500 to 5,000 items this compression serves to reduce index searching. However, it yields items which have to be examined for the exact data wanted. Figure 11.3 is a sample index card for reference retrieval.

The 8" × 5" card is probably the most useful for a manual reference index system. The characteristics for storing having been chosen, the items containing that information are listed on the cards by description and location. The user searches the index and retrieves the items indicated. Then he must review each item for the particular information wanted on each characteristic.

## Putting It All Together

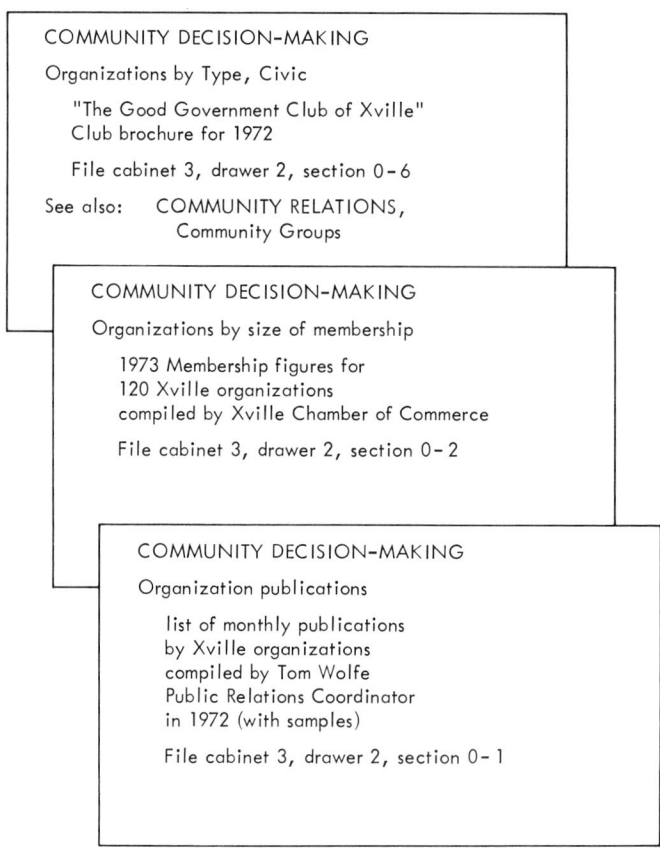

**Figure 11.2**
Sample index cards for item retrieval.

There are several disadvantages to a reference retrieval system. The listing by characteristic such as size of membership of organizations, as in Figure 11.3, tells the user that membership figures are contained in each item. Several of the items are described well enough by title to direct the user. However, one item, a listing of registered nonprofit organizations, will have to be reviewed first to see what it consists of and, second, if it includes organizations about which the user wants membership information. This problem can be lessened by adding further description on the index card or by attaching an abstract to the cover of the item. Listing several items on a card also means added work in updating the index. If a new item is substituted, the entire card must be remade. When new items are added, several cards for two or more characteristics may have to be removed and new cards made up.

While a usable card indexing system can be devised, standard commercial cards with sorting features are available from office stationery firms. The choice

```
COMMUNITY DECISION-MAKING

Organizations by size of membership

    "Businessmens' Organizations in Xville"
    Xville Chamber of Commerce, 1974 (brochure)
    cabinet 3, drawer 1

    "Xville Salutes Its Veterans' Groups"
    Xville Daily Clarion, July 4, 1973
    cabinet 3, drawer 2

    "Non-Profit Organizations Registered With
    the State Division of Taxation, 1972"
    The Division, 1973
    cabinet 8, drawer 2

    Alumni Associations of Xville
    Public and Private Schools (abstract of survey
    by Tom Wolfe, Public Relations Coordinator
    Xville Central Schools, 1971)
    cabinet 3, drawer 2

    See also: COMMUNITY RELATIONS, Alumni
```

**Figure 11.3**
Sample index card for reference retrieval.

will depend on the administrator's needs and availability of funds. Whatever system is adopted should be highly usable, flexible, and easily maintained by district personnel.

*OPERATING CONSIDERATIONS*

**Updating the Bank.** The data bank should be efficient to use and up-to-date. In addition to a highly accurate index, an efficient data bank has a maximum of concise but sufficient data and information. This means that data collapse, collation, abstracts, and summaries of original items are necessary. Charts or trend analysis sheets may be used to display data gleaned from lengthy documents. There is a need for constant review of materials and the establishment of criteria for removing superseded items. For example, the receipt of the latest annual report of the county executive permits the removal of the previous year's report. An abstract of the old report and the retention of certain tables from it might, however, be desirable for comparison purposes. How much summarizing is done and what criteria are established for removal of items depends on several factors, including the nature and frequency of use for certain data; the multiple uses which they have, the subjects on which trend data is desirable, and the staff time available for updating tasks.

**Equipment and Supplies.** The equipment and supplies needs are relatively standard: regular file cabinets for items, small cabinets for microfiche (see p. 202) and index cards, shelves for source materials, a microfiche reader, and photo-copying capability. While a data bank room with reader facilities is desirable, storage cabinets and reference shelves can be set up in an existing office easily accessible to users.

**Administration.** The administrator who is in charge of the data bank must know the intricacies and problems of community analysis. The most logical choice is probably the administrator responsible for school-community relations. Whoever is assigned this task should have the major role in setting up the system, reviewing the sources of data and information, selecting items for inclusion, and overseeing the operation of the bank. It will be his task to determine the needs of the other users, devise the means of abstracting and maintaining trend data, set criteria for updating the bank, The clerical staff assigned to the data bank operation for indexing, storing, and retrieving items should be under his supervision.

**Ethical Considerations.** A word about ethical considerations in data bank operation is necessary. Some materials will undoubtedly be of a confidential nature, e.g., drafts of town planning documents or a local industrial plant's manpower needs. Many items will contain names of individuals, e.g., club rosters, alumni lists, boards of directors of companies. Then there may be the results of local power structure studies or protocols of interviews with citizens on file. Not only must physical security be maintained but use of materials will have to be conducted in ways which do not breach the privileged nature of the information. Policies and procedures should be devised by the administrator in charge of the data bank to meet these considerations. But these measures should not be so cumbersome that they interfere with data bank operation.

The next section of the chapter will help the administrator identify and gain access to the sources of data and information for storage in the data bank. As will be seen, there is a multitude of sources which can be utilized.

sources

The data and information sources which follow indicate where the administrator may start the locating task, largely through the use of reference materials: inventories, checklists, and catalogs. Review of his own questions will help him to further refine, select, and gain access to materials for storage in the data bank. He will also have to take into account the unique sources within his own school and community. Finally, he will want to reexamine some sources already known to him but not yet viewed as aids to understanding the community.

## WITHIN THE SCHOOL

Chief school officers and other administrators have a good knowledge of the information and data generated within the school, at least as it exists in final form. These sources have been reviewed in Chapter 4 under the discussion of documents. This section will suggest solutions to the problems of making school-generated items available through the data bank.

There are three rather universal difficulties with school-generated items. First, the items are usually scattered in several places and there is usually no single listing of where specific information is located. Second, there are only meager indications of exactly what data and information is in any given item. Finally, many reports and other materials prepared for specific purposes may not provide the data and information in forms which serve other purposes.

The solutions to the first two difficulties are in the systematization of data collection and a careful indexing of items in the data bank. This may be started by reviewing files or making an inventory of reports and other materials on hand by title, subject, and location. Once this intial listing has been made, the administrator and his staff can begin to determine what items should be regularly routed into the data bank.

The third difficulty, usability of data and information, has to be contended with almost immediately if maximum use is to be made of generated information. The solution is to capture data and information at the point in its development where it can be applied to several questions. There is no easy short-cut available. The anticipating of data needs, the data bank vocabulary, and index development, done earlier, will provide some clues. However, maximum efficiency will be attained only through experience.

## WITHIN THE COMMUNITY

The school community is rich in sources of data and information that are useful in the examination of school-community problems. These sources were listed and discussed in Chapter 4 (see Figure 4.1). This section will present ways of monitoring local sources for information to be included in the data bank.

Identification of central locations and getting on mailing lists, plus letters of inquiry and personal contact, will develop access points to this information. It is highly desirable to obtain a flow of regularly gathered and updated information. It is also highly desirable to obtain data in the form most usable by the school system. Each consideration can be met without sacrificing the other but the number of sources utilized may be increased. These are time-consuming tasks and there are few short-cuts.

Except for the major U.S. cities and some of the more populous towns, there are few systematic listings of local agency publications or reports issued for reviewing what is available. The interested user must find his own ways of monitoring output from local groups. The search for sources should begin by looking for the central locations, places where the output of local agencies and groups are concentrated. The office of the city manager or mayor or the clerk of the local legislative body may receive the file agency reports. The public relations office for the city or county often maintains voluminous files for its own and public use. County and regional libraries are another central location with the added advantage of an indexing system.

Gaining access to a number of sources may be as simple as discussing the kinds of items wanted with an agency head or writing him a letter of request. Some governments and organizations maintain mailing lists, especially those with public relations offices. Many government agencies will readily supply materials to other governments such as the school district as a courtesy. Others are willing to exchange information and data. A few will require in-person examination and copying of what they have.

Using private organization sources is a matter of estimating time involvement and benefits of such efforts. Many private sources are highly irregular in their output or frequently change their form of reporting. In some instances, output reflects biases in organization objectives. Private sources can close off the flow of information in situations where there are major policy changes impending or where industrial secrecy or confidentiality of records is deemed more important than sharing with the school.

## STATE AND NATIONAL SOURCES

Turning to state and national governments, service organizations, and private suppliers of information, there are different problems of selection, access, and usability. There are literally tons of material, often free, published by state and federal agencies. National associations provide brochures and reports. Commercial service organizations supply selected information on a fee basis and mailing lists abound. For the school administrator to make effective use of these sources, he must develop a careful strategy of selection and intake.

The first consideration is to avoid overloading the system. Items which cannot be brought to bear on school problems, or which cannot be absorbed into the data bank through receiving and indexing, are useless. An effort must be made to balance the amount and types of items received with the potential uses they will have.

The second consideration is economy. Selection strategy must include identification of the most appropriate sources at reasonable cost. While information from governmental sources is relatively low in cost, subscriptions to private service organizations can be expensive. Yet, subscriptions may be economical if they save the cost of converting or summarizing data. In addition, it must be remembered that there are costs attached to reviewing, obtaining, receiving, filing, and indexing which increase with the number of items handled.

Fortunately for the schoolman, there are means of reviewing what is available as an aid to selecting. After the anticipated data needs have been identified, published catalogs, checklists, and services' descriptions provide a place to start finding what is needed. These listings and descriptions should be kept on a reference shelf in the data bank office. By reading through them on a regular basis, items of interest can be noted and ordered for the data bank. It will take a while to become familiar with these guides but some basic descriptions are provided here.

At the state level, over 40 states issue checklists of publications originating in state agencies (see Appendix A for a listing by states). Some lists appear quarterly, others are issued annually. However, the contents are generally the same: a listing of reports, charts, booklets, and bulletins available to the public. Materials are listed either alphabetically by titles or under the agency name. Disappointingly few are indexed by subject. Each entry gives the title of the publication, number of pages, and cost. Some entries include descriptions of the content but most do not. For some items there are two entries: one for the report text, another for accompanying statistical data. Order forms are rarely enclosed but there are usually instructions on how to order materials.

What state publications might be of use to the school administrator in understanding the community? Some illustrative titles follow:

> North Carolina Department of Local Affairs, Division of Community Planning, *Manpower Needs and Resources: Norwood, North Carolina.* July 30, 1971, 11 pp. (processed).
>
> New Hampshire Department of Education, *Valuations, Property Tax Assessments, and School Tax Rates of School Districts, 1967-68.* 1968, 11 pp.
>
> Ohio Department of Mental Hygiene and Correction, *Juvenile Court Statistics.* 1970, 46 pp., map.
>
> Vermont Agricultural Experiment Station Bulletin No. 665. Ellis, Mary J., *Vermont Families: Income and Expenditures.* 1970, 37 pp.
>
> Texas Employment Commission, *A Labor Market Report on Calhoun County, Texas.* August, 1971, 16 pp., map.

In addition to checklists there are special catalogs and indexes available. State libraries' gifts and exchange divisions frequently publish lists of items received from sources both in and out of state. State education agencies, as schoolmen are aware, often make available lists of reports, studies, and publicity materials developed by the agency. This is also true of other state agencies.

Another helpful source is the land grant unversity or public university in the state. The land grant institutions publish technical and popular documents in a variety of fields as part of their public service function. Many state colleges and universities have educational field service units. Each may have listings of information available to administrators.

At the national level the largest gatherer and disseminator of data and information is the federal government. It is also the supplier of the most complete indexes and catalogs of its materials, providing the user with relatively easy means of review. (See Appendix A for a partial listing.)

First, there is the *Monthly Catalog of U.S. Government Publications* available from the Superintendent of Documents, Washington, D.C. 20402. Publications are listed by title and department, with the number of pages and costs noted. There is a subject index. The catalog and periodic supplements can be obtained by subscription, if desired. Order forms are included.

The Library of Congress publishes a *Monthly Checklist of State Documents* which lists all materials received or noted. There is an annual index.

The Bureau of the Census publishes a quarterly catalog of its materials, supplemented monthly. This is an annotated guide containing geographic and subject indexes to the contents of the publications listed. It also includes data files (computer tapes and punchcards), special tabulations, and computer programs available for use with census data. Order forms are included.

Also available directly from the Bureau is a monthly publication, *Small Area Notes,* containing census data, information, services, and programs for use at the state, regional, county, and city levels.

Then there are special indexes and catalogs published by separate agencies. The most familiar to educators is *Research in Education,* an ERIC (Educational Resources Information Center) index. Published monthly, it contains abstracts of recently completed research in education. Nearly all ERIC material is available at low cost in microfiche form, which reduces the storage problem. (Simple desk microfiche readers are now on the market for about $40.00.) The following sample listing of ERIC descriptors indicates its potential use for school-community study.

| | |
|---|---|
| community attitudes | disadvantaged groups |
| community leaders | employment patterns |
| community organization | rural families |
| community survey | school redistricting |

Turning next to national nongovernment sources, associations of businesses, public service organizations, and specialized information services, there are numerous products available. Their outputs range from publicity materials to technical abstracts. Costs range from a few dollars for a single report copy to several hundred dollars for a year's service (see Appendix A for a partial listing of sources).

An association service familiar to educators is the Research Division of the National Education Association. Its several publications provide reports of studies by Division personnel on such topics as teachers' salaries, school finance, racial integration, school law, and basic educational statistics. The *NEA Research Bulletin,* issued four times a year, carries seven to ten reports in each issue, while

*Research Memos* and *Research Summaries,* published several times a year, carry briefer reports on these topics.

There are service agencies which publish materials in bulletin form, focusing on current issues or bringing together the pertinent information on a topic. Such service agencies simply send fliers to potential users on their mailing list announcing the offerings. For example, occasional bibliographies in planning are announced by the Council of Planning Librarians, Monticello, Illinois. The Committee for Economic Development (CED), New York City, sends lists on request and sells single copies of its statements or reports.

There is also a growing field of abstracting services whereby a standardized list of publications in a specialized field is reviewed and pertinent articles abstracted or the tables of contents are duplicated. The best known to school administrators is *Educational Administration Abstracts* presenting abstracts of articles from journals as selected by competent reviewers. *Current Contents* is an example of the second type. The weekly issues reproduce, in their original format and frequently in advance of publication, the tables of contents of more than 1,106 journals reporting research and practice in behavioral, social, and management sciences, and in educational theory and content.

In addition, there are educational services organizations which provide packages of information about such topics as administration, curriculum, and school board policy-making, as summarized opinion from the national scene. Crofts Educational Services of New London, Connecticut, is a well-known example. Most organizations permit users to subscribe to all or part of the service by topic or area of interest with fees scaled accordingly.

## summary

The chapter focused on the development of a school-community data bank and the strategies for tapping sources of information to be stored in it. The anticipation of information needs for problem-solving was noted as the key to data bank development. The basic considerations in establishing an efficient data bank were choosing an appropriate level of retrieval, providing for multiple entry, and devising a flexible indexing system. The size of the school district and the anticipated amount of usage were pointed out as factors in meeting these considerations.

Selecting and accessing sources of information which might be needed in the data bank was seen as a process of inquiry and review. Within the school and the local community, the basic strategy was to find out what information is available and to arrange for its acquisition. At the state and national levels, the review of checklists and catalogs, published by agencies and organizations, was suggested. Brief descriptions of these materials were provided.

references

HOLM, BART E., *How to Manage Your Information*. New York: Van Nostrand Reinhold, 1968.

MARTINO, R. L., *MIS—Management Information Systems*, Wayne, Pa.: Management Development Institute, 1969.

National Archives and Record Services (GSA), *Information Retrieval Systems*. Washington, D.C.: Government Printing Office, 1970.

REES, ALAN, M., "Information Needs and Patterns of Usage," in *Information Retrieval in Action*, Center for Documentation and Communication Research, Western Reserve University, Cleveland: Press of Western Reserve University, 1963.

SHARP, JOHN R., *Some Fundamentals of Information Retrieval*, London: Andre Deutsch, Ltd., 1965.

# Sharing the Findings

*twelve*

In this final chapter four themes will be explored. First, to highlight the place of information feedback in decision-making, the idea of sharing findings will be placed in a policy process perspective. Second, to introduce the idea of information dissemination, groups with whom it might be relevant to share the findings will be considered. Third, to assure that the information developed is clearly presented, several suggestions will be made for organizing the feedback report. Finally, to bring together the concepts presented the book will be concluded with a brief summarization of the process of understanding communities.

## the policy process and information

Educational leaders need to be aware of citizens' expectations if they hope to develop policies which will be supported by their communities. This has always been true, but as school districts move toward more complex definitions of task, and communities become more heterogeneous in composition and, in consequence, more heterogeneous in expectations, the need for such information becomes ever more imperative. Thus, the search for information is predicated on the belief that clear, accurate, and relevant information concerning communities is required for educational leaders to be able to cope with change.

Educational leaders' responses to community demands in the past have often been gross and rather nonspecific. In large measure this has been true because of the assumption that community members would acquiesce to the views of school boards and educators. It has also been true, at least in part, because educators were not acquainted with methods of gathering accurate and complete information concerning the opinions and attitudes of citizens as a basis for action. The situation has changed; citizens are less prone to acquiesce to educators' and school boards' views today. Fortunately, and perhaps as a consequence of this, methods of information-gathering have become more widely available and more clearly understood by educators. It is now possible to ascertain the direction and intensity of citizens' expectations.

Citizens' expectations influence policy-making at all stages of the policy process. Therefore information about these expectations must be made available to policy-makers at the point in the policy process where it can be most helpful. This can be most clearly depicted by summarizing the information-gathering activity which takes place at each of the policy stages:[1]

1. *Formulation.* Ideas or proposals are initiated. Often these ideas or proposals emerge from citizens' judgments of how well the schools are performing. At this stage educational leaders need to know what is being proposed and the problems behind the proposals.
2. *Deliberation.* Points of view emerge relative to proposals. Counter demands are raised and community forces begin to coalesce. At this stage educational leaders must know who is proposing what.
3. *Organization of Support.* Groups form and bring influence to bear in support of or against particular proposals. At this point educational leaders must know what groups are developing and the reasons that they are being formed.
4. *Consideration by Authority.* As selections from among alternative courses of action emerge, community members speak out in support of or against such choices. At this stage educational leaders must know the bases, direction, and intensity of support and opposition to the selected alternatives so that they can assess the proposals against educational criteria and decide which to support.
5. *Promulgation.* With alternatives selected and decisions made public, citizens begin to express positions of support or rejection. At this stage educational leaders must know, on the basis of insights about their community, how best to publicize the choices made.
6. *Effectuation.* Once a policy is implemented it is possible for community members to establish positions on the appropriateness of the alternative chosen. At this stage educational leaders must be able to communicate the effects of the decision to the community and ascertain the perceptions of community members toward the new policy.

[1] For a more complete policy discussion the reader is referred to Chapter 1. See especially Table 1.1.

Establishing policies which are educationally sound and which also reflect the expectations of the community requires that there be information feedback from and to the community at each of the stages of the policy process. The techniques presented herein of clarifying information needs, securing the required information and, finally, analyzing it, should provide a basis for such feedback. With the information gathered and organized, it is necessary to make it available to policy-makers as a rational basis for decision-making.

Sharing the results is a critical task, bringing together the information gathered with action toward problem resolution. Thus there remain two tasks for the schoolman. First, he must be able to identify and reach appropriate groups with whom to share the information. Second, he must be able to organize the information so that it can be clearly communicated to these groups.

### possible audiences

There are several different groups with whom the findings might be shared. Most obviously the information must be made available to those within the system who will have to make necessary decisions in order to resolve problems. These individuals, whether administrators, teachers, or school board members, will be better decision-makers if their decisions are based upon clear and full information. Second, for public relations purposes it may be desirable to disseminate results of the study to the general community or at least to those who participated in the study. Such sharing tells citizens that the school system is aware of its obligation to keep them informed. A side benefit can accrue from this effort in the form of further problem clarification if community members who read the results feed back their perceptions of the problem and its resolution. Finally, it may be appropriate to share the findings with educators outside of the community. There are many problems in school districts which have implications for other educational settings. We encourage administrators to disseminate their findings to educators in the field and to university researchers who are always looking for problem-based empirical findings to help them to understand current and emerging educational issues.

The audience with whom the results are to be shared should be considered before deciding what information to report and how to report it. The several audiences will vary in their familiarity with the problem being explored; in their interest in the information being shared; and in their ability to read and understand summary reports. Administrators and teachers in the school district, being highly concerned about school-related issues, will probably want detailed reports about the problem and the results obtained. Further, because of their academic preparation, most of them are quite capable of digesting complex concepts and detailed evidence.

School boards will probably be as interested in the issues as teachers and administrators, but most often school board members vary greatly in their capacity to digest such reports. Generally it is advisable to write at a level which can be comprehended by the least educated board member. For example, avoid use of complex words and phrases where simple words and phrases can be used. This is good writing style at any time, but especially when it is known that some readers will not otherwise understand the report. In addition, the report should be scrupulously free of the writer's biases unless explicitly so noted, especially when it is to be used by the school board for problem resolution.

The report should be written in the same straightforward manner for the general community. In addition, the administrator must always remember that there are many activities which compete for the attention of citizens. As such, the report should be succinctly written. Possibly an abstract or summary of the report can be written for this purpose. Persons in the community will want to understand the general message without having to read a voluminous report. Finally, as one way of furthering understanding about the community it may be a good idea to invite responses to the report. If feasible, provide a stamped, self-addressed card with the report to facilitate such responses.

The last audience, educators beyond the confines of the school district, can be reached in several ways. The vehicles traditionally employed for such sharing include the reading of papers at practitioner and researcher conferences (e.g., the American Association of School Administrators, the American Educational Research Association, and the many regional research conferences); journals which are read by schoolmen (e.g., *Phi Delta Kappan, Educational Administration Quarterly,* the *Clearinghouse,* and the *NEA Journal* and its state affiliates' periodicals); monographs; and books. Those who judge papers, manuscripts for journals, and proposed monographs and books, demand high standards for the materials they will print. It is a good idea to review similar published findings to learn what these expectations are. Further, seeking the advice and criticisms of others who have had their findings published may save the administrator many problems in such writing.

In this chapter we can do no more than discuss general report format. It is incumbent upon the administrator to modify these general recommendations to meet the needs and preferences of his specific audience. Taking the intended audience into consideration while writing the findings enhances the possibility that the final product will have maximum effect.

organizing the report<br>for information feedback

The primary consideration in feedback is to structure information in a way that provides a basis for clarifying citizens' positions on policy issues. The structuring of information for feedback is a vital aspect of the total process of understanding communities. Therefore, it may be well to pause and highlight the major components of the feedback report.

Reports of information searches are usually organized so that they proceed in a manner which parallels the chronology of the search effort. After the reader is introduced to the contents of the report he is then told what the problem is, the methods used to obtain information about the problem, the results of the search and, finally, the conclusions and implications which have been drawn. Often there are also materials appended which the reader might want to refer to. These sections of the report will be discussed below.

## INTRODUCTION

At the outset the reader has to be convinced that there will be information in the report that is important to him. Thus this section is composed of one or more paragraphs which introduce the reader to the report and let him know what to expect in it. It should be brief, to the point, and interesting.

## PROBLEM SPECIFICATION

The report's purposes should next be clearly described. The reader should be told what led to the gathering of such information; i.e., *why you did what you did*. To attach meaning to information he must have an understanding of the initial problem. Description of the general problem should be followed by some discussion of the major concerns. For example, the general problem may have been voter rejection of the latest school budget. Major concerns about this problem may have included belief that certain groups in the community were particularly opposed to the budget and suspicion that certain items in the budget triggered its defeat. The more fully and clearly the problem and the major concerns are presented to the reader, the more he will understand why you did what you did.

To help the reader further it is recommended that the discussion of the problem be followed by a listing of the questions which were designed in order to isolate the information needed to understand the problem. For example, regarding the hypothetical school budget defeat, the following questions may have guided the collection of information:

1. Is this the first time that a school budget has been defeated?
2. Is there a trend toward less support for school budgets?
3. Are particular neighborhoods especially negative about the last budget request?
4. Did those voting against the budget have particular criticisms of it as it was presented?
5. Was the budget defeat related to a "taxpayers' revolt"?

By listing these questions after stating the problem, the writer provides additional help for the reader as he seeks understanding about the problem explored.

## METHODS OR PROCEDURES USED

Once the reader knows *why* the search was made he should be told *how* it was done. What methods were used to obtain the information which was needed to understand the problem? The reader will probably have more confidence in the information presented if he knows that the schoolman has followed a systematic and well-tested methodological approach. Therefore the procedures employed should be described. If document search was part of the process, the documents studied and the subsequent grouping of the information obtained should be summarized. If trend analysis was included, the trend sources and how they were compiled should be portrayed. If interviews or questionnaires were employed then instrument development, number of respondents and how they were selected as well as the way that information was reduced and analyzed should be described. Besides providing a service for the reader, a report of the procedures used serves a second purpose: It can be of help in future information-gathering efforts. If it is decided to employ the methods used in further problem specifications, it will be possible to turn to the report and be quickly reminded of the process employed.

Whatever limited the schoolman's information search should also be shared with readers in this section. There are almost always some limitations which arise when seeking information. These limitations might take the form of insufficient funds, scarcity of qualified personnel, or inadequate time to fully analyze the information obtained. It is only ethical to share these realities with readers so that they can properly weigh the evidence to be presented in the results section.

## THE RESULTS

The information obtained should be presented in a cogent and succinct manner. Often more information is obtained than can possibly be included in the written report. A balance must be attained between brevity and completeness. The reader must have sufficient information if he is to understand the problem, but he should not be overwhelmed by the findings or he may feel incapable of digesting them. This delicate balance will vary with the audience for whom the report is intended, but there are several general guidelines that can help the writer to achieve it.

To begin, a logical organization of the findings can be achieved by grouping them around the major questions stated at the outset of the report. For example, the questions related to the school budget defeat could become the basis for subdividing the findings of the search. Since the major questions stated at the outset of the project will have been introduced earlier in the report, the reader should be well prepared for such an organizational system.

Second, information which is not directly related to an understanding of the problem should be excluded from the body of the report. Such information can only distract the reader from the problem being explored. It might be appropriate, as noted later, to append some of this information to the report if it is economically feasible and if it is suspected that such information might eventually prove to be relevant.

Finally, whenever possible summaries, rather than lengthy accounts of the findings, should be provided. This can best be done by presenting the findings in visual form with supporting textual statements. Visual forms such as tables, charts, and figures can sharply reduce the amount of space required, thus allowing the text to focus on the major findings rather than presenting a tedious cataloging of all evidence obtained. The visual forms provide the detailed information for the reader to pursue *if he desires*. He can, however, choose to limit his reading to the accompanying text and still understand the problem. Chapters 8, 9, and 10 focus on analysis of information. These should be reviewed for suggestions regarding the reduction of information. Chapter 9 in particular, which focuses on ways of ordering information into visual forms, may be pertinent to the report writer's needs.

## CONCLUSIONS AND IMPLICATIONS

This section serves two functions: summarizing the information gathered and drawing implications for problem resolution. It is a vital section of the report because it is the only place where a synthesis of the information obtained can be presented. Often readers, through lack of time or interest, skip or skim read the earlier sections, concentrating their efforts on the conclusions and implications section.[2]

The first conclusions component, the *summary of the project,* should begin with a brief reiteration of the problem and the methods employed. Next, the information obtained should be summarized. This might well be done according to the initial questions posed. In whatever way this information is organized, it should not merely be a duplication of the findings section. Rather, it should be in the form of general statements and serve the purpose of clarifying the problem explored.

The second conclusions component, the *drawing of implications for problem resolution,* should turn to the question of "What does it all mean?" Here the writer states his interpretations of the findings, recommending alternative

---

[2]Sometimes it may be useful to list the major conclusions at the outset of the report as well as in this section to give the reader advanced notice of what is to come and increase his interest in pursuing the report.

courses of action to the reader. The writer should offer only alternative suggestions which can be fully supported by the information obtained. Further, he should leave room for the reader to develop his own interpretations. That is, the implications noted in the report should act as a stimulus for debate and further insights, not as the final word on the issue.

When drawing implications be wary of exceeding the findings. Where trends are unclear, do not leave the reader with the belief that definite directions can be seen. Overstatements often creep into reports because writers want to be able to present some definite findings. Therefore, take a red pencil to the first draft of the report and mercilessly remove such statements.

Further, some questions about a problem may not be answered in an information-gathering effort. Sometimes the expected sources of information prove to be unavailable to the schoolman. At other times they are available but do not provide sufficient information to answer the initiating questions. If the writer finds that one or more questions cannot be answered, he should say so! We believe that it is as important to describe what was not answered as it is to report what was answered. Ethically, the reader should have this information as he draws his own conclusions about the problem. Further, by maintaining a record of what is still unknown, direction can be provided for further information-gathering.

Finally, as information is collected new insights into the problem should follow. As a result further questions may be formulated. When this happens the new and unanswered questions should be noted. These questions may be helpful to the reader as he considers the report. In addition, they should be helpful to the schoolman if he plans further information-gathering efforts concerning the problem.

## APPENDED MATERIALS

Usually the writer will possess more information than he can or should include in the main body of the report. However, if this information can facilitate problem resolution or make future information-gathering efforts a bit easier, it might justifiably be appended to the report. For example, results which are too lengthy to include in the findings section may have been gathered. Examples include lengthy quotations from survey instruments and the full text of pertinent documents which were reviewed. Another type of information to append might be methodological; e.g., questionnaires, interview schedules, respondent selection systems, and sources of documents reviewed. A third kind of information might be bibliographical citations if the schoolman has reviewed sources in the literature and has used ideas from these sources to develop questions, select methods, or draw conclusions. In short, any information which can help the reader who wants further specification should be considered for inclusion in an appendix.

## some writing concerns

There are many writing concerns which we could dwell on, most of which practicing administrators are fully acquainted with as a result of developing memos, summaries, evaluations, and other reports on an almost daily basis. The special demands of sharing information which result from a major study of the community, however, require that we highlight three particular writing concerns.

First, besides having some facility for writing and being willing to take on the task, the person selected to compile the report should have played a role in problem specification and information search. Only those persons who have been closely involved with the project can possibly be sufficiently knowledgeable about the processes pursued and the information obtained. If he is to condense and interpret material for the report, the writer should be fully versed in the entire information-seeking effort.

Second, the writer should take care to provide linkages to make the report flow smoothly. This applies not only to sentence-to-sentence and paragraph-to-paragraph links, but also to section-to-section links. The writer has been through the entire process and probably visualizes it fairly well. The reader, on the other hand, has not shared in the experience and will need whatever conceptual bridges the writer can provide. Often it will be necessary to be a bit repetitive for these bridging activities to be accomplished. The writer should feel free to be repetitious when this serves a useful purpose. The principles associated with repetition in the classroom have valid application to report writing.

Finally, by planning for all contingencies at the outset of the writing, the administrator will avoid the onerous task of extensive rewrites.[3] By thinking ahead toward writing during the problem specification and information collection stages, it is possible to minimize the need for recall and, further, to reduce the unpleasantnesses of report writing by spacing it over time. Certainly the introduction, problem specification, and methods sections can be written before the information is totally analyzed. In addition, seeking criticism as the writing progresses can help to overcome format and composition shortcomings,[4] as well as the perceptual limitations that any one person will have about the problem and the findings. For these reasons it is a good idea to ask others who write well and have some understanding of the problem to critique the manuscript at its various stages.

[3] Realistically, some rewriting will be required. It is inevitable that some points will be unclear or less than fully presented. It is better at the outset to accept this reality of writing than to attempt short-cuts which usually end up costing much more in terms of the time consumed and the quality of writing which results than they save.

[4] Most writers keep a style handbook at their side while writing the report. As questions arise concerning style, answers can usually be found in the style book. There are many such books available on the market. We recommend Rudolf Franz Flesch, *The Art of Readable Writing,* New York: Harper & Row, 1949, and William Strunk, Jr., and E. G. White, *The Elements of Style,* New York: Macmillan, 2nd ed., 1972.

Report writing is not an easy task. Rather, it is a demanding process which requires a feeling for organization, writing skills, and the ability to accept criticism. Fortunately most schoolmen have had extensive experience with similar tasks such as writing annual reports, summarizing school achievement test score results, and developing written justifications for resource requests. Therefore they should find that, with persistence, it is possible to become proficient at writing up the results of information-gathering efforts.

## a few parting words on understanding communities

Most school administrators, through experience, are aware that the quickening pace of change in society is making it increasingly difficult to predict community opinion. It is becoming more apparent to educational policy-makers that their decisions are not always consonant with the needs and desires of their communities. Consequently, in increasing numbers, administrators are being asked to assemble complete and accurate information about their communities to help policy-makers plan for the education of children in their school districts. To get this information, schoolmen must have a basic acquaintance with the techniques employed in understanding communities.

Because gathering information is such an important administrative function we take this last opportunity to encourage schoolmen to use the techniques for understanding communities described in the book. We feel that administrators should become their school districts' best information-gathering resources, providing expertise from *within* rather than constantly resorting to the omnipresent research consultant whose reports are often filed rather than acted upon. There is every reason to believe that administrators can learn how to employ these techniques effectively. The myth that gathering information about communities requires an expert knowledge of complex research methods should be laid permanently to rest.

Schoolmen have an initial advantage in learning these techniques in that they are already well acquainted with problem-solving, the basic process which is employed in understanding communities. They already use this process in performing their daily activities. All that is necessary is that problem-solving skills be combined with appropriate methodological and analytical skills.

Let us review the stages of the problem-solving process as described in the book. The initial stage is to specify the problem. General concerns have to be translated into specific problems before they can be explored. We have suggested ways of conceptualizing community concerns and organizing what is known about them that should help schoolmen to clarify and specify their particular community concerns as clearly defined problems. They should also be able to use these ideas to monitor emerging problems and take appropriate action *before* they become major concerns.

The second problem-solving stage is to gather information about these problems. As we have noted, in some instances a search of documents will suffice while in other instances a survey of community opinions may also be required. In either case the methods used to collect such information are not nearly so complex as many schoolmen have been led to believe. We have tried them and taught them to others — they work.

The third problem-solving stage is coding and analysis of information. Schoolmen have been particularly apprehensive of these tasks. Experience has led us to believe that they can easily learn to organize information into useful findings with only a minimum of study. If they can employ the relatively simple analysis procedures noted herein, schoolmen should be able to discover trends, differences, and associations which exist in the information collected. At times statistical treatment may be desirable. If so, statistical tests such as chi-square can be employed. These tests and the other procedures explored in the book should be sufficient to meet the analysis needs of most school-related research problems.

The fourth problem-solving stage calls for writing and disseminating the findings which have been established. Reporting findings should be a manageable task for administrators. They presently are required to write similar kinds of formal reports for other administrators, teachers, school boards, and state education agencies. They should be able to apply this experience to the task of reporting the results obtained in their study of communities. The suggestions contained in this chapter should reinforce and add to their experience, helping schoolmen to produce clear and lucid reports.

What remains in problem-solving is to explore alternative solutions, develop and implement courses of action, and evaluate the effectiveness of these actions. We fully realize that fiscal, human, and political constraints affect such action decisions. However, these constraints make it all the more relevant to possess accurate and complete information about the community. The demands and needs which exist in the community must be known if decisions are to be made which will result in viable educational programs.

By now it should be clear that we view the monitoring of communities as a critical function of the school administrator. The effectiveness of the administrator is directly related to his understanding of the community he serves. The future holds uncertainties which must be clarified if school districts are to fulfill the educational objectives for which they were created. Periodic probes can provide educational decision-makers with an understanding of changing expectations of communities over time. In other words, the information gathered today can also help administrators to understand their communities tomorrow. Building a usable data bank of information about the community and about the state of education in general should give administrators a useful tool for following trends.

Our belief that schoolmen should extend their internal capacity for monitoring their communities cannot be overemphasized. This should not be viewed as just one more task which further complicates administrators' lives, but as a way of making their jobs more manageable. Mastering these techniques will ultimately help schoolmen to reduce the time spent on pursuing remedial courses of action and, we hope, result in a better batting average for correct decisions. The payoffs from understanding communities, in the form of better school-community relations and more effective and acceptable educational programs, should make the effort well worth while.

We would like to leave the reader with a request. We would like to hear from you concerning experiences you have when employing the techniques described to understand your own community. Has a particular technique proven particularly useful? Do you have any specific suggestions which could lead to better use of any techniques? Are there any particularly interesting or humorous anecdotes which you can share with us? In short, we are interested in knowing how the ideas explored here work out in practice in your own school district. Any ideas you might want to share would be most welcome.

# Data and Information Sources

*appendix a*

This appendix contains the addresses of organizations useful as information sources for the school community data bank discussed in Chapter 11. National governmental, association, and commercial sources are listed first. State publication checklist titles and publishing agencies are shown in Table A.1.

## FEDERAL GOVERNMENT

Bureau of the U.S. Census
Suitland, Maryland 20233

Publishes *Bureau of the Census Catalog* quarterly with monthly supplements. Also *Small Area Notes* for use by county, city, and other local agencies. Computer tapes, other publications available are described in the *Catalog*.

ERIC Document Reproduction Service
Leasco Information
4827 Rugby Avenue
Bethesda, Maryland 20014

Publishes monthly ERIC Index and abstract journal *Research in Education*. Documents cited are available from the Reproduction Service in hard copy and microfiche, except as otherwise noted in the abstract.

Library of Congress
Exchange and Gifts Division
Washington, D.C. 20540

Publishes the *Monthly Checklist of State Documents*.

Superintendent of Documents
United States Government Printing Office
Washington, D.C. 20402

Publishes the *Monthly Catalog of U.S. Government Publications*. Nearly all federal government publications are available through the Superintendent of Documents.

## OTHER GOVERNMENT

The New York City
Urban Research Inventory
Office of the Mayor
250 Broadway
New York, New York 10007

Compilation of over 2,000 urban-related research projects in 87 city agencies and 56 colleges and universities in New York City. Abstracts describe project objectives and current status. Listing available in announcement.

220   Appendix A

*ASSOCIATIONS*

Council of Planning Libraries
P.O. Box 229
Monticello, Illinois   61856
Publishes occasional annotated bibliographies on planning in several fields. Listings are available.

National Industrial Conference Board
845 Third Avenue
New York, New York   10002
Publishes *Road Maps of Industry* containing economic and demographic data.

Research Division
National Education Association
1201 Sixteenth Street, N.W.
Washington, D.C.   20036
Publishes *NEA Research Bulletin* four times a year and *Research Memos* and *Research Summaries* several times a year, reporting studies conducted by Division staff.

*COMMERCIAL*

Committee for Economic Development
477 Madison Avenue
New York, New York   10022
Publishes occasional studies of national policy questions in several fields of business and public endeavor. Available on request or by subscription. Listings available.

Crofts Educational Services
100 Garfield Avenue
New London, Connecticut   26320
Several separate services, which can be subscribed to separately, provide summaries of national opinions on educational, administration, curriculum, school board policies, and federal aids.

*Current Contents:* Behavioral, Social, and Educational Sciences
Institute for Scientific Information
325 Chestnut Street
Philadelphia, Pennsylvania   19106
Weekly issues reproduce the tables of contents of more than 1,106 journals reporting research and practice in these fields.

*Educational Administration Abstracts*
Circulation Office
E.A. Publications
3100 Sullivan Avenue — Suite D
Columbus, Ohio   43204

Published three times a year, *Abstracts* reviews articles from nearly 100 journals in education, political science, sociology, public administration, and business which are pertinent to the tasks and processes of administration and social factors influencing education.

Institute for Development of Educational Activities, Inc. (I/D/E/A)
Information and Services Division
P.O. Box 446
Melbourne, Florida 32901

Publishes the annual report of CFK, Ltd. *Annual Gallup Poll on How the Nation Views the Public Schools* and other information about schools. Listings available.

### Table A.1
**State Publications Checklists and Indexes**[a]

| State | Publication | Published By | Issued | Cumulative |
|---|---|---|---|---|
| Alabama | None | | | |
| Alaska | State Publications Received | Alaska Division of State Libraries, Juneau | Annually | |
| Arizona | Checklist of Publications of the State of Arizona | State Department of Library and Archives, Phoenix | Annually | |
| Arkansas | Checklist of Arkansas State Publications | University of Arkansas Library, Fayetteville | Semiannually | |
| California | California State Publications | State Printing Division, Sacramento | Quarterly | Annually |
| Colorado | Checklist, Colorado Publications Received | Division of State Archives and Records, Denver | Quarterly | |
| Connecticut | Checklist of Publications of Connecticut | Connecticut State Library, Hartford | Monthly | |
| Delaware | Accessions List | Public Archives Commission, Dover | Quarterly | |
| Florida | Short Title Checklist of Official Florida Publications | University of Florida Libraries, Gainesville | Bimonthly | |
| Georgia | Checklist of Official Publications of the State of Georgia | Georgia State Library, Atlanta | Quarterly | |
| Hawaii | Hawaii Documents[b] | Hawaii State Library, Honolulu | Bimonthly | |
| Idaho | The Idaho Librarian | Idaho Library Association, Boise | Annually | Annually |
| Illinois | Publications of the State of Illinois | Government Documents Branch, Illinois State Library, Springfield | Semiannually | |
| Indiana | Library Occurrent | State Library, Indianapolis | Quarterly | |
| Iowa | Iowa Documents | Iowa State University Library, Ames | Quarterly | |
| Kansas | Checklist of Official Publications | The Kansas State Library, Topeka | Biennially | |

| State | Publication | Source | Frequency | Notes |
|---|---|---|---|---|
| Kentucky | Checklist of Kentucky State Publications | Archives and Records Service, Frankfort | Annually | |
| Louisiana | State of Louisiana Official Publications | The Department of State, Baton Rouge | Monthly | Semiannual |
| Maine | Checklist of State of Maine Publications | The State Library, Augusta | Quarterly | |
| Maryland | Maryland Manual | Hall of Records Commission, Annapolis | Annually | For previous year |
| Massachusetts | Commonwealth of Massachusetts Publications | State Library, Boston | Monthly | |
| Michigan | Michigan Documents | State Library of Michigan, Lansing | Bimonthly | Annually |
| Minnesota | Minnesota State Publications | Document Department, St. Paul | 9 months/year | |
| Mississippi | None | | | |
| Missouri | Monthly List, Missouri State Government Documents | Missouri State Library, Jefferson City | Monthly | |
| Montana | Montana State Publications | Montana State Library, Helena | Annually | |
| Nebraska | Annual Checklist | State Library, Lincoln | Annually | |
| Nevada | Official Publications List | State Library, Carson City | Monthly | |
| New Hampshire | New Hampshire State Department Publications | New Hampshire State Library, Concord | Biennially | |
| New Jersey | Checklist of Official New Jersey Publications | New Jersey State Library, Trenton | Bimonthly | |
| New Mexico | Publications of New Mexico State Agencies | State Record Center and Archives, Santa Fe | Monthly | |
| New York | Checklist of Official Publications of the State of New York | State Library, Albany | Monthly | |
| North Carolina | Checklist of Official North Carolina Publications | University of North Carolina, Chapel Hill and North Carolina State Library | Bimonthly | |
| North Dakota | North Dakota State Publications | State Library Commission, Bismark | Semiannually | |
| Ohio | Ohio Documents: A List of Publications of State Departments | State Library of Ohio, Columbus | Quarterly | |
| Oklahoma | None | | | |
| Oregon | Checklist of Official Publications of the State of Oregon | Oregon State Library, Salem | Quarterly | |

Table A.1 (continued)

| State | Publication | Published By | Issued | Cumulative |
|---|---|---|---|---|
| Pennsylvania | Checklist of Official Pennsylvania Publications | State Library, Harrisburg | Monthly | |
| Rhode Island | Checklist of Publications of State Agencies | The Rhode Island State Library, Providence | Annually | |
| South Carolina | Checklist of South Carolina State Publications | South Carolina State Library, Columbia | Annually | Planned for each 5 years |
| South Dakota | None | | | |
| Tennessee | List of Tennessee State Publications | State Library, Nashville | Annually | |
| Texas | Texas State Documents | Archives Division, Texas State Library, Austin | Monthly | |
| Utah | Checklist of Utah State Documents | Utah State Library and Utah State Archives, Salt Lake City | Semiannually | |
| Vermont | Checklist of Available Vermont State Publications | Department of Libraries, Montpelier | Annually | |
| Virginia | Checklist of Virginia State Publications | Virginia State Library, Richmond | Annually | |
| Washington | Washington State Publications | State Library, Olympia | Monthly | Annually |
| West Virginia | Short Title Checklist of West Virginia State Publications | West Virginia Department of Archives and History, Charleston | Quarterly | |
| Wisconsin | Wisconsin Public Documents | State Historical Society of Wisconsin, Madison | Monthly | Annually |
| Wyoming | None | | | |

[a] Compiled by the authors through a survey of the states, 1972.
[b] Publication of "Hawaii Documents" has been suspended since 1970 due to plans to computerize.

# Table of Random Numbers

*appendix b*

Table of Random Numbers

| | | | | | |
|---|---|---|---|---|---|
| 00000 | 10097 32533 | 76520 13586 | 34673 54876 | 80959 09117 | 39292 74945 |
| 00001 | 37542 04805 | 64894 74296 | 24805 24037 | 20636 10402 | 00822 91665 |
| 00002 | 08422 68953 | 19645 09303 | 23209 02560 | 15953 34764 | 35080 33606 |
| 00003 | 99019 02529 | 09376 70715 | 38311 31165 | 88676 74397 | 04436 27659 |
| 00004 | 12807 99970 | 80157 36147 | 64032 36653 | 98951 16877 | 12171 76833 |
| 00005 | 66065 74717 | 34072 76850 | 36697 36170 | 65813 39885 | 11199 29170 |
| 00006 | 31060 10805 | 45571 82406 | 35303 42614 | 86799 07439 | 23403 09732 |
| 00007 | 85269 77602 | 02051 65692 | 68665 74818 | 73053 85247 | 18623 88579 |
| 00008 | 63573 32135 | 05325 47048 | 90553 57548 | 28468 28709 | 83491 25624 |
| 00009 | 73796 45753 | 03529 64778 | 35808 34282 | 60935 20344 | 35273 88435 |
| 00010 | 98520 17767 | 14905 68607 | 22109 40558 | 60970 93433 | 50500 73998 |
| 00011 | 11805 05431 | 39808 27732 | 50725 68248 | 29405 24201 | 52775 67851 |
| 00012 | 83452 99634 | 06288 98083 | 13746 70078 | 18475 40610 | 68711 77817 |
| 00013 | 88685 40200 | 86507 58401 | 36766 67951 | 90364 76493 | 29609 11062 |
| 00014 | 99594 67348 | 87517 64969 | 91826 08928 | 93785 61368 | 23478 34113 |
| 00015 | 65481 17674 | 17468 50950 | 58047 76974 | 73039 57186 | 40218 16544 |
| 00016 | 80124 35635 | 17727 08015 | 45318 22374 | 21115 78253 | 14385 53763 |
| 00017 | 74350 99817 | 77402 77214 | 43236 00210 | 45521 64237 | 96286 02655 |
| 00018 | 69916 26803 | 66252 29148 | 36936 87203 | 76621 13990 | 94400 56418 |
| 00019 | 09893 20505 | 14225 68514 | 46427 56788 | 96297 78822 | 54382 14598 |
| 00020 | 91499 14523 | 68479 27686 | 46162 83554 | 94750 89923 | 37089 20048 |
| 00021 | 80336 94598 | 26940 36858 | 70297 34135 | 53140 33340 | 42050 82341 |
| 00022 | 44104 81949 | 85157 47954 | 32979 26575 | 57600 40881 | 22222 06413 |
| 00023 | 12550 73742 | 11100 02040 | 12860 74697 | 96644 89439 | 28707 25815 |
| 00024 | 63606 49329 | 16505 34484 | 40219 52563 | 43651 77082 | 07207 31790 |
| 00025 | 61196 90446 | 26457 47774 | 51924 33729 | 65394 59593 | 42582 60527 |
| 00026 | 15474 45266 | 95270 79953 | 59367 83848 | 82396 10118 | 33211 59466 |
| 00027 | 94557 28573 | 67897 54387 | 54622 44431 | 91190 42592 | 92927 45973 |
| 00028 | 42481 16213 | 97344 08721 | 16868 48767 | 03071 12059 | 25701 46670 |
| 00029 | 23523 78317 | 73208 89837 | 68935 91416 | 26252 29663 | 05522 82562 |
| 00030 | 04493 52494 | 75246 33824 | 45862 51025 | 61962 79335 | 65337 12472 |
| 00031 | 00549 97654 | 64051 88159 | 96119 63896 | 54692 82391 | 23287 29529 |
| 00032 | 35963 15307 | 26898 09354 | 33351 35462 | 77974 50024 | 90103 39333 |
| 00033 | 59808 08391 | 45427 26842 | 83609 49700 | 13021 24892 | 78565 20106 |
| 00034 | 46058 85236 | 01390 92286 | 77281 44077 | 93910 83647 | 70617 42941 |
| 00035 | 32179 00597 | 87379 25241 | 05567 07007 | 86743 17157 | 85394 11838 |
| 00036 | 69234 61406 | 20117 45204 | 15956 60000 | 18743 92423 | 97118 96338 |
| 00037 | 19565 41430 | 01758 75379 | 40419 21585 | 66674 36806 | 84962 85207 |
| 00038 | 45155 14938 | 19476 07246 | 43667 94543 | 59047 90033 | 20826 69541 |
| 00039 | 94864 31994 | 36168 10851 | 34888 81553 | 01540 35456 | 05014 51176 |
| 00040 | 98086 24826 | 45240 28404 | 44999 08896 | 39094 73407 | 35441 31880 |
| 00041 | 33185 16232 | 41941 50949 | 89435 48581 | 88695 41994 | 37548 73043 |
| 00042 | 80951 00406 | 96382 70774 | 20151 23387 | 25016 25298 | 94624 61171 |
| 00043 | 79752 49140 | 71961 28296 | 69861 02591 | 74852 20539 | 00387 59579 |
| 00044 | 18633 32537 | 98145 06571 | 31010 24674 | 05455 61427 | 77938 91936 |
| 00045 | 74029 43902 | 77557 32270 | 97790 17119 | 52527 58021 | 80814 51748 |
| 00046 | 54178 45611 | 80993 37143 | 05335 12969 | 56127 19255 | 36040 90324 |
| 00047 | 11664 49883 | 52079 84827 | 59381 71539 | 09973 33440 | 88461 23356 |
| 00048 | 48324 77928 | 31249 64710 | 02295 36870 | 32307 57546 | 15020 09994 |
| 00049 | 69074 94138 | 87637 91976 | 35584 04401 | 10518 21615 | 01848 76938 |

Reproduced by permission of Rand Corporation, *A Million Random Digits with 100,000 Normal Deviates,* New York: Free Press, 1965.

**Table of Random Numbers** *(continued)*

| | | | | | | | | | | |
|---|---|---|---|---|---|---|---|---|---|---|
| 00050 | 09188 | 20097 | 32825 | 39527 | 04220 | 86304 | 83389 | 87374 | 64278 | 58044 |
| 00051 | 90045 | 85497 | 51981 | 50654 | 94938 | 81997 | 91870 | 76150 | 68476 | 64659 |
| 00052 | 73189 | 50207 | 47677 | 26269 | 62290 | 64464 | 27124 | 67018 | 41361 | 82760 |
| 00053 | 75768 | 76490 | 20971 | 87749 | 90429 | 12272 | 95375 | 05871 | 93823 | 43178 |
| 00054 | 54016 | 44056 | 66281 | 31003 | 00682 | 27398 | 20714 | 53295 | 07706 | 17813 |
| 00055 | 08358 | 69910 | 78542 | 42785 | 13661 | 58873 | 04618 | 97553 | 31223 | 08420 |
| 00056 | 28306 | 03264 | 81333 | 10591 | 40510 | 07893 | 32604 | 60475 | 94119 | 01840 |
| 00057 | 53840 | 86233 | 81594 | 13628 | 51215 | 90290 | 28466 | 68795 | 77762 | 20791 |
| 00058 | 91757 | 53741 | 61613 | 62269 | 50263 | 90212 | 55781 | 76514 | 83483 | 47055 |
| 00059 | 89415 | 92694 | 00397 | 58391 | 12607 | 17646 | 48949 | 72306 | 94541 | 37408 |
| 00060 | 77513 | 03820 | 86864 | 29901 | 68414 | 82774 | 51908 | 13980 | 72893 | 55507 |
| 00061 | 19502 | 37174 | 69979 | 20288 | 55210 | 29773 | 74287 | 75251 | 65344 | 67415 |
| 00062 | 21818 | 59313 | 93278 | 81757 | 05686 | 73156 | 07082 | 85046 | 31853 | 38452 |
| 00063 | 51474 | 66499 | 68107 | 23621 | 94049 | 91345 | 42836 | 09191 | 08007 | 45449 |
| 00064 | 99559 | 68331 | 62535 | 24170 | 69777 | 12830 | 74819 | 78142 | 43860 | 72834 |
| 00065 | 33713 | 48007 | 93584 | 72869 | 51926 | 64721 | 58303 | 29822 | 93174 | 93972 |
| 00066 | 85274 | 86893 | 11303 | 22970 | 28834 | 34137 | 73515 | 90400 | 71148 | 43643 |
| 00067 | 84133 | 89640 | 44035 | 52166 | 73852 | 70091 | 61222 | 60561 | 62327 | 18423 |
| 00068 | 56732 | 16234 | 17395 | 96131 | 10123 | 91622 | 85496 | 57560 | 81604 | 18880 |
| 00069 | 65138 | 56806 | 87648 | 85261 | 34313 | 65861 | 45875 | 21069 | 85644 | 47277 |
| 00070 | 38001 | 02176 | 81719 | 11711 | 71602 | 92937 | 74219 | 64049 | 65584 | 49698 |
| 00071 | 37402 | 96397 | 01304 | 77586 | 56271 | 10086 | 47324 | 62605 | 40030 | 37438 |
| 00072 | 97125 | 40348 | 87083 | 31417 | 21815 | 39250 | 75237 | 62047 | 15501 | 29578 |
| 00073 | 21826 | 41134 | 47143 | 34072 | 64638 | 85902 | 49139 | 06441 | 03856 | 54552 |
| 00074 | 73135 | 42742 | 95719 | 09035 | 85794 | 74296 | 08789 | 88156 | 64691 | 19202 |
| 00075 | 07638 | 77929 | 03061 | 18072 | 96207 | 44156 | 23821 | 99538 | 04713 | 66994 |
| 00076 | 60528 | 83441 | 07954 | 19814 | 59175 | 20695 | 05533 | 52139 | 61212 | 06455 |
| 00077 | 83596 | 35655 | 06958 | 92983 | 05128 | 09719 | 77433 | 53783 | 92301 | 50498 |
| 00078 | 10850 | 62746 | 99599 | 10507 | 13499 | 06319 | 53075 | 71839 | 06410 | 19362 |
| 00079 | 39820 | 98952 | 43622 | 63147 | 64421 | 80814 | 43800 | 09351 | 31024 | 73167 |
| 00080 | 59580 | 06478 | 75569 | 78800 | 88835 | 54486 | 23768 | 06156 | 04111 | 08408 |
| 00081 | 38508 | 07341 | 23793 | 48763 | 90822 | 97022 | 17719 | 04207 | 95954 | 49953 |
| 00082 | 30692 | 70668 | 94688 | 16127 | 56196 | 80091 | 82067 | 63400 | 05462 | 69200 |
| 00083 | 65443 | 95659 | 18288 | 27437 | 49632 | 24041 | 08337 | 65676 | 96299 | 90836 |
| 00084 | 27267 | 50264 | 13192 | 72294 | 07477 | 44606 | 17985 | 48911 | 97341 | 30358 |
| 00085 | 91307 | 06991 | 19072 | 24210 | 36699 | 53728 | 28825 | 35793 | 28976 | 66252 |
| 00086 | 68434 | 94688 | 84473 | 13622 | 62126 | 98408 | 12843 | 82590 | 09815 | 93146 |
| 00087 | 48908 | 15877 | 54745 | 24591 | 35700 | 04754 | 83824 | 52692 | 54130 | 55160 |
| 00088 | 06913 | 45197 | 42672 | 78601 | 11883 | 09528 | 63011 | 98901 | 14974 | 40344 |
| 00089 | 10455 | 16019 | 14210 | 33712 | 91342 | 37821 | 88325 | 80851 | 43667 | 70883 |
| 00090 | 12883 | 97343 | 65027 | 61184 | 04285 | 01392 | 17974 | 15077 | 90712 | 26769 |
| 00091 | 21778 | 30976 | 38807 | 36961 | 31649 | 42096 | 63281 | 02023 | 08816 | 47449 |
| 00092 | 19523 | 59515 | 65122 | 59659 | 86283 | 68258 | 69572 | 13798 | 16435 | 91529 |
| 00093 | 67245 | 52670 | 35583 | 16563 | 79246 | 86686 | 76463 | 34222 | 26655 | 90802 |
| 00094 | 60584 | 47377 | 07500 | 37992 | 45134 | 26529 | 26760 | 83637 | 41326 | 44344 |
| 00095 | 53853 | 41377 | 36066 | 94850 | 58838 | 73859 | 49364 | 73331 | 96240 | 43642 |
| 00096 | 24637 | 38736 | 74384 | 89342 | 52623 | 07992 | 12369 | 18601 | 03742 | 83873 |
| 00097 | 83080 | 12451 | 38992 | 22815 | 07759 | 51777 | 97377 | 27585 | 51972 | 37867 |
| 00098 | 16444 | 24334 | 36151 | 99073 | 27493 | 70939 | 85130 | 32552 | 54846 | 54759 |
| 00099 | 60790 | 18157 | 57178 | 65762 | 11161 | 78576 | 45819 | 52979 | 65130 | 04860 |

Table of Random Numbers *(continued)*

| | | | | | |
|---|---|---|---|---|---|
| 00100 | 03991 10461 | 93716 16894 | 66083 24653 | 84609 58232 | 88618 19161 |
| 00101 | 38555 95554 | 32886 59780 | 08355 60860 | 29735 47762 | 71299 23853 |
| 00102 | 17546 73704 | 92052 46215 | 55121 29281 | 59076 07936 | 27954 58909 |
| 00103 | 32643 52861 | 95819 06831 | 00911 98936 | 76355 93779 | 80863 00514 |
| 00104 | 69572 68777 | 39510 35905 | 14060 40619 | 29549 69616 | 33564 60780 |
| 00105 | 24122 66591 | 27699 06494 | 14845 46672 | 61958 77100 | 90899 75754 |
| 00106 | 61196 30231 | 92962 61773 | 41839 55382 | 17267 70943 | 78038 70267 |
| 00107 | 30532 21704 | 10274 12202 | 39685 23309 | 10061 68829 | 55986 66485 |
| 00108 | 03788 97599 | 75867 20717 | 74416 53166 | 35208 33374 | 87539 08823 |
| 00109 | 48228 63379 | 85783 47619 | 53152 67433 | 35663 52972 | 16818 60311 |
| 00110 | 60365 94653 | 35075 33949 | 42614 29297 | 01918 28316 | 98953 73231 |
| 00111 | 83799 42402 | 56623 34442 | 34994 41374 | 70071 14736 | 09958 18065 |
| 00112 | 32960 07405 | 36409 83232 | 99385 41600 | 11133 07586 | 15917 06253 |
| 00113 | 19322 53845 | 57620 52606 | 66497 68646 | 78138 66559 | 19640 99413 |
| 00114 | 11220 94747 | 07399 37408 | 48509 23929 | 27482 45476 | 85244 35159 |
| 00115 | 31751 57260 | 68980 05339 | 15470 48355 | 88651 22596 | 03152 19121 |
| 00116 | 88492 99382 | 14454 04504 | 20094 98977 | 74843 93413 | 22109 78508 |
| 00117 | 30934 47744 | 07481 83828 | 73788 06533 | 28597 20405 | 94205 20380 |
| 00118 | 22888 48893 | 27499 98748 | 60530 45128 | 74022 84617 | 82037 10268 |
| 00119 | 78212 16993 | 35902 91386 | 44372 15486 | 65741 14014 | 87481 37220 |
| 00120 | 41849 84547 | 46850 52326 | 34677 58300 | 74910 64345 | 19325 81549 |
| 00121 | 46352 33049 | 69248 93460 | 45305 07521 | 61318 31855 | 14413 70951 |
| 00122 | 11087 96294 | 14013 31792 | 59747 67277 | 76503 34513 | 39663 77544 |
| 00123 | 52701 08337 | 56303 87315 | 16520 69676 | 11654 99893 | 02181 68161 |
| 00124 | 57275 36898 | 81304 48585 | 68652 27376 | 92852 55866 | 88448 03584 |
| 00125 | 20857 73156 | 70284 24326 | 79375 95220 | 01159 63267 | 10622 48391 |
| 00126 | 15633 84924 | 90415 93614 | 33521 26665 | 55823 47641 | 86225 31704 |
| 00127 | 92694 48297 | 39904 02115 | 59589 49067 | 66821 41575 | 49767 04037 |
| 00128 | 77613 19019 | 88152 00080 | 20554 91409 | 96277 48257 | 50816 97616 |
| 00129 | 38688 32486 | 45134 63545 | 59404 72059 | 43947 51680 | 43852 59693 |
| 00130 | 25163 01889 | 70014 15021 | 41290 67312 | 71857 15957 | 68971 11403 |
| 00131 | 65251 07629 | 37239 33295 | 05870 01119 | 92784 26340 | 18477 65622 |
| 00132 | 36815 43625 | 18637 37509 | 82444 99005 | 04921 73701 | 14707 93997 |
| 00133 | 64397 11692 | 05327 82162 | 20247 81759 | 45197 25332 | 83745 22567 |
| 00134 | 04515 25624 | 95096 67946 | 48460 85558 | 15191 18782 | 16930 33361 |
| 00135 | 83761 60873 | 43253 84145 | 60833 25983 | 01291 41349 | 20368 07126 |
| 00136 | 14387 06345 | 80854 09279 | 43529 06318 | 38384 ˜74761 | 41196 37480 |
| 00137 | 51321 92246 | 80088 77074 | 88722 56736 | 66164 49431 | 66919 31678 |
| 00138 | 72472 00008 | 80890 18002 | 94813 31900 | 54155 83436 | 35352 54131 |
| 00139 | 05466 55306 | 93128 18464 | 74457 90561 | 72848 11834 | 79982 68416 |
| 00140 | 39528 72484 | 82474 25593 | 48545 35247 | 18619 13674 | 18611 19241 |
| 00141 | 81616 18711 | 53342 44276 | 75122 11724 | 74627 73707 | 58319 15997 |
| 00142 | 07586 16120 | 82641 22820 | 92904 13141 | 32392 19763 | 61199 67940 |
| 00143 | 90767 04235 | 13574 17200 | 69902 63742 | 78464 22501 | 18627 90872 |
| 00144 | 40188 28193 | 29593 88627 | 94972 11598 | 62095 36787 | 00441 58997 |
| 00145 | 34414 82157 | 86887 55087 | 19152 00023 | 12302 80783 | 32624 68691 |
| 00146 | 63439 75363 | 44989 16822 | 36024 00867 | 76378 41605 | 65961 73488 |
| 00147 | 67049 09070 | 93399 45547 | 94458 74284 | 05041 49807 | 20288 34060 |
| 00148 | 79495 04146 | 52162 90286 | 54158 34243 | 46978 35482 | 59362 95938 |
| 00149 | 91704 30552 | 04737 21031 | 75051 93029 | 47665 64382 | 99782 93478 |

**Table of Random Numbers** *(continued)*

| | | | | | | | | | |
|---|---|---|---|---|---|---|---|---|---|
| 00150 | 94015 | 46874 | 32444 | 48277 | 59820 | 96163 | 64654 | 25843 | 41145 | 42820 |
| 00151 | 74108 | 88222 | 88570 | 74015 | 25704 | 91035 | 01755 | 14750 | 48968 | 38603 |
| 00152 | 62880 | 87873 | 95160 | 59221 | 22304 | 90314 | 72877 | 17334 | 39283 | 04149 |
| 00153 | 11748 | 12102 | 80580 | 41867 | 17710 | 59621 | 06554 | 07850 | 73950 | 79552 |
| 00154 | 17944 | 05600 | 60478 | 03343 | 25852 | 58905 | 57216 | 39618 | 49856 | 99326 |
| 00155 | 66067 | 42792 | 95043 | 52680 | 46780 | 56487 | 09971 | 59481 | 37006 | 22186 |
| 00156 | 54244 | 91030 | 45547 | 70818 | 59849 | 96169 | 61459 | 21647 | 87417 | 17198 |
| 00157 | 30945 | 57589 | 31732 | 57260 | 47670 | 07654 | 46376 | 25366 | 94746 | 49580 |
| 00158 | 69170 | 37403 | 86995 | 90307 | 94304 | 71803 | 26825 | 05511 | 12459 | 91314 |
| 00159 | 08345 | 88975 | 35841 | 85771 | 08105 | 59987 | 87112 | 21476 | 14713 | 71181 |
| 00160 | 27767 | 43584 | 85301 | 88977 | 29490 | 69714 | 73035 | 41207 | 74699 | 09310 |
| 00161 | 13025 | 14338 | 54066 | 15243 | 47724 | 66733 | 47431 | 43905 | 31048 | 56699 |
| 00162 | 80217 | 36292 | 98525 | 24335 | 24432 | 24896 | 43277 | 58874 | 11466 | 16082 |
| 00163 | 10875 | 62004 | 90391 | 61105 | 57411 | 06368 | 53856 | 30743 | 08670 | 84741 |
| 00164 | 54127 | 57326 | 26629 | 19087 | 24472 | 88779 | 30540 | 27886 | 61732 | 75454 |
| 00165 | 60311 | 42824 | 37301 | 42678 | 45990 | 43242 | 17374 | 52003 | 70707 | 70214 |
| 00166 | 49739 | 71484 | 92003 | 98086 | 76668 | 73209 | 59202 | 11973 | 02902 | 33250 |
| 00167 | 78626 | 51594 | 16453 | 94614 | 39014 | 97066 | 83012 | 09832 | 25571 | 77628 |
| 00168 | 66692 | 13986 | 99837 | 00582 | 81232 | 44987 | 09504 | 96412 | 90193 | 79568 |
| 00169 | 44071 | 28091 | 07362 | 97703 | 76447 | 42537 | 98524 | 97831 | 65704 | 09514 |
| 00170 | 41468 | 85149 | 49554 | 17994 | 14924 | 39650 | 95294 | 00556 | 70481 | 06905 |
| 00171 | 94559 | 37559 | 49678 | 53119 | 70312 | 05682 | 66986 | 34099 | 74474 | 20740 |
| 00172 | 41615 | 70360 | 64114 | 58660 | 90850 | 64618 | 80620 | 51790 | 11436 | 38072 |
| 00173 | 50273 | 93113 | 41794 | 86861 | 24781 | 89683 | 55411 | 85667 | 77535 | 99892 |
| 00174 | 41396 | 80504 | 90670 | 08289 | 40902 | 05069 | 95083 | 06783 | 28102 | 57816 |
| 00175 | 25807 | 24260 | 71529 | 78920 | 72682 | 07385 | 90726 | 57166 | 98884 | 08583 |
| 00176 | 06170 | 97965 | 88302 | 98041 | 21443 | 41808 | 68984 | 83620 | 89747 | 98882 |
| 00177 | 60808 | 54444 | 74412 | 81105 | 01176 | 28838 | 36421 | 16489 | 18059 | 51061 |
| 00178 | 80940 | 44893 | 10408 | 36222 | 80582 | 71944 | 92638 | 40333 | 67054 | 16067 |
| 00179 | 19516 | 90120 | 46759 | 71643 | 13177 | 55292 | 21036 | 82808 | 77501 | 97427 |
| 00180 | 49386 | 54480 | 23604 | 23554 | 21785 | 41101 | 91178 | 10174 | 29420 | 90438 |
| 00181 | 06312 | 88940 | 15995 | 69321 | 47458 | 64809 | 98189 | 81851 | 29651 | 84215 |
| 00182 | 60942 | 00307 | 11897 | 92674 | 40405 | 68032 | 96717 | 54244 | 10701 | 41393 |
| 00183 | 92329 | 98932 | 78284 | 46347 | 71209 | 92061 | 39448 | 93136 | 25722 | 08564 |
| 00184 | 77936 | 63574 | 31384 | 51924 | 85561 | 29671 | 58137 | 17820 | 22751 | 36518 |
| 00185 | 38101 | 77756 | 11657 | 13897 | 95889 | 57067 | 47648 | 13885 | 70669 | 93406 |
| 00186 | 39641 | 69457 | 91339 | 22502 | 92613 | 89719 | 11947 | 56203 | 19324 | 20504 |
| 00187 | 84054 | 40455 | 99396 | 63680 | 67667 | 60631 | 69181 | 96845 | 38525 | 11600 |
| 00188 | 47468 | 03577 | 57649 | 63266 | 24700 | 71594 | 14004 | 23153 | 69249 | 05747 |
| 00189 | 43321 | 31370 | 28977 | 23896 | 76479 | 68562 | 62342 | 07589 | 08899 | 05985 |
| 00190 | 64281 | 61826 | 18555 | 64937 | 13173 | 33365 | 78851 | 16499 | 87064 | 13075 |
| 00191 | 66847 | 70495 | 32350 | 02985 | 86716 | 38746 | 26313 | 77463 | 55387 | 72681 |
| 00192 | 72461 | 33230 | 21529 | 53424 | 92581 | 02262 | 78438 | 66276 | 18396 | 73538 |
| 00193 | 21032 | 91050 | 13058 | 16218 | 12470 | 56500 | 15292 | 76139 | 59526 | 52113 |
| 00194 | 95362 | 67011 | 06651 | 16136 | 01016 | 00857 | 55018 | 56374 | 35824 | 71708 |
| 00195 | 49712 | 97380 | 10404 | 55452 | 34030 | 60726 | 75211 | 10271 | 36633 | 68424 |
| 00196 | 58275 | 61764 | 97586 | 54716 | 50259 | 46345 | 87195 | 46092 | 26787 | 60939 |
| 00197 | 89514 | 11788 | 68224 | 23417 | 73959 | 76145 | 30342 | 40277 | 11049 | 72049 |
| 00198 | 15472 | 50669 | 48139 | 36732 | 46874 | 37088 | 73465 | 09819 | 58869 | 35220 |
| 00199 | 12120 | 86124 | 51247 | 44302 | 60883 | 52109 | 21437 | 36786 | 49226 | 77837 |

# Table of Chi-Square

*appendix c*

## Table of Chi-Square

| Degrees of Freedom df | P = .99 | .98 | .95 | .90 | .80 | .70 | .50 | .30 | .20 | .10 | .05 | .02 | .01 |
|---|---|---|---|---|---|---|---|---|---|---|---|---|---|
| 1 | .000157 | .000628 | .00393 | .0158 | .0642 | .148 | .455 | 1.074 | 1.642 | 2.706 | 3.841 | 5.412 | 6.635 |
| 2 | .0201 | .0404 | .103 | .211 | .446 | .713 | 1.386 | 2.408 | 3.219 | 4.605 | 5.991 | 7.824 | 9.210 |
| 3 | .115 | .185 | .352 | .584 | 1.005 | 1.424 | 2.366 | 3.665 | 4.642 | 6.251 | 7.815 | 9.837 | 11.341 |
| 4 | .297 | .429 | .711 | 1.064 | 1.649 | 2.195 | 3.357 | 4.878 | 5.989 | 7.779 | 9.488 | 11.668 | 13.277 |
| 5 | .554 | .752 | 1.145 | 1.610 | 2.343 | 3.000 | 4.351 | 6.064 | 7.289 | 9.236 | 11.070 | 13.388 | 15.086 |
| 6 | .872 | 1.134 | 1.635 | 2.204 | 3.070 | 3.828 | 5.348 | 7.231 | 8.558 | 10.645 | 12.592 | 15.033 | 16.812 |
| 7 | 1.239 | 1.564 | 2.167 | 2.833 | 3.822 | 4.671 | 6.346 | 8.383 | 9.803 | 12.017 | 14.067 | 16.622 | 18.475 |
| 8 | 1.646 | 2.032 | 2.733 | 3.490 | 4.594 | 5.527 | 7.344 | 9.524 | 11.030 | 13.362 | 15.507 | 18.168 | 20.090 |
| 9 | 2.088 | 2.532 | 3.325 | 4.168 | 5.380 | 6.393 | 8.343 | 10.656 | 12.242 | 14.684 | 16.919 | 19.679 | 21.666 |
| 10 | 2.558 | 3.059 | 3.940 | 4.865 | 6.179 | 7.267 | 9.342 | 11.781 | 13.442 | 15.987 | 18.307 | 21.161 | 23.209 |
| 11 | 3.053 | 3.609 | 4.575 | 5.578 | 6.989 | 8.148 | 10.341 | 12.899 | 14.631 | 17.275 | 19.675 | 22.618 | 24.725 |
| 12 | 3.571 | 4.178 | 5.226 | 6.304 | 7.807 | 9.034 | 11.340 | 14.011 | 15.812 | 18.549 | 21.026 | 24.054 | 26.217 |
| 13 | 4.107 | 4.765 | 5.892 | 7.042 | 8.634 | 9.026 | 12.340 | 15.119 | 16.985 | 19.812 | 22.362 | 25.472 | 27.688 |
| 14 | 4.660 | 5.368 | 6.571 | 7.790 | 9.467 | 10.821 | 13.339 | 16.222 | 18.151 | 21.064 | 23.685 | 26.873 | 29.141 |
| 15 | 5.229 | 5.985 | 7.261 | 8.547 | 10.307 | 11.721 | 14.339 | 17.322 | 19.311 | 22.307 | 24.996 | 28.259 | 30.578 |
| 16 | 5.812 | 6.614 | 7.962 | 9.312 | 11.152 | 12.624 | 15.338 | 18.418 | 20.465 | 23.542 | 26.296 | 29.633 | 32.000 |
| 17 | 6.408 | 7.255 | 8.672 | 10.085 | 12.002 | 13.531 | 16.338 | 19.511 | 21.615 | 24.769 | 27.587 | 30.995 | 33.409 |
| 18 | 7.015 | 7.906 | 9.390 | 10.865 | 12.857 | 14.440 | 17.338 | 20.601 | 22.760 | 25.989 | 28.869 | 32.346 | 34.805 |
| 19 | 7.633 | 8.567 | 10.117 | 11.651 | 13.716 | 15.352 | 18.338 | 21.689 | 23.900 | 27.204 | 30.144 | 33.687 | 36.191 |
| 20 | 8.260 | 9.237 | 10.851 | 12.443 | 14.578 | 16.266 | 19.337 | 22.775 | 25.038 | 28.412 | 31.410 | 35.020 | 37.566 |
| 21 | 8.897 | 9.915 | 11.591 | 13.240 | 15.445 | 17.182 | 20.337 | 23.858 | 26.171 | 29.615 | 32.671 | 36.343 | 38.932 |
| 22 | 9.542 | 10.600 | 12.338 | 14.041 | 16.314 | 18.101 | 21.337 | 24.939 | 27.301 | 30.813 | 33.924 | 37.659 | 40.289 |
| 23 | 10.196 | 11.293 | 13.091 | 14.848 | 17.187 | 19.021 | 22.337 | 26.018 | 28.429 | 32.007 | 35.172 | 38.968 | 41.638 |
| 24 | 10.856 | 11.992 | 13.848 | 15.659 | 18.062 | 19.943 | 23.337 | 27.096 | 29.553 | 33.196 | 36.415 | 40.270 | 42.980 |
| 25 | 11.524 | 12.697 | 14.611 | 16.473 | 18.940 | 20.867 | 24.337 | 24.172 | 30.075 | 34.382 | 37.652 | 41.568 | 44.314 |
| 26 | 12.198 | 13.409 | 15.379 | 17.292 | 19.820 | 21.792 | 25.336 | 29.246 | 31.795 | 35.563 | 38.885 | 42.856 | 45.642 |
| 27 | 12.879 | 14.125 | 16.151 | 18.114 | 20.703 | 22.719 | 26.536 | 30.319 | 32.912 | 36.741 | 40.113 | 44.140 | 46.963 |
| 28 | 13.565 | 14.847 | 16.928 | 18.939 | 21.588 | 23.647 | 27.336 | 31.391 | 34.027 | 37.916 | 41.337 | 45.419 | 48.278 |
| 29 | 14.256 | 15.574 | 17.708 | 19.768 | 22.475 | 24.577 | 28.336 | 32.461 | 35.139 | 39.087 | 42.557 | 46.693 | 49.588 |
| 30 | 14.953 | 16.306 | 18.493 | 20.599 | 23.364 | 25.508 | 29.336 | 33.530 | 36.250 | 40.256 | 43.773 | 47.962 | 50.892 |

[a]This Table of Chi-Square is taken from Table IV of Fisher and Yates: *Statistical Tables for Biological, Agricultural and Medical Research*, published by Oliver & Boyd, Edinburgh, and by permission of the authors and publishers.

# Annotated Readings

The processes and techniques explained in the book are sufficient for *beginning* to understand communities, but further knowledge may be necessary for ascertaining differences and associations. As confidence in the approaches is achieved, school administrators may want to explore additional techniques or gain in-depth knowledge of existing avenues of understanding. In this bibliography we have annotated a number of reading sources which may be helpful for such purposes. The readings have been grouped in categories that generally parallel the organization of the book. Within those categories the readings are arranged in alphabetical order by author.

## BUILDING A FRAMEWORK

Aiken, Michael, and Paul E. Mott (eds.), *The Structure of Community Power*. New York: Random House, 1970. In a single volume this work brings the best of the knowledge about community power structures together. Included are historical perspectives, identification of critical factors in the employment of power, relationships of formal and informal centers of power, and comparative studies across diverse settings. Most immediately relevant for the administrator is the section dealing with methodological bases for identifying power centers in the community. Each of the major schools of thought is identified and the means employed are presented in some detail.

Kepner, Charles H., Benjamin B. Tregoe, *The Rational Manager.* New York: McGraw-Hill, 1965. A highly readable book that highlights the need to understand problems and their causes. While written for the business world, the approaches and techniques for problem specification, decision-making, and problem avoidance are highly relevant for school related problems. There are many "tips" and "forms" provided for each of the main processes.

Nunnery, Michael Y., and Ralph B. Kimbrough, *Politics, Power, Polls and School Elections.* Berkeley, Calif.: McCutchan Publishing Corporation, 1971. Political activity by school officials is essential to the improvement of educational opportunity at the district level. Political processes and the political system must be understood by those who would embark on this route. Public opinion polling and the techniques of campaigning are skills which need to be developed as part of the two-way communication system vital to the political process.

Summerfield, Harry L., *The Neighborhood-Based Politics of Education.* Columbus, Ohio: Charles E. Merrill, 1971. The notion that local educational decision systems are closed is attacked as faulty. Decision elites are not impervious to public opinion and demand. Conflict between elites and the general public can be managed but not controlled in the educational political system. It is public demand that initiates change or adherence to the status quo.

Sumption, Merle R., and Yvonne Engstrom, *School-Community Relations.* New York: McGraw-Hill, 1966. The authors present a view of school-community relations through the concept of the "changing school in the changing community." Social, economic, and political change keep the community in a constant state of flux. Effective communication between school and community is necessary for monitoring these changes and their meaning. The community survey is one basic tool in the development of such communication.

*GENERAL METHODOLOGY*

Costner, Herbert L., ed., *Sociological Methodology 1971.* San Francisco: Jossey-Bass, Inc. Publishers, 1971. The third volume in a series sponsored by the American Sociological Association, this book presents perspectives on social research methods with guidance on certain methodological problems. Part One concentrates on data production; Part Two on measurement errors in regression and path analysis; Part Three on certain process models; and Part Four on measures of association and prediction research. This is a highly complex work but could be valuable for deeper understanding of the research tools of sociology.

Kerlinger, Fred N., *Foundations of Behavioral Research,* 2nd ed. New York: Holt, Rinehart & Winston, 1973. An excellent overview of research and research techniques that have general application. The section dealing with techniques for ascertaining attitudes, details, approaches, like the "Q" Sort," which may have value for community survey approaches. There is also a highly readable set of chapters dealing with analysis and analytic techniques.

Lutz, Frank W., and Laurence Iannaccone, *Understanding Educational Organizations: A Field Study Approach.* Columbus, Ohio: Charles E. Merrill, 1969. A book on research methodology focusing on system-environment relations. It presents approaches to the study of power in communities and attaches the approaches to methodological procedures. Particularly useful are: Chapter V on observation methods; Chapter VI on analyzing data; and Chapter VII which deals with the organization of findings.

Riker, William H., *The Study of Local Politics.* New York: Random House, 1955. Riker's particular objective is to provide undergraduate students in the area of political science with field research methods to study local politics. As such, he has much to say for the schoolman who would try to discover the political status of his local community. The author gives suggestions of questions to ask and develops a series of interviewing approaches and tips.

Warren, Roland L., *Studying Your Community.* New York: Russell Sage Foundation, 1955. Though somewhat outdated, the book covers the various sectors of community life (e.g., background, economic structure, government, housing, and education.) It provides a useful guide to the ways into the vast amount of information available within the local community. With a basic understanding of the community institutions and their modes of operation described in this book, the reader is in a better position for tracking down needed information. Chapter 18 carries through the basic steps involved in surveying citizens but little detail is provided.

## METHODS OF SURVEY RESEARCH

Backstrom, Charles H., and Gerald D. Hursh, *Survey Research.* Evanston, Ill.: Northwestern University Press, 1963. This book was written for political scientists and political sociologists but applies equally well to community study by school personnel. It is a practical primer on how to carry out a survey. The authors take the reader, step by step, through the entire process from drawing a sample, through question writing, to fieldwork, and data processing. Many useful ideas are offered. This is a highly recommended book for reinforced understandings of the survey.

Good, Carter V., *Essentials of Educational Research.* New York: Appleton-Century-Crofts, 1966. Chapter V (pp. 190-281), entitled "Survey: Description, Analysis, Classification," offers many valuable ideas concerning the school-community survey. Included is historical development of the uses of the survey for educational analysis in local communities, contrasts and comparisons between interviews and questionnaires, and a variety of techniques for discovering facts about the community. A useful background chapter with a good bibliography up to the mid-1960s.

Hennessy, Bernard C., *Public Opinion.* Belmont Calif.: Wadsworth, 1965. In a democracy, the process from opinion to policy is an important one. *How* and *why* opinions are formed, held, and changed are topics explored through concept and theory. The dynamics of opinion change, viewed in a political context, make the book valuable to the schoolman. The measurement of opinion through polls and surveys is discussed. The methodology of survey research is presented in detail.

Parten, Mildred, *Surveys, Polls, and Samples.* New York: Harper & Row, 1950. A pioneering book in the field of survey research process. Provides in-depth explorations of all facets of surveying from planning, to doing the fieldwork, to preparing the report of the findings. Highly readable, it includes both advantages and disadvantages of various procedures. A thorough bibliography of works related to survey research up to 1950 is included.

Young, Pauline V., *Scientific Social Surveys and Research,* 4th ed. Englewood Cliffs, N.J.: Prentice-Hall, 1966. This book treats the total survey process with good detail in selected areas. It also includes some topics not usually found in overviews of this nature. For example, Chapter 13 by Calvin Schmid has an excellent discussion of "Graphic Presentations." The chapters dealing with interviewing and questionnaires have some helpful cues for consideration.

## SAMPLING

Kish, Leslie, *Survey Sampling.* New York: John Wiley, 1965. A sophisticated and complete text that focuses on the processes and theories of sampling. Requires a fairly substantial familiarity with probability and statistics.

Stephan, Frederick F., and Philip J. McCarthy, *Sampling Opinions: An Analysis of Survey Procedure.* New York: John Wiley, 1963. An excellent sourcebook that systematically develops understandings of sampling. Part I deals with background material for conceptual understanding and application. Part II concentrates on analyses and empirical studies; and Part III is a synthesis, reviewing understandings and interpreting for application.

Yates, Frank, *Sampling Methods for Censuses and Surveys,* 3rd ed. New York: Hafner, 1960. This book has very complete coverage of sampling and sampling methods with an excellent bibliographic section. Application and examples are, unfortunately, rather far removed from the concerns of schools and school administration.

## QUESTIONNAIRES AND THEIR CONSTRUCTION

Likert, Rensis, "A Technique for the Measurement of Attitudes," *Archives of Psychology,* No. 140 (1938). This is a classic in technique for attitude measurement. It provides the background and theory for Likert's measurement approaches that have been successfully extended and employed over the years.

Oppenheim, A. N., *Questionnaire Design and Attitude Measurement.* New York: Basic Books, 1966. The author uses the term "questionnaire" to fit both the interview and questionnaire formats. As such, there is much valuable information for the schoolman whether he is constructing an interview schedule or a questionnaire. The book focuses upon design problems, question wording, ways of establishing attitudes, and ways of quantifying the resultant information for analysis. At the end of each chapter there is a useful bibliography that provides access to further sources for the interested reader.

Payne, Stanley I., *The Art of Asking Questions*. Princeton, N.J.: Princeton University Press, 1951. An excellent "do's and don'ts" book on question stating. As the author notes in his preface, "The art of asking questions is not likely ever to be reduced to easy formulas." All that he offers the reader is his substantial observations as a researcher on the most common problems encountered by those who write survey questions and some practical ways to avoid pitfalls. The book probably presents one of the most complete treatments of this topic available.

Webb, Eugene J., Donald T. Campbell, Richard D. Schwartz, and Lee Sechrest, *Unobtrusive Measures: Nonreactive Research in the Social Sciences*. Skokie, Ill.: Rand McNally, 1966. An excellent source for understanding the theory and application of those measures that do *not* involve a direct contact with respondents or subjects. As an example of an unobtrusive measure the number of broken windows in a school building may indicate a level of student alienation. The authors explore types of unobtrusive measures as well as the problems in interpreting such indicators.

## INTERVIEWING

"The Interview in Social Research," *American Journal of Sociology*. LXII, No. 2 (Sept. 1956), 137-94. The entire issue is devoted to interviewing and includes some of the thinking of outstanding researchers about various aspects of this process. For example, one article focuses on age and sex problems, another on role relations and neutrality in the interview setting, and another on a classification scheme for biased questions.

Gorden, Raymond L., *Interviewing: Strategy, Techniques, and Tactics*. Homewood, Ill.: Dorsey, 1969. This book is a must! The author has gathered together a wealth of information and techniques for this specialized area of gathering information. "The intent is to increase sensitivity to a broad spectrum of communication problems, to present a wide assortment of interviewing tools, and to introduce a frame of reference useful in bringing the tools to bear on these problems." This quotation from the Preface is not mere boast; it has been well achieved in this highly readable book. As a further bonus there is an excellent bibliography. Highly recommended!

Hyman, Herbert Hiram, *Interviewing in Social Research*. Chicago, Ill.: University of Chicago Press, 1954. The focus of this book is a study of factors that operate within the interview to produce error. The book treats interviewing as a method of inquiry – highlighting errors, their sources, and their control. It is well documented and highly authoritative.

Richardson, Stephen A., Barbara Snell Dobrehnwend, and David Klein, *Interviewing*. New York: Basic Books, 1965. An in-depth analysis of the interview process. Focus is on interviewer-interviewee relationships, how they develop, constraints, and construction of a "facilitating" environment. The authors cover a wide range of interviewing situations, discussing the impacts of content, personality, geographical locus, and the structure of the interview instrument itself.

Survey Research Center, *Interviewer's Manual.* Ann Arbor, Mich.: Institute for Social Research, May 1969. Constructed as a guide book for interviews in the Survey Research Center, the manual covers interviews and sampling "do's and don'ts." The contents of the manual reflect the extensive experiences of the Center. It can well be used by school district personnel to gain insights into the surveying and interviewing processes.

*ANALYSIS*

Berelson, Bernard, *Content Analysis in Communications Research.* Glencoe, Ill.: Free Press, 1952. This is one of the first books in the area and one that is still an excellent overview and basic source. It highlights the uses of content analysis as a research tool. Since it is an early work, later sources by other writers extend the techniques and applications developed.

Budd, Richard W., Robert K. Thorp, and Lewis Donohew, *Content Analysis of Communications.* New York and London: Crowell Collier and Macmillan, 1967. There is an excellent annotated bibliography of over 300 works in the field of content analysis included in this work. The purpose of the book is to indicate ways that content analysis can be used or applied. Many of its examples are drawn from the mass media although a wider scope of application is implied. A good resource book for basic understandings and techniques.

Davis, James A., *Elementary Survey Analysis.* Englewood Cliffs, N.J.: Prentice-Hall, 1971. This book is part of a series dealing with the methods of the social sciences. The emphasis is restricted to those analytic tools of a nonparametric nature (as Yule's Q and Gamma). The approach is for a nonmathematical understanding with sufficient explanation so that the technique can be applied. This is a helpful supplement to our analytic chapters.

Holsti, Ole R., *Content Analysis for the Social Sciences and Humanities.* Reading, Mass.: Addison-Wesley, 1969. The book is viewed as an introduction as well as a guide to documentary research. The author presents an historical development and overview; designs for content analyses; uses; inferences and cause and effect; coding; sampling-reliability-validity; and the uses of computers. This is an excellent work for understanding the field of analysis and a highly recommended resource.

Lohnes, Paul R., and William W. Cooley, *Introduction to Statistical Procedures: With Computer Exercises.* New York: John Wiley, 1968. For the staff person in the schools looking for a book that integrates elementary statistics with computer thinking, this is it. This is a highly recommended text for integrating the machine and the technique.

Nie, Norman, Dale H. Bent, and C. Hadlai Hull, *SPSS: Statistical Package for the Social Sciences.* New York: McGraw-Hill, 1970. This is an essential manual for employing the computer with those statistical techniques that are frequently helpful in survey analysis. It is an excellent companion text for developing an understanding of the computer, reading and interpreting computer printouts, and understanding the arrangements and use of certain statistical programs. Highly recommended for those who have computer resources available.

Olsen, John A., *Mapping: A Method for Organizing Data About Your School Attendance Area,* Bulletin of the Oregon School Study Council, Vol. 12, No. 7 (March 1969). A detailed method of graphically presenting physical and cultural data in spatial patterns. Mapping has the advantage of showing relationships of community features, thus providing the schoolman with readily available information in an easily understood form. Observation is a key method in making maps, but written records also provide data for inclusion.

Rosenberg, Morris, *The Logic of Survey Analysis.* New York: Basic Books, 1968. This book is devoted to that segment of the survey process that is concerned with abstracting meaning from the data. The author highlights the logic or reasoning behind the operations of analysis. Since it deals specifically with surveys and survey analysis, it is very appropriate for the schoolman. It is well written with good examples and does *not* assume advanced knowledge of mathematics. This is another book that is highly recommended for advancing the knowledge-base and understandings of analysis.

Schmid, Calvin F., *Handbook of Graphic Presentation.* New York: Ronald Press, 1954. In this handbook there are techniques, clues, problems, and examples of a variety of ways for presenting statistical data in graphic form. A chapter is devoted to each of the most important types of charts. In each case the advantages and disadvantages, distortions, special difficulties and problems are listed for the particular approaches presented. The book is quite detailed and includes excellent examples.

Siegel, Sidney, *Nonparametric Statistics for the Behavioral Sciences.* New York: McGraw-Hill, 1956. This is one of the classic texts in the field. What makes it even more important is that it is well written so that the techniques may be easily learned and applied from the descriptions given. It will make an excellent reference for extending the competencies in nonparametric analytic tools.

Wallis, W. Allen, and Harry V. Roberts, *The Nature of Statistics.* New York: Free Press, 1965. The authors have done the almost impossible – they have written an entertaining book about statistics. Chapter 9 is particularly helpful as it describes the art of reading statistical tables. As a general aid for those who are forced into the use and understanding of statistics, this book is a must.

*INFORMATION: SHARING, STORAGE, AND RETRIEVAL*

Holm, Bart E., *How to Manage Your Information.* New York: Van Nostrand Reinhold, 1968. This book sets out the basic principles of information storage and retrieval and then illustrates them as they apply to several professions. The same principles are applied in examining record management and data systems, as well as in discussing the pros and cons of mechanization of data handling. Written for the nontechnical reader, it is free of jargon and well illustrated.

Lott, Richard W., *Basic Data Processing,* 2nd ed. Englewood Cliffs, N.J.: Prentice-Hall, 1971. While written primarily for the business student this book provides a good introduction to all aspects of data processing for students in any field. The author moves the reader into the technical parts gradually with well presented information. Topics treated include the various machines associated with processing data.

Ross, Joel E., *Management by Information System.* Englewood Cliffs, N.J.: Prentice-Hall, 1970. The intent of the author is to close the communication gap between the manager and the computer specialist, an intent which seems to have been achieved in this well prepared book. He approaches management and information from a systems perspective. The work is well written and well illustrated.

Wynne, Edward, *The Politics of School Accountability: Public Information about Public Schools.* Berkeley, Calif.: McCutchan Publishing Corporation, 1972. In general, this book provides a framework for the need for keeping the community informed as well as for a continuous feedback from the community into the schools. The focus is on the concept of "accountability" with its implications for topics such as: "the impact of the public on public school policy making," "attitudes and patterns of reporting," and "forces attempting to generate school feedback systems."

# Index

## A

Abstracting services, 203
Ackoff, Russell L., 97
Accountability, 5
Accuracy:
  of data bank indexes, 197
  of information 40–41
  of population lists, 90
  of survey results, 108–9
Advantages:
  of cluster sampling, 103
  of drop off-pickup questionnaires, 130
  of interviews, 123–24, 131
  of mailed questionnaires, 130
  of reference retrieval systems, 196–97
  of simple random sampling, 97
  of stratified random sampling, 99
  of systematic samples, 100
  of telephone interviews, 131
  (see also Disadvantages)
Advertising, 5
Age:
  and cluster sampling, 102–3
  coding of, 115
  in population definition, 90, 93
  in stratified sampling, 97–98
Alumni interviews, 56

American Indians, 4
Analysis:
  chi square tests in, 146
  "code-key" in, 144
  computers in, 144–46
  content, 140–44, 151
  of data:
    density maps in, 158–60
    descriptive statistics in, 160
    histograms in, 149–50
    line graphs in, 151–54
    means in, 160
    medians in, 160
    mode in, 160
    readings about, 236–37, 240–41
    scattergrams in, 154–60
    "scenarios" in, 160
  desk-sized computers in, 146
  of documents, *53–63*
  goal of 135–36, 148
  "hand," *135–44*
  keys in, 144
  needlesort in, 146
  personnel for, 145
  of survey results, 108
  and Trend Analysis Sheets, 151
  of trends, 148 151–54
  (see also Interpretation)

*243*

244  Index

Area sampling (*see* Cluster sampling)
Article reprints, 56
*Art of Asking Questions, The* (Payne), 75
*Art of Readable Writing, The* (Flesch), 213
Arts, the, 4
Attitude Scale, the, 140
Authenticy of documents, 54, 56-59, 63

**B**

Bachrach, Peter, 87
Backstrom, Charles H., 103
Band of tolerance, 18-20, 33
Baratz, Morton S., 87
Bar graphs (*see* Histograms)
Bendiner, Robert S., 8
"Best guess," 30
Bias:
   in documents, 58
   in interviews, 124, 125, 127
   in motivational techniques, 123
   in random selection, 94, 96
   in reports, 208
   in systematic sampling, 100-101
   in telephone interviews, 129
   in weighted samples, 138
Black power, 4
Bond issues, 8, 18, 25, 29, 42-48, 89-90
Boroko, Harold, 145
Boycotts, 4, 86
Bross, Irwin D. J., 154
Brown, Francis E., 154
Budgeting:
   and community expectations, 5, 8, 18
   for fieldwork, 118
Bureau of Census, the, 202
Bursk, Edward C., 154
Bursk, Parker J., 154

**C**

Call-backs:
   for interviews, 116, 126, 127
   for questionnaires, 121
Carter, Richard F., 8
Categories:
   in chi-square tests, 166, 170-74, 177-80
   in coding, 68
   of data, *91-97*, 135
   dichotomous, 108
   identification of, 149-50
   multiple chi-square, 177-80
CED (*see* the Committee for Economic Development)
Census figures, 190
Census tracts, 23

CFK, Ltd., 63
Chambers of Commerce, 62
Champion, Dean J., 180
Change (*see* Social change)
Chapman, John F., 154
Chi-square test:
   in analysis, 146
   a priori expectations in, 169-71
   categories in, 166, 170-74, 177-80
   computation rules for, 166-68, 170, 173 177, 180
   "contingency coefficient" in, 180
   degrees of freedom in, 168, 170-81 passim
   *Gamma* coefficients in, 180
   "goodness of fit" in, 169, 174, 180-82
   "indifference" in, 167, 169
   introduction to, 166-69
   levels of confidence in, 168
   levels of probability in, 168, 170, 173, 182
   multiple categories in, 177-80
   the Phi coefficient in, 176
   and sample goodness, 137-38
   strength of agreement in, 178
   and the "Table of Chi-square," 177, 181 233
   values in,
   Yates' Correction in, 176
Church groups, 10
Civil rights, 4
Clelland, Richard C., 154
Cluster sampling, 101-9
"Code-key," 144
Coding:
   of age, 115
   in content analysis, 141-44
   of data, *135-44*
   of demographic questions, 68
   in fieldwork, 114-15, 124
   of survey respondents' sex, 115
Commercial survey organizations, 111
Committee for Economic Development, the, 203
Community, the:
   consensus in, 8-9, 14
   dissent in, 4
   documents of, 60-62
   expectations of, 6-12, 14-16, 56, 206
   "major sectors" of, 23
   "non-decisions" in, 87
   opinions of, 8
   orientation to, 122
   and policy, 7-12, 14-16
   population growth of, 27
   reactions of, 112
   readings about, 235-36

and social change, 4–10, 15
  values of, 6–11, 87–88
  voting patterns of, 10–12, 14, 23–27, 40, 60, 98, 99
Comparability of documents, 57–58
Computers:
  in analysis, 115, 144–46
  in data retrieval, 190
  desk-sized, 146
  regional, 190
Confidence:
  in chi-square tests, levels of, 168
  of survey respondents, 123
  in survey results, 104–6, 107, 109
Confidentiality:
  of data banks, 198
  of data sources, 200
  of questionnaires, 120
  of survey responses, 112
Confrontations, 4
Content analysis (*see* Analysis, content)
"Contingency coefficient," 180
Control cards, 114, 118, 120, 122, 126, 128, 129
Conway, James A., 53
Cooperation, respondent, 108
Coordinating center, the, 118, 122
Costs:
  of mail surveys, 107
  of questionnaires, 119–23
  of sample surveys, 111, 112
  of telephone surveys, 107
Council of Planning Librarians, the, 203
Cover letters, 120
Criteria:
  for data, 197
  for demographic questions, 78–79
  for methodology selection, 36, *37–48*
Crofts Educational Service, 203
*Current Contents,* 203
Curriculum reports, 56, 58
Curriculum research centers, 62

# D

Dahl, Robert A., 87
Data:
  analysis of:
    content, 140–44
    density maps in, 158–60
    descriptive statistics in, 148–49, 160
    histograms in, 149–54
    line graphs in, 151–54
    mean in, 160
    median in, 160
    mode in, 160

  newspapers in, 160
  personnel for, 161
  range in, 160
  scattergrams in, 154–60
  "scenarios" in, 160
  summary sheets in, 160
  "topographically" equivalent maps in, 158–59
  variables in, 154–55
anticipating needs for, 188
arrangement of, 148
criteria for, 197
classification of, 135
coding of, *135–44*
collection of, 135–40
concept of, 135–36
content analysis of, 140–44
conversion of, 188
generalization of, 140
indexing, 188, 199
  chi-square test in, 165, 166–69, 170–84
  Pearson Product Moment Correlation in, 165
  respondents' perceptions in, 114
  scattergrams in, 165
  significance in, 182–83
  statistician's aid in, 165
  "t test" in, 165
location of, 190
missing, 138
objectivity toward, 140
in problem specification, 23–29
"qualitative," 135
"quantitative," 135
retrieval (*see* Data retrieval)
review of, 197
sources of:
  abstracting services, 203
  budget reports, 190
  the Bureau of the Census, 190, 202
  businesses, 187, 199–200
  the Committee for Economic Development, 203
  the Council of Planning Librarians, 203
  Crofts Education Services, 203
  *Current Contents,* 203
  *Educational Administration Abstracts,* 203
  the federal government, 200–203
  the Library of Congress, 202
  local government, 187, 199
  the *Monthly Catalog of U. S. Government Publications,* 202
  the *Monthly Checklist of State Documents,* 202
  the *NEA Research Bulletin,* 202

246  Index

newspapers, 40, 56, 62, 87, 116, 140, 143, 160, 190
private organizations, 187, 199-200
the Research Division of the National Education Association, 202
*Research in Education,* 202
*Research Memos,* 203
*Research Summaries,* 203
school administrations, 187, 199
*Small Area Notes,* 202
state government, 187, 200-203
tax rates, 190
storage of, *187-200*
structured, 135, 138-40
   depiction of, *148-60*
   interpretation of, *165-84*
   variables in, 165
unstructured, 135, 140-44
   depiction of, *148-61*
   interpretation of, 164-65
usability of, 199-200
(*see also* Information)
Data banks:
   confidentiality of, 198
   costs of, 200
   criteria for, 197
   entry descriptors for, 191
   indexing for, 191-97
   and input-output parity, 190-91
   and manual sorting systems, 190
   personnel for, 198
   readings about, 241-42
   retrieval indexes in, 195
   school-community, *188-203*
   security of, 198
   updating of, 197
Data collapse, 197
Data retrieval:
   computers in, 190
   criteria for, 197
   indexing for, 191-97
   and input-output parity, 190-91
   and item retrieval, 190, 195
   levels of, 190
   and manual sorting systems, 190
   personnel for, 198
   readings about, 241-42
   reference retrieval in, 190, 195-97
   thermofax in, 198
   Xerox in, 198
Davis, James A., 180
DeCani, John S., 154
Decision-making, *10-16,* 104-8, 114
Degrees of freedom, 168, 170-81 passim
Demographic description, 141
Demographic questions, 46, 66-68, 69, 78-79, 82

Density maps, 158-60
Descriptive statistics, 148-49, 160
Deviation:
   and bands of tolerance, 18-20
   correction of, 21ff.
   and expectations, 17-18
   explanations of, 29-33
   factors in, 23
   location of, 23-27
   negative, 20-21
   participants in, 27
   positive, 20-21
   and problem specification, 23
   progressive action toward, 21
   time of, 27
   (*see also* Problems)
Dichotomous-choice questions, 72
Disadvantages:
   of cluster sampling, 103
   of drop off-pickup questionnaires, 130
   of interviews, 123-24, 131
   of mailed questionnaires, 130
   of reference retrieval systems, 196-97
   of simple random sampling, 97
   of stratified random sampling, 99
   of systematic sampling, 100-101
   of telephone interviews, 131
   (*see also* Advantages)
Dissent, 25
Document research, 36-38, 40-41, 43-48, 53-54
Documents:
   analysis of, *53-63*
   article reprints, 56
   authenticity of, 54, 56-57, 63
   from banks, 62
   bias in, 58
   Board of Education reports, 60
   CFK, Ltd., 63
   Chamber of Commerce, 62
   city directories, 90
   comparability of, 57-58
   completeness of, 57-58
   curriculum committee reports, 58
   curriculum research centers, 62
   *Educational Administration Quarterly,* 63
   *Educational Leadership,* 63
   Educational Resources and Information Center, 62, 202
   *Education Index,* 63
   historical societies, 62
   job placement records, 57
   the Kettering Foundation, 63
   kinds of, *55-63*
   the League of Women Voters, 62
   location of, 60-63
   mailing lists, 90

maps, 60
National Census of Occupations, 53
newspapers, 56, 62, 87
the *Phi Delta Kappan Magazine,* 63
primary sources, 56
the *Readers Guide to Periodical Literature,* 63
*Research in Education,* 62
secondary sources, 56
state educational agency reports, 60, 62-63
summary of, 58-60
in survey respondent selection, 87
tax rates, 58, 60, 61
usefulness of, 53, 54, 57-58, 63
voting records, 60
Drop off-pickup questionnaires, 121-23
Drug problem, the, 4
Dyckman, T. R., 154

# E

Earle, Ralph B., 65
*Educational Administration Quarterly,* 63
*Educational Leadership,* 63
Educational Resources and Information Center, the, 62, 202
*Education Index,* 63
*Elements of Style, The* (Strunk and White), 213
Entry descriptors, 190
Environment, 5-6, 15, 20
ERIC (*see* Educational Resources and Information Center)
Error:
 in histograms, 150
 in sample lists, 113
 tolerance of, 18-20
Expectations:
 a priori, in chi-square test, 169-71
 of business groups, 9-10
 of church groups, 10
 community, 6-12, 14-16, 56, 206
 of ethnic groups, 9
 and ideologies, 7
 of performance in schools, 7, 17-18
 plurality of, 10
 and protest actions, 10
 and social change, 9, 15, 21
 and taxpayers' groups, 9
 and tradition, 7

# F

Factual questions, 66, 68, 69, 79, 82
Feedback (*see* Information feedback)

Fieldwork:
 call-backs in, 116, 121, 126, 127
 codes in, 114-25
 control cards in, 114, 118, 122, 126, 128, 129
 coordination of, 115-16, 118, 120
 costs of, 118-19
 follow-ups in, 112, 116, 120, 154, 155
 maps in, 122
 objectives of, 112-13
 personnel for (*see* Fieldworkers)
 preparation for, 113-19
 and pretests, 116
 for questionnaires, 119-23
 scheduling of, 116-18
 supervision of, 115-16
 tact in, 112
 time requirements of, 114, 115
 timing of, 118
Fieldworkers:
 college graduates as, 127
 and community orientation, 122
 female, 127
 male, 127
 middle-class, 127
 paid, 115
 recruitment of, 115, 127
 requirements for, 127-29
 supervision of, 115
 training of, 111-12, 115, 116-18, 121, 122, 127-29
 volunteer, 115, 123
 working-class, 115, 123
Flesch, R. F., 213
Follow-up survey, 112, 116, 120, 154, 155
Fox, David J., 140
"Future shock," 3

# G

Games, Paul A., 149, 154, 160, 177
*Gamma* coefficients, 180
Glass, Gene V., 149, 154
Goldrich, Daniel, 11
Good, Carter V., 57
"Goodness of fit," 169, 174, 180-82
Graphs (*see* Line graphs)
Guttman, Louis, 74
Guttman Scale, the, 74

# H

"Hand analysis, *135-44*
Head, Kendra B., 65
Hennessey, Bernard, 11, 112
Histograms, 148-54

248  Index

Holm, Bert E., 190
Holsti, Ole R., 140
Huff, Darrell, 160
Hunter, Floyd, 87
Hursch, Gerald D., 103

**I**

Ideology, 7
Income:
 in population definition, 93
 in stratified sampling, 97-98
 in systematic sampling, 100
Indexing, 191-97
"Indifference," 167, 169
Information:
 accessibility of, 40
 accuracy of, 40-41
 background, 54
 bibliographic, 56
 coding of, 82
 demographic, 125-26
 diagramming of, 58-60
 gathering of, 43-48
 geographic, 57
 needs for, 54-56
 parallel lists of, 29-30
 and policy, 14-16
 population, 57
 relevance of, 40
 for sample size, 103-4
 tax, 57
 (see also Data)
Information feedback, *205-14*
Information retrieval, 190 (see also Data retrieval)
Input-output parity, 190-91
Institute for Social Research, 92
Instrument, survey (see Survey instrument)
Interpretation:
 chi-square test in, 165, 166-69, *170-84*
 Pearson Product Moment Correlation in, 165
 respondents' perceptions in, 164
 scattergrams in, 105
 significance in, 182-83
 statistician's aid in, 165
 "t test" in, 165
 variables in, 165ff.
 (see also Analysis)
Interview respondents, selection of, *85-109*
Interviews:
 advantages of, 123-24, 131
 alumni, 56

analysis, 107
appointments for, 125
appropriateness of, *85-109*
arrangement of, 124-27
assignment of, 126-27
bias in, 124, 127, 129
call-backs for, 126, 127
conduct of, 124-27
control of, 125
control cards in, 126, 128, 129
cost of, 107
disadvantages of, 124, 131
and key participants, 123-24
note-taking in, 126, 128
opinion probes in, 123
personnel requirements for, 112, 127-29
personnel training for, 127-29
practice of, 128
preparations for, 111
pretest of, 127
rapport in, 124, 125, 129
readings about, 239-40
sequential, 164-65
structured, 123-24
and survey respondents, 108, 124, 125, 129
telephone, 129, 131
time requirements for, 107, 126
unstructured, 123-24
Item retrieval, 190 (see also Data retrieval)

**K**

Kaplan, Abraham, 163-64
Kepner, Charles H., 22, 29, 30
Kerlinger, Fred N., 93
Kettering Foundation, the, 63
Klare, George R., 149, 154, 160, 177
Koenkers, Robert H., 169
Key participants, 86, 87, 116, 123-24
Knill, William D., 11

**L**

Lake, Dale G., 65
League of Women Voters, the, 62
Line graphs, 148, 151, 152, 161

**M**

McKelvey, Troy, 53
Mail-back questionnaires, 120-21
Male-female ratios, 93
Manual sorting systems, 190

Maps:
  in cluster sampling, 101-2
  density, 158
  in document analysis, 60
  in fieldwork, 122
  in interviews, 126
  in respondent selection, 91
  "topologically" equivalent, 158-59
Mass media, 3, 10
Mean, 160
Median, 160
Methodologies:
  advantages of, 36
  descriptions of, 56
  disadvantages of, 36
  in document search, 36-38, 40-41, 43-48
  economy of, 41
  readings about, 236-37
  results of, 35, 37, 40
  skills required for, 35, 41-42
  in survey research, 36, 39
  in survey respondent selection, 85ff.
  in tandem, 36, 40
  time requirements of, 41-42
Migrant workers, 57
*Million Random Digits with 100,000 Normal Deviates, A* (Rand Corporation), 94-95
Mode, 160
Models, 29-33, 34, 86
Monroe desk computers, 146
*Monthly Catalog of U. S. Government Publications,* the, 202
*Monthly Checklist of State Documents,* the, 202
Motivation, in interviews, 120, 121, 123, 124
Mouly, George J., 107
Multiple-choice questions, 72, 75, 82
Murray, Donald S., 154

## N

National Census of Occupations, the, 57
National Opinion Research Center, the, 118
NEA Research Bulletin, the, 202
Needlesort, 146
Newspapers:
  in content analysis, 140, 143, 160
  as documents, 40, 56, 52, 87, 190
  in sample surveys, 116
"Non-decisions," 87
Non-scaled multiple-choice questions, 75
Norm-maintenance, 33
Norm-transformation, 33

Norms, 17, 21, 33
North, Robert C., 140

## O

Open-ended questions (*see* Questions, open-ended)
Opinion probes, 66, 68-69, 79, 82, 123, 124, 125
Osgood, Charles E., 74

## P

"Packaged" survey instruments, 63
Parten, Mildred R., 105, 107
Patterns (*see* Trends)
Payne, Stanley, 75
Pearson Product Moment Correlation, the, 165
Personnel:
  clerical, 116-18
  college graduates as, 127
  and community orientation, 122
  computer, 145
  for data analysis, 161
  for data banks, 198
  female, 127
  for fieldwork, 111-12, 115-18, *121-29*
  local, 146
  male, 127
  middle-class, 127
  paid, 115
  for questionnaires, 120-21
  recruitment of, 115, 127
  requirements for, 127-29
  for sample surveys, 111-12, 121
  supervision of, 115
  training of, 111-12, 115, 116-18, 121, 122, 127-29
  volunteer, 115, 123, 129
  working class, 127
Phi coefficient, the, 176
*Phi Delta Kappan,* the, 63
Pilot studies, 86, 87, 109
Pluralism, 4-5, 10
Policy:
  and authority, 14-15
  board of education, 55, 56
  and the community, 7-12, 14-16, 206
  and consensus, 10, 14
  effectuation of, 11, 15, 26
  formulation of, 12, 26, 39, 206
  information requirements for, 15, 206
  and public relations, 14
  and school administration, 7-12, 14-16
  statement of, 14

stages of, 206
support of, 12–14
textbook, 56
Political change, 3–4
Political participation, 4
Polsby, Nelson W., 87
Population, respondent:
  arrangement of, 100
  composition of, 88–91
  characteristics of, 89–91, 93, 97–99, 109, 115
  definition of, 88–93
  geographic distribution of, 89
  and representative samples, 88, 89, 93
  strata of, 98–99, 101
  weighted, 98–99
Population growth, 27
Population lists, 90–91
Possible-probable models, 30–33
Pretest, the, 80–82, 83, 116, 127
Probability, levels of, 93, 168, 170, 173, 182
Probes (see Opinion probes)
Problems:
  as deviations, 14–17
  and expectations, 17–18, 21
  explanation of, 29–33
  factors in, 23
  location of, 23–27
  negative, 20–21
  as neutral, 20–21
  of pluralism, 4–5
  positive, 20–21
  specification of:
    "best guess" in, 30
    case histories in, 21–22
    charts in, 60
    comparison and contrast analysis in, 29–30
    demographic questions in, 46
    dissent in, 25
    document search in, 36–38, 40–41 43–48, 53–63
    forms in, 29–33
    goals in, 58–59
    information for, 22–33, 43–48
    Kepner and Tregoe model in, 29–30
    maps in, 60
    methodologies for, 35–49
    models in, 29–33, 34
    and norm-maintenance, 21
    and norm-transformation, 21
    possible-probable model in, 30–33
    process of, 22–33
    questions for, 27–29
    research specialists in, 46
    "social mapping" in, 27
  survey research in, 36–39, 43–48
  voting patterns in, 23–27
  time of, 27
Programmers, 145
Protest action, 4, 10
Purposeful selection (see Survey respondents, purposeful selection of)

## Q

"Quality of life," 3
Questionnaires:
  appropriateness of, 85–109
  bias in, 123
  call-backs for, 121
  confidentiality of, 120
  control cards in, 120
  costs of, 119–20, 121, 122–23
  distribution of, 120–23
  drop off-pickup, 121–23
  fieldwork for, 119–23
  follow-up of, 112
  hand-delivered, 107, 108
  mail, 107, 111–12, 120–21
  personnel for, 120–21
  preparations for, 111–12
  in problem specification, 43–48
  readings about, 238–38
  self-administering, 111
  and stratified samples, 123
  in survey research, 37–39
  telephone, 107
  time requirements for, 121
  timing of, 112
Questions:
  ambiguity in, 76, 80, 82
  appropriateness of, 85–109
  clarity of, 75, 80, 82
  demographic, 66–68, 69, 78–79, 82, 125–26
  development of, 66–80
  dichotomous choice, 71, 82, 108
  emotional reactions to, 76, 77–78
  formats of, 139–40
  levels of complexity in, 75–76
  loaded, 76, 80
  multiple-choice, 72, 82
  non-scaled multiple-choice, 75, 82
  open-ended, 70–75, 82, 140
  opinion, 66, 68–69, 79, 82, 123, 124, 125
  scaled multiple-choice, 72–75, 82
  structured, 70–75, 82
  of survey respondents, 118, 124, 125
  threatening, 78
  types of, 66–69
  wording of, 66, 69, 75–77, 82

Index    251

## R

Race:
  in population definition, 93
  in stratified random sampling, 97-98
  in systematic sampling, 100
Rand Corporation, the, 94-95
Random appointments, 127
Random distribution, 155
Random Numbers, Tables of, 93-96
Random sampling:
  bias in, 94, 96
  and random numbers, 93-96
  and representativeness, 93
  and sample surveys, 93, 96-103
  simple, 96-97
  stratified, 97-99
Random telephone calls, 113
Range, 116
Rapport, 124, 125, 129
*Readers Guide to Periodical Literature,* the, 63
"Reality test" (*see* Pretest)
Reference retrieval, 190, 195-97 (*see also* Data retrieval)
Reich, Charles, 3
Relevance:
  of descriptive techniques, 160
  of information, 40
  of methodologies, 39ff.
  of the survey instrument, *85-109*
  in trend analysis, 152
Report of findings, the *205-14*
Reports:
  of CFK, Ltd., 63
  community, 61
  of curriculum committees, 58
  of the Kettering Foundations, 63
  of the *Phi Delta Kappan Magazine,* 63
  reading achievement, 58
  state education agency, 60
  tax, 57, 58, 66, 67
Representativeness, 92, 93, 137, 180
Research, survey (*see* Survey research)
Research Division of the National Education Association, the, 202
*Research in Education,* 62
*Research Memos,* 203
Research specialists, 46
*Research Summaries,* 203
Respondents, survey (*see* Survey respondents)
Richardson, Stephen A., 39, 42, 127
Robinson, John P., 65
Rossi, Peter, 10
Rummel, J. Francis, 36
Rusk, Jerrold G., 65

## S

Sample, the:
  characteristics of, 101-2
  and the chi-square test, 137-38
  contamination of, 116
  demographic variables in, 137
  "goodness" of, 137
  observation of, 113
  organization of, 114-15
  representative, 88, 89, 93, 137, 180
  selection of, 80-81
  sequential, 138
  size of:
    accuracy, factor in, 107, 108
    and confidence, 104-6, 107
    estimating the, 111
    and personnel requirements, 121
    and personnel training, 115
    and resources, 107-8
    and time requirements, 121
    and tolerance of error, 104, 105-7
    and "uncertainty," 105
  stratified, 114
  substitutions in, 114
  verification of 111, 113-14
  weighted, 138
Sample surveys (*see* Surveys, sample)
Sampling, area (*see* Cluster sampling)
Sax, Gilbert, 127
Scaled multiple-choice questions, 72-75
Scatter diagrams (*see* Scattergrams)
Scattergrams:
  in data depiction, 148, 154-61, 165
  as density maps, 158-60
  random distribution in, 155
  and "topologically" equivalent maps, 158-59
  variables in, 154-55
"Scenarios," 160
School administration:
  accountability in, 5
  budgeting in, 5, 8, 18, 118
  and the community, 8-12, 14-16
  conflict in, 7
  and consensus, 10
  as data source, 187, 199
  and expectations, 15, 16
  feedback in, 15, 205-14 passim
  problem specification in, *23-33*
  public relations in, 14
  skepticism in, 19-20
  systems approach to, 5
Semantic Differential Scale, the, 73, 74
Sex, factor of:
  in cluster sampling, 102-3
  in coding, 115

## 252  Index

in population definition, 90
in sample verification, 113
in stratified random sampling, 97–98
in systematic sampling, 100
Sex education, 7, 8, 40
Shaver, Phillip R., 65
Significance, definition of, 182–83
Simon, Julian L., 138, 151
Simple random sampling, 96–97, 109
*Simplified Statistics* (Koenker), 109
Skepticism, 19–20
Skills:
  methodological, 41–42
  in questionnaire administration, 120
  in sample measurement, 106–7
Slonim, Morris James, 92, 100
*Small Area Notes*, 202
Smidt, S., 154
Social change:
  and advertising, 5
  and the community, 4–10, 15
  and ethnic groups, 4, 10
  and expectations, 9, 15, 16, 21
  and "future shock" 3
  and the mass media, 3, 10
  and political participation, 4
  and population growth, 27
  Reich, Charles, on, 3
  Toffler, Alvin, on, 3
  and tradition, 10
  and values, 4–5
"Social mapping," 27
Social movements, 4
"software," 145
Stanley, Julian C., 149, 154
State education agencies, 60, 62–63, 187, 190, 200–203
Statistics, descriptive (*see* Descriptive statistics)
Stratified random sampling, 97–99, 109, 123
Strength of agreement, 178
Structured data (*see* Data, structured)
Structured interviews (*see* Interviews, structured)
Structured questions (*see* Questions, structured)
Strunk, William J., 213
"Summary sheets," 138–39, 160
Survey coordinator, the, 127–28, 141
Survey instrument, the:
  choice of, 111
  construction of, 66, 77–83
  demographic questions in, 66–68, 69, 78–79, 82
  dichotomous-choice questions in, 72
  factual questions in, 66, 68, 69, 79, 82
  and the Guttman Scale, 74
  inclusiveness of, 78
  instructions for, 82
  introduction to, 77, 79, 83
  length of, 79
  multiple-choice questions in, 72
  non-scaled multiple-choice questions in, 75
  open-ended questions in, 70–75
  opinion probes in, 68–69, 79, 82, 123
  "packaged," 65
  pretest of, 80–82, 83, 116, 127
  reactions to, 76, 77–78, 112
  relevance of, *85–109*
  scaled multiple-choice questions in, 72–75
  sections of, 77–78
  self-administering, 119–20
  and the Semantic Differential Scale, 73, 74
  structured questions in, 70–75
  transitions in, 79, 80
  types of questions in, 66–69
  wording of, 66, 69, 75–77, 82
Survey research, 36, 37, 43
*Survey Research* (Blackstrom and Hursh), 103
Survey respondents:
  anticipatory responses of, 79
  appointments with, 124
  coding of, 124
  complaints of, 118
  confidence of, 123
  cooperation of, 78, 108
  educational level of, 76
  geographical distribution of, 115, 122
  interviews of, 37, 39, 43–48, 78, 120–24, 125, 129
  "key participants" among, 86, 87
  middle-aged, 127
  motivation of, 120–24
  order of, 103
  questions of, 118, 124, 125
  random selection of, *88–108*
  rapport with, 124, 125, 129
  reactions of, 76, 77–78, 112, 164
  resistence of, 116
  subgroups of, 66
  threats to, 77, 78
  values of, 68, 76, 78, 83
  working class, 127
*Surveys, Polls and Samples* (Parten), 105
Surveys, sample:
  advantages of, 92
  and analytic-mode decisions, 108
  bias in, 94, 96
  call-backs in, 116

Index  253

cluster sampling in, 101-2
coding in, 114, 124
complaints about, 118
and concomitant purposes, 108
confidence in, 104-6, 107
confidentiality in, 112
cooperation decisions in, 108
costs of, 111, 112
follow-ups in, 116, 154-55
implementation of, 107-8
income, factor of, in, 97-98, 100
"key participants" in, 116
personnel for, 146
preparation for, 113-19
as public relations, 108
questions about, 118
race, factor of, in, 97-98, 100
random selection in, 93, 96-103
reactions to, 76, 77-78, 112, 116
readings about, 237-38
representativeness of, 92-93
resistance to, 116
rumors about, 116
sample size in, 103-7
sex, factor of, in, 97-98, 100
simple random sampling in, 96-97
stratified random sampling in, 97-99
systematic sampling in, 99-101
tolerance of error in, 104, 105-7
"uncertainty" in, 105
and urban renewal, 103
and voting patterns, 98, 99
Surveys, saturation, 40
Surveys, telephone, 107
Swanson, Bert, 11
Systematic sampling, 99-101
Systems approaches, 5

## T

"Table of Chi-square," the, 177, 181, 233
Table of Sample Sizes, the, 104
Tax information, 58, 60, 61
Telephone checks, 113
Television, 3, 116
Thermofax, 197
Time requirements:
　for demographic questions, 67-68
　for fieldwork, 115
　for interviews, 126
　for respondent contact, 122-23
　and sample size, 121
　for sample surveys, 112
Toffler, Alvin, 3

Tolerance, band of (*see* Band of tolerance)
Tolerance limits, 18-20
Tradition, 6-8, 10
Tregoe, Benjamin B., 22, 29, 30
Trend Analysis Sheets, 151
Trends, 148, 151, 152-53
"T test," the, 165-66

## U

"Uncertainty," 105
Universe (*see* Population, respondent)
University survey centers, 111
Urban blight, 4
Urban renewal, 103

## V

Value positions, 76, 83
Values:
　in chi-square tests, 168
　community, 4-11, 68
　and policy, 11
　and social change, 4-10
Variables:
　in interpretation, 165ff.
　in scattergrams, 154-55
　in trend analysis, 151
Volunteers, 115, 123, 129
Voting patterns, 10-12, 14, 23-27, 40, 60, 98, 99

## W

Weighted samples, 138
White, E. G., 213
Women's liberation, 4
Wording of questions, 66, 69, 75-77, 82

## X

Xerox, 197

## Y

Yates' Correction, 176

## Z

Zanovich, George, 140
Zinnes, Dina A., 140